From Cows to Space
With GOD as My Copilot

From Cows to Space
With GOD as My Copilot
MY CAREER And FAMILY LIFE

ALFRED MILLER

Copyright © 2019 by Alfred Miller.

Library of Congress Control Number:	2019910533
ISBN: Hardcover	978-1-7960-4836-0
Softcover	978-1-7960-4835-3
eBook	978-1-7960-4834-6

All rights reserved. No part of this book may be reproduced or transmitted in any form or by any means, electronic or mechanical, including photocopying, recording, or by any information storage and retrieval system, without permission in writing from the copyright owner.

Scripture quotations marked NIV are taken from the Holy Bible, New International Version®. NIV®. Copyright © 1973, 1978, 1984 by International Bible Society. Used by permission of Zondervan. All rights reserved. [Biblica]

Unless otherwise indicated, all scripture quotations are from The Holy Bible, English Standard Version® (ESV®). Copyright ©2001 by Crossway Bibles, a division of Good News Publishers. Used by permission. All rights reserved.

Any people depicted in stock imagery provided by Getty Images are models, and such images are being used for illustrative purposes only. Certain stock imagery © Getty Images.

Print information available on the last page.

Rev. date: 07/26/2019

To order additional copies of this book, contact:
Xlibris
1-888-795-4274
www.Xlibris.com
Orders@Xlibris.com
800347

Dedication

I dedicate this book to my lovely spouse Dorothy who has been at my my side for over 66 faithful years as my earthly Co-Pilot.

Contents

Preface ix
Acknowledgments xvii

Chapter 1   The Early Years and World War II 1
Chapter 2   My Teenage Years 17
Chapter 3   How My Parents Came to America 24
Chapter 4   Milking Cows 32
Chapter 5   Airplanes, Rockets, Jets, and German V-2s 37
Chapter 6   High School Sports and Activities 45
Chapter 7   My Early Dating Years...52
Chapter 8   Joe Miller and Sons and Miller Brothers 55
Chapter 9   Sisters, Fun, Music, and Mary 66
Chapter 10 Hunting, Fishing, Pearl Harbor, and the Wasco
                Rifle Club..71
Chapter 11 Finally, College 79
Chapter 12 Dorothy Enters College, Relationships, and Courtship....85
Chapter 13 Dorothy Alice Worley 91
Chapter 14 John Rogers's Pioneer Family 98
Chapter 15 Grandpa John Rogers's Sons Were Also Pioneers...........110
Chapter 16 Dorothy's Return to College and Studies......................120
Chapter 17 Shake, Rattle, and Roll 125
Chapter 18 The Wedding 133
Chapter 19 Senior Year at the University..141
Chapter 20 The Right Place at the Right Time.................................147
Chapter 21 All You Need to Know about Edwards Air Force Base ..155

Chapter 22	YF-100A Supersonic Sabre	161
Chapter 23	XB-52 Stratofortress Bomber	167
Chapter 24	New Computer and X-2 Computer Support	173
Chapter 25	Fatal X-2 Rocket Crash	178
Chapter 26	Chief, Computer Programming Section	181
Chapter 27	Mr. Bill Adams, Data Reduction Branch Chief	192
Chapter 28	As Chief, Mr. Phillips Applied His Vast Flight Test Knowledge	195
Chapter 29	My Promotion to Data Reduction Branch Chief	200
Chapter 30	Share	210
Chapter 31	Range Commanders Council	214
Chapter 32	Little Kids, Fun, Anniversaries, and Family Photos	217
Chapter 33	Long-Term, Full-Time Study	226
Chapter 34	Promotion to Deputy Technical Support Division	231
Chapter 35	NF-104 Crash, President Reagan Policies, and New Developments	238
Chapter 36	Family Reunions and Memories	247
Chapter 37	Technical Support Division	255
Chapter 38	Hill/Wendover/Dugway Program Office (Utah Test and Training Range Formation)	268
Chapter 39	Space	275
Chapter 40	God Is the Way, the Truth, and the Life	284
Chapter 41	My Last Day	293
Chapter 42	Contract Management and Party Time	296

Epilogue 311

Preface

This is a human story about a freckle-faced, bashful, stuttering boy raised on a dairy farm prior to and during World War II. I am eighty-eight years old and telling my story about the way I grew up with four brothers and three sisters—with me in the middle—and how I wondered about life. I was raised by God-centered parents who were both immigrants from Switzerland in the early 1900s. This is not only my story; it is also, more importantly, a God story. Furthermore, it is also a story about immigrants in this country and early pioneering families that made significant contributions to making this country a great nation. My story demonstrates how one can excel in life with God's help. I grew up on a secluded dairy farm in Wasco, California, in the humble regions of the southern San Juaquin Valley in Central California and went to the edges of space. I feel that God wants me to tell my life's story. With his help, I hope that I can convey this story as meaningful and helpful for anyone who wonders about life and how to cope with basically a Godless, immoral, selfish, and almost anything-goes society.

Besides my accomplishments on the job, I have something to say about a life that God asks and challenges us to live. With my experiences in life, I have something to say about God and my life to my children, grandchildren, including my great-grandchildren, great-great grandchildren, siblings, relatives, friends, and anyone who has struggled or is struggling with the meaning of life. I have strived and lived a God-fearing life that I feel is worthy of being showcased. It is a long convoluted and fascinating story that demonstrates what God can accomplish.

Even though I am quite old, I still have something to say about my life's story. I wondered about life and struggled to raise eight kids on loan from God with a wonderful spouse, Dorothy. In addition, God gave me a fantastic career that allowed me to assist the United States of America in making aircraft and space history without fully realizing its significance. I thank God for permitting me to pioneer the use of scientific computers for flight test and evaluation purposes.

My family life's journey took me from milking about one hundred cows as a teenager during World War II to experiencing an adventurous career at the very famous and prestigious Air Force Flight Test Center (AFFTC) at Edwards Air Force Base in California. I was involved and engaged in practically all the air force test activity at Edwards AFB and the National Aeronautics and Space Administration (NASA). I was heavily involved in the first recovery of the space shuttle landing and many others on the Rogers dry lakebed, thereby entitling my memoir *From Cows to Space with God as My Copilot*.

My involvement in flight testing at Edwards AFB spanned thirty-two years. I graduated from the University of California at Berkeley in June 1953 with a BS degree in mathematics and statistics. I was assigned to support the highest-priority program, the prototype YF-100A super Sabre, which was the first aircraft to fly supersonic in level flight.

As a mathematician assigned to a highly expert and competent flight test team, I had a front-row seat and a bird's-eye view of flight testing. In addition, I was very fortunate to support many other test programs, which involved the testing of various bombers, fighters, cruise missiles, and many more weapon systems. I suffered from and endured three serious depressions along the way.

I feel that my life needs to be told not for my benefit and adulation but for my family. They wondered what I did at Edwards as I went off to work in a suit, white shirt, and tie. I remember my dad, in overalls, going to work in the cold, wet cow barns. He was milking cows and working on the farm virtually 24/7.

God, early in my life, dangled trainer aircraft flown by air cadets in training from Minter Field, near Bakersfield, during World War II, in full view. The pilots used the farm's huge silo as a ground reference point. I could see their faces as they flew directly over the farm. I watched in awe as I fell in love with airplanes.

This is not only my story. It is a story about how God works wonders. I feel compelled to write it for anyone who is interested in what God can do for you if you join God, hand in hand, in living a God-fearing life both on and off the job. I submit that you too can work wonders. I encourage you to read it. I would be most pleased if my story convinces just one person by changing their lifestyle.

Society needs to put God first in order to restore this country to its founding fathers' values that praise God and make God number one. If you decide to read this book, ask God to assist you as your copilot. God can work wonders with anyone. God put me in the right place at the right time. I can attest to that. I rest my case.

Enjoy the read—and may God bless you. His will be done. Amen.

Alfred F. Miller
Lancaster, California

From Cows to Space with God as My Copilot provides an insider's view of activities at the Air Force Flight Test Center and Edwards Air Force Base during the exciting second half of the twentieth century. Testing and evaluation require a true team effort of engineers, pilots, aircrew, maintainers, technical support personnel of myriad disciplines, and tons of complex data acquisition, transmission, and processing equipment. Fritz Miller's observations of these activities from the perspective of a key member of the technical support community is enlightening.

During his career, data gathering progressed from kneepad notes, photo panel pictures, and oscillograph rolls dumped on the flight test engineer's desk to thousands of parameters transmitted and displayed in real time to dozens of engineers manning mission control centers. Data-processing equipment progressed from slide rules and calculators (add, subtract, multiply, and divide only) to supercomputers. Systems under test progressed from the early jet aircraft to the space shuttle.

Coming from a rural, agricultural upbringing (as did a great many aeronautical practitioners of the day, including myself), Fritz conveys the sense of awe we all felt as part of this golden age of aviation. His relationship with God shines through the narrative and his life. Enjoy!

—Richard Hildebrand, former technical and executive director,
  Air Force Flight Test Center

One of the most interesting things about this book by Fritz Miller is that he started writing when he was eighty-eight years old and had celebrated his sixty-sixth wedding anniversary. Eighty-eight years is an age when most seniors get tired and are retired. In the case of Fritz, this is the time he had gathered the most explosive energy and inspiration to write this piece without getting tired. It was written in less than eleven months. This points to the fact that God blessed him for this purpose, and I am glad this dream has been accomplished.

In his book, Fritz uses his personal life experiences to convey the message of God's love—personified in Jesus Christ—to his family and to the entire humanity. As such, his personal testimony is a way to share the gospel of Christ by explaining his career and faith experiences. He has convincingly argued that life does not make sense unless we accept Jesus as our Lord and savior and embrace Jesus's teachings as the central feature of our lives. Most spectacularly, Fritz wittingly acknowledged the fact that he was able to get to this point because of his firm faith and absolute trust in God.

From Cows to Space with God as My Copilot is a book that appeals to every genre in society. It appeals to the younger generations who are so eager to engage in life and career, middle-aged people who are swimming in the euphoria of materialism, and the older generations who are still exploring the reality of God's hand in their life experiences. This book gives moral insights and provides us the opportunity to rethink our lifestyles and discover that God can work with someone.

Most books are acquired to be used in decorating bookshelves. Some are acquired to read and gain knowledge. Few books are acquired to read and gain wisdom. *From Cows to Space with God as My Copilot* is one of the few books from which one can gain wisdom. It is informative, formative, and transformative. I strongly recommend this book to all. Do not miss it.

—Rev. Gerald Osuagwu, associate pastor,
    Sacred Heart Catholic Church, Lancaster, California

Acknowledgments

First, I would like to thank my beautiful wife, Dorothy, for being my faithful partner as we traveled our journey together and for being a fantastic and caring mother for our eight lovely children.

A special thanks to Natalie, my second daughter, who is a wiz at Microsoft word who got me quick-started by teaching me the basic fundamentals of Microsoft word and for jokingly giving me a great theme for my book: "Daddy, you were at the right place at the right time." Natalie also assisted me in designing my cover page.

Melissa, my oldest daughter, carried me through to the final landing—when I needed her most. My special thanks to Melissa for being at the other end of the cell phone and always present at our home, as needed. Melissa and Meribeth, my youngest daughter, greatly assisted me in collecting and inserting all the pictures for my manuscript.

Thanks to all the family members, living siblings, relatives, and dear friends who pushed me along. A heartfelt thanks to all my wonderful lady friends who I count money with at church weekly for their strong encouragement and support by nudging me continuously along the way. They are referred to as my "countesses."

My kind and wonderful thanks to a very special and dear friend for greatly assisting me in staying focused on my story and for keeping me on the flight path. She was a constant reminder for me to stick to my story. She always told me to "get back to work" with an occasional encouraging word by sending me a thumbs-up or a welcome kind "well done."

Last, but certainly not least, a Godly thanks to Father Gerald Osuagwu, the associate pastor of Sacred Heart Church for encouraging me to express my God-centered approach to life in writing about my life's journey. After reading a few chapters of my book and getting his advice on some spiritual topics, he said, "Fritz, you are writing your gospel."

That almost floored me. It sounded blasphemous.

He said, "Absolutely not. This is your story, and it's your gospel." He put a whole new perspective on my approach to writing my memoirs. Thank you so much, Father. Absolutely!

Chapter 1

The Early Years and World War II

Josef and Marie (Marty) Miller family with Richard, Alfred, Aloise, Josef Jr., Mary (L to R) and Rose in her mother's arms

Miller Family in 1935

Who is this guy? Well, Fritz is Alfred Frank Miller. Fritz is the little guy in the first row, second from the left, looking down at my younger brother Richard. Top right is dad, and baby Rose is being held by mom. The first row, starting from the right is Mary, Joe, Aloise, myself, and then Richard on the far left.

Mom always called me Alfred. Dad had all kinds of names for me. One of which was "Guglehupf." One of the hired hands on the ranch, Gus Kloeppel, called me Fritz because I reminded him of the katzenjammer kids in a cartoon page of the local paper.

Mom kept saying, "His name is Alfred," in her very strong Swiss accent.

Anyway, Gus kept calling me Fritz.

Mom thought she had picked a name that was hard to nickname. My brothers and sisters began calling me Fritz. Eventually, mom started to call me Fritz too. Regardless what I was called, I am the same young redheaded, freckle-faced, bashful, shy, stuttering kid who wondered and lived like any other young person growing up. I thought and wondered about life. Why are we here? I was always interested in the stars, the universe, and space in general.

Born and Raised in the Family Home

I was born on September 21, 1930, in the farm home where I was raised. It was also my brother Joe's sixth birthday. Sharing birthdays with my oldest brother is deposited in a bank full of memories. God was always in the family. There was a collage of religious pictures and crucifixes displayed throughout the home. Besides saying all the prayers before meals, we were introduced to all the basic prayers. Mom taught us the rosary. Mom's favorite mantra was "Vatter unser" ("Let us pray"). We all learned the Lord's Prayer, in Swiss, and all the other prayers, including how to make and say the sign of the cross in "Schwyz."

The God-Centered Family

It was instilled in us loud and clear why God made us and why we are here. The answer is outlined in the *Baltimore Catechism*: "God made me to know him, to love him, and to serve him in this world and to be happy with him forever in the next." *Forever* is the operative word. I was certainly born and raised in a wonderful Catholic family that fostered the main principles of a good Catholic life. I was kick-started and propelled in the right direction from the very beginning. God is good.

My Catholic Upbringing

My Catholic education continued to grow. We always went to Sunday Mass. I went to confession almost weekly, performed altar boy duties on Sundays, and learned all of the Mass responses in Latin. Yes, we rang the bells at consecration. I learned how to genuflect and when to genuflect. It was so ingrained in me that I would genuflect before I would sit down at the movies, which someone pointed out to me for my embarrassment. It goes to show how Catholic I was. I got the best Catholic training from the strict Franciscan nuns.

Franciscan Nuns

Saint John the Evangelist Church was truly blessed to have nuns available to teach there. I got a good religious education, and they served me well in preparing me for an overall grammar school education. I was very prepared for high school.

My Young Teenage Social Experience

The only thing I wasn't prepared to do was socialize with anyone other than family, friends, and relatives. I was somewhat isolated on the farm. I used to say that I could not get in trouble—even if I wanted to. Going out always meant going to church on Sundays and occasional Saturday-night confessions. In addition, I would go to movies that were approved by mom, shopping trips to Wasco and Bakersfield, or travel around the farm and Wasco with my dad. I might go chumming around with my older brothers or fish and get involved in other activities with my dad, my brothers, and my church and school friends.

Boy Scouts

In order to get broader social involvements, I wanted to join the Boy Scouts—but Dad turned me down. I think he didn't want me to get involved in other public activities. At times, Dad was very strict and set in his ways, but he had good intentions. Dad was very European in his approach. All families being raised today would be better off if they got more discipline, particularly the latchkey children.

My First Paying Job

My first paying job was digging up worms for my dad's many fishermen friends. They would always pay me in change. I liked the coins because I could hear the jingle and the feel of money in my pocket, unlike paper money. I worked on my own, knowing where the worms were. My first paying job made me feel good about myself. I harvested a lot of kinds of worms. I saved my money and was very pleased with my bankroll, as sparse as it was.

My Eighth-Grade Mentor

My eighth-grade teacher, Sister Lucida, had the greatest influence on me. I thought I wanted to become a Catholic priest. World War II started a year or two before. Things were happening in the world. The Doolittle raid took place, and *Thirty Seconds over Tokyo* was written by one of the survivors. Sister exposed us to the outside world of events, including some information about World War II, and she would read excerpts from the book. I started to pay a little more attention to World War II by reading the newspapers and watching Movietone newsclips at the local theater. I read the *Battle of Tarawa*, which was about the deadliest battle in the Pacific prior to Iwo Jima. War, battles, suffering, and deaths really affected me.

Early World War II Battles

The Battle of El-Alamein

I remember seeing war movie clips about the battles in North Africa. The first battle of El-Alamein was disastrous for the allies. The gigantic cannons firing huge explosive shells and dismembering and scattering bodies on either side of the conflict were unbearable to watch. In addition, there were aircraft, bombs, infantry, and tanks blasting away in concert. This basically left me in tears, and I tried desperately to cover them up. By the time the movie clips were over, I was almost petrified with fright. Movies at the time were still a novelty and had a special appeal to me. The moving pictures could mesmerize with their vivid realism. War literally woke me up to the worst elements that exist in an evil world. Witnessing war vicariously, as I was able to, had a profound effect on me. I was not quite twelve years old at the time. It was a very impressionable age, particularly for me. I was a sensitive, gullible boy who, in large part, was living in isolation with a wonderful large family on a farm.

More War and Human Loss

For the latter part of my grammar school years and the two first years of high school, I lived with daily reminders of this very human costly war. Young Wasco soldiers returned in caskets draped with the American flag, under the watchful eye of my oldest brother Joe, who had a farm deferment. It was unbearable for him to have so many friends die during the war. Joe finally convinced dad to let him join the service, and he was inducted in the navy as a pharmacist mate. Joe spent the war stateside, tending to badly wounded soldiers at the famous Oak Knoll Navy Hospital in Oakland, California. Many soldiers were killed or wounded each week. It was a very sad time in America.

Sergeant Raymond Schroeder Was a Hero

The newspaper clippings within this chapter are from the old Wasco *News*, which was sold to the Wasco *Tribune* in 1980. All the records for Wasco *News* have been destroyed. I have spoken to the owner of the Wasco *Tribune*, and he is reluctant to provide approval to use the newspaper articles in my book since he was not the owner during World War II. I am using these newspaper articles based on the situation described above. I hope this will suffice.

The Frank Schroeder family

The Frank and Genevieve Schroeder family moved from Freeburg, Missouri, to Wasco, California in the 1930s. He was a farmer and a registered member of the Saint John Evangelist Catholic Church. They had seven children, and many were about the same ages as the Miller family. The Schroeders had four sons and three daughters. The families were parishioners at Saint John's and knew each other very well. In addition, most of the family members attended Saint John's Grammar School. Raymond joined the army in early 1941—before the Japanese attack on Pearl Harbor. Two younger brothers, Richard and Arthur, served during World War II. Another brother, Clarence, called Sam, was a little younger than me. He served in the navy during the Korean War. Imagine the worry and deep concern the Schroeder family experienced with their three sons fighting in a number of combat zones over a span of five years. They were suffering from grief with no stars on their home windows. However, they could be delivered at any time. They all survived the wars. They had God in their foxholes and on their warships and passenger ships. One of Ray's combat support ships sank prior to entering the African campaign, and he doesn't know how to swim.

Sergeant Schroeder Fought Three Major Battles

He fought with General George Patton in the battle of North Africa. He fought with General Mark Clark during the invasion of mainland Italy with the American and British amphibious invasion forces at Salerno, Italy. In addition, he followed the invasion of Normandy to participate in the liberation of France and Western Europe with the third army, which was commanded by General George S. Patton. In many ways, he has been there and done that many times over. The following is a list of pictures and notes he kept during the war years. He was an unsung hero. Ray must have thought, *I know God won't give me anything I can't handle. I just wish that he didn't trust me so much.*

Raymond Schroeder

Sergeant Schroeder fought battles in many undesirable combat situations, and he was very disciplined and meticulous in how he carried out his affairs. He planted a neat garden and landscaped and maintained a well-kept yard. My first used car, which dad bought for me, was Ray's 1948 Dodge coupe.

When Mary and Ray had their first daughter, Karen, they visited me at the University of California Berkeley on their way up to Northern

California to visit his sister Bernice and his brother-in-law, Gus. I kidded him that he came up to see the 1948 Dodge he had owned. It was hard to play one-upmanship with Ray. He responded, "You got that about right." I really appreciated the visit. It was my first time I was away from home, and Mary was special. Ray had excellent handwriting. He dressed neatly and conservatively and had a good appearance. He could be a little ornery at times. After I was married to Dorothy for about five years, he found out I had never been drunk before. Dad kept cold beer in the refrigerator, but I never touched it for my own sake.

His plan was to get me smashed. In the army, I am sure that Ray got quite a bit of training in that regard. The annual family Thanksgiving gathering was being celebrated at Mary and Ray's new home. After stuffing ourselves, Ray invited my brothers and I to follow him out to garage and see what we could find. He found two bottles of vodka stashed away. He immediately said, "Let's belly up to the bar." There was no bar, but it demonstrated his type of humor. He showed us how to drink without a bar or stool. He proceeded to chug a few gulps straight out of the bottle and invited the other brothers, including me, to join him. My oldest brother, Joe, obliged him with a couple of gulps and a grimace. Aloise reluctantly followed suit.

When it was my turn, Ray looked at me as if I was a sissy. I shied away from the situation. He kept after me. I found out what peer pressure was all about. My older brothers finally talked me into having a swig. I took a little sip. That wasn't good enough. By that time, I realized that all the older brothers were in on it. I thought, *This is a learning experience—have at it. After I take a robust charge at the bottle and take an average-sized drink, that will satisfy them. No way.*

I drank a little more, and round two got underway. I had to join in the repeat process. I didn't feel the effects of the first blast yet. *What the hell?* This time, I swallowed more than I should have. As I began to feel a little tipsy, I left the garage and went into the house. All of the ladies were there, including my mom, Dorothy, her mother, my sisters, and my brothers' wives.

The only seat left was the ottoman somewhat out of view. I sat down, listened to the conversation, and started to giggle. There wasn't anything to giggle about, but there I was. The more I tried to stop giggling, the more obvious it was to everybody in the room that something was amiss.

Dorothy told me later that she knew we were up to no good in the garage. She had never seen me drunk, and she became suspicious.

Dorothy's mother always spoke her mind and blurted out, "He is drunk."

The plan succeeded, and Ray put another notch in his combat rifle, so to speak. He won a friendly family battle of his own. I was the victim.

Sergeant Raymond Schroeder

Sergeant Raymond Schroeder returned from the war after serving in the army for more than five years and exhibited all the symptoms of post-traumatic stress disorder (PSTD). It can be triggered by a terrifying encounter that can be psychologically absorbed by experiencing or witnessing a devastating event or events. Symptoms include flashbacks, nightmares, severe anxiety, and uncontrollable thoughts about the event, which can be manifested at almost any time.

Mary discretely revealed to my family that Ray would literally wake up at night and try to climb the walls. Ray put on a mask of being a happy-go-lucky guy. He didn't like his picture being taken or movies being made of him making faces at the camera. I am sure it was one of his defense mechanisms to possibly hide his true feelings and lingering suffering.

I always liked Ray. Deep down, past all of his war experiences and dramatic consequences, Ray was a good person. God, of course, knew his true nature and rewarded him with a marriage to my fantastic sister. They raised six children, including twin daughters, Francine and Christine. They had two other daughters. Karen was the oldest, and Susan was the youngest daughter. They had two sons, Philip and Steven, and Ray lived a long life and died at the age of eighty-nine.

Letter to His Parents from a War Zone

Ray wrote a letter to his parents and family from a foxhole. Knowing Ray, I could sense his sincerity and true self as a lonely soldier missing all of his family. Ray wasn't one to reveal too many feelings and emotions.

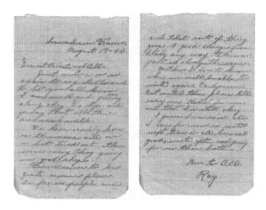

Ray was very meticulous. One of his duties after the war was being a gravedigger. Was he told to document his grave-digging assignment—or was he just accomplishing his normal way of doing things? His historical notebooks describe what a soldier has to experience during wartime. His powerful, succinct records reveal a firsthand account of how horrendous and difficult it is to be engaged in wartime combat and deal with the aftermaths of war.

Ray, in my estimation, is a true hero for fighting and liberating many European cities, putting enemy soldiers in their graves, and digging up his comrades' graves after the truce. Ray suffered physical and other psychological battle scars. Ray paid the price. He received a small disability payment for his physical wounds—but not for his long bout with PTSD. His psychological battle scars rubbed off on his spouse and family, but we can be very proud of him. The tears I have in my eyes as I write this chapter about his very sad story are for you Ray. May you rest in peace. Amen.

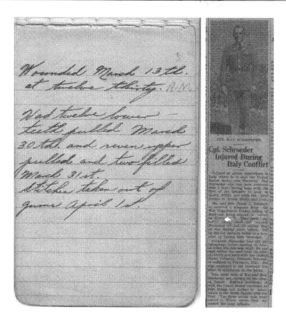

In his notebook, he reveals the day and hour that he was wounded, when he got his teeth pulled, and when he got his false teeth. The newspaper clips reveal more information regarding the circumstances of his wounds in action. He also listed his comrades by name and rank. His notebooks are replete with bloodstains, cigarette burns, mud stains, and smears—possibly tears—that tell their own story.

Silk Maps

Some war maps were made out of silk to be used in battle. These silk maps were made for clarity, durability, and availability. They can be rolled up, forced into a pack, withstand rain, mud, snow, and the like, and be readily available for a soldier's reference in battle. Ray documented his arrival into France. On the next page is a silk map.

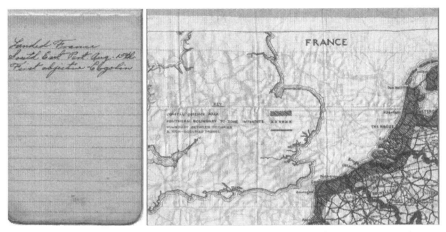

World War II infantry map for soldiers in battle (US army map)
Ray's battle locations

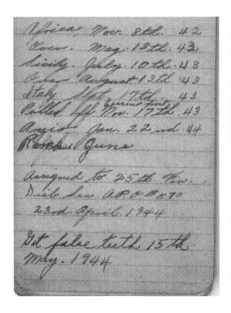

Grave-Digging Assignment

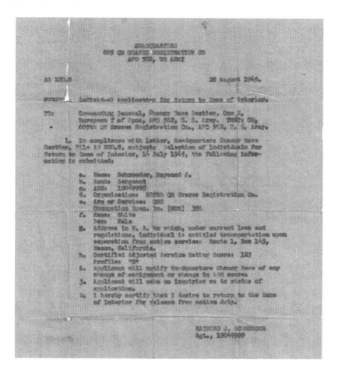

Ray became a hero during the war. He volunteered to—or was assigned to—perform grave-digging duty. He participated in the removal of soldiers buried or reburied in the battlefield, to be given a proper and honorable burial at military cemeteries. Ray took his grave-digging assignment very seriously. He described, recorded, and documented the condition of the bodies in the graves and their personal items. In addition, he assisted in their relocation and reinternment.

His brother Sam got a hold of his notebook and showed it to me when we were in high school. No pictures, but Ray had outlines, diagrams, and descriptions of decayed bodies. I didn't need to look at that notebook with all of its descriptions of deteriorating bodies. Knowing that they died in battle was enough as far as I was concerned. The war had a profound impact on me, which unknowingly had some impact on my psyche. In my late high school years, I had minor bouts with anxiety and depression. I might have had a minor case of PTSD, which manifested again and intensified in my first year of college.

Ray dug many graves and documented a number of grave contents and conditions. Many were American and British soldiers including noncommissioned officers and officers still in tattered battle uniforms with cigarette lighters and cases and other personal items. No one knows how many graves he assisted in relocating. Many graves were in such horrible condition that the remains were reburied. The following are two detailed accounts. One describes the grave contents without body descriptions, and the other is one of the less gruesome of many absolutely horrible-looking human remains.

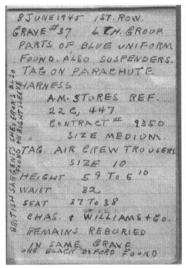 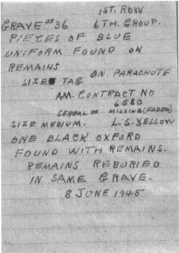

Returning Home

I do not understand why a twice-wounded veteran soldier, awarded a Purple Heart, who fought five years in and out of the trenches, was assigned grave-digging duty. The army should have known that years of almost continuous battle would have some psychological effects on a combat soldier. To the contrary, was he assigned because he was battle-experienced, seasoned veteran able to withstand the horrible rigors of war. Would Ray cope much better than an average soldier? Unfortunately, the job had to be done. Ray did it. Not knowing very much about PTSD, the army did what it had to do. I am absolutely convinced that his last assignment contributed to his PTSD. Another long-ending war tragedy.

The reason I included my brother-in-law's war story early in my life's story is twofold. First, I became aware of the tragedies of war at a very young age, which had a very profound effect on me. For almost half of my grammar school and high school years, World War II was dominant. Second, later in my life and after a couple of more wars, PTSD was finally observed, studied, analyzed, and finally understood for what it is.

As my story unfolds, I too had three serious episodes of clinical depression—not unlike some soldiers returning from war. Could it be that I suffered some form of PTSD? I only came to that conclusion, right or wrong, in writing about Ray's war experiences and my story. Showcasing Sergeant Schroeder's personal handwritten diaries, battle locations, awards, and horrific duties as a grave-digger are extremely powerful and need to be told.

A Self-Made Amateur War Historian

Returning soldiers do not tell their children much about their war experiences. I came to that conclusion when I would talk to my oldest daughter Melissa's father-in-law. She was married to his son, Rodger Gaudi. By that time, I was a self-made historian. I have watched practically all the movies and television war series about World War II, read books and magazines, and had conversations with war veterans.

I have had many conversations with Bernard Gaudi. He was a marine who fought the complete Battle of Iwo Jima. He was battling his way up to Mount Suribachi and was within one hundred yards of the making of the famous Rosenthal picture of the seven marines raising the flag on Mount Suribachi. Babe, as he was called, was a nineteen-year-old rifleman who performed every duty in his squad of fifteen.

Rodger's dad is the only fighting marine in his squad who survived. We talked about many things—much about his accomplishments but not much about his personal emotions and feelings. I got the best information from him after a few beers that we both enjoyed. I would relate to Rodger some of the things that he told me. Rodger would respond, "He never told me that."

After the Battle of Iwo Jima, he was assigned to another marine unit that was preparing for the invasion of mainland Japan. Upon receiving the wonderful news of the Japanese surrender, he did express his feelings and deep emotion. He went to Japan, made a friendly invasion, and was greeted by most of the Japanese villagers with acknowledgment and applause.

What a fantastic turnaround in emotion, sentiment, and feelings that Babe and Ray experienced when they were told about V-J Day. Babe was being prepared to invade Japan with total estimated casualties of one million for both sides of the conflict. That was when he expressed his emotions and relief. He still advocates that President Truman made the right decision by dropping the atom bomb.

I hope, in some way, that I can be a stand-in for sergeant Raymond Schroeder by sewing together the unknown pieces for his immediate family, relatives, and friends to know more about their father's untold story about being a true World War II hero.

A Taste of War

My first real taste of war—or maybe I should say the smell of war—was watching a Movietone newsclip about the war in North Africa. All that war making and killing on display in the middle of the church hall was too much to comprehend. What kind of a world are we living in? What is the world becoming? Regardless to what is happening today, we are headed toward Christ's Second Coming. Stop this nonsense and be ready was my innermost feeling.

Regarding my next stage in my life, what now? Seminary at St. Josephina's in Ohio? No. They turned me down due to my heart murmur. Looking back, it was the right decision for the wrong reason. Sending a country boy far off to become a priest at age fourteen, with virtually no life experience, was and is not advisable. Back in the old days, a flood of teenage boys was sent off to the seminary. Many became priests, and some were caught up in the recent church scandals. Some, not a few, ended up with identity crises in more ways than one. That has led to many church scandals that have been ameliorated but not totally eliminated. The Catholic Church is not perfect; it is, to some extent, a lot like all of us. We are all in a journey together. There are a number of lay Catholics entering the seminary at much older ages to seek second careers. God bless them all.

So what do I do now? I continue on. I continued my education at Wasco High School, beginning my freshman year in September 1944.

Chapter 2

My Teenage Years

1939 family portrait

There were advantages of living on the farm during wartime. I remember the days when gas was rationed. Since dad had a lot of farm tractors and vehicles that needed gas, he had a C sticker, which meant no restrictions on fuel. Dad did not take advantage of no-gas restrictions by rarely going fishing. An A sticker meant an allotment of four gallons a week. Many other items were rationed. You could buy only two pairs of shoes each year. Meat was somewhat scarce along with coffee.

I remember my sister Mary working at the local malt shop, where she made fantastic vanilla milk shakes, which were now made out of soybeans.

Ugh. No Hershey bars. Dentyne gum was hard to get. I remember my dad buying savings bonds. At school, the good nuns set up a program where we could save our dimes to buy twenty-five-dollar savings bonds.

Mom maintained a very healthy victory garden where she raised all kinds of vegetables and the like. We had fruit, walnut, pomegranate, orange, and pecan trees. We also had grapes, some of which were fermented into wine. Dad made beer and root beer as well. Dad occasionally invited the farmhands to join in a few meetings near the wine cellar for a little libation and employee bonding.

Dad was an amateur butcher, and he would supplement the meat needed by raising animals—but no pigs since they were too dirty and not compatible with a dairy farm. Good liquor and wine were scarce. He had two cellars that were used for making beer, wine, and soda pop, and Mom made good use of the leftover storage space for canning. We made out very well despite the restrictions, and we all took advantage of the benefits of living on a dairy farm during wartime.

Life on the Farm

The picture above was taken in 1939, where I was about nine years old. Family life on the farm was a great experience. In the large Miller family, Mom, Dad and all eight siblings played a role in forming family life on the farm. Being the middle sibling, in my view, was particularly challenging. That jokingly means that I had to respond as a slave to my elders, but by the same token, I could lord it over my younger siblings. That was definitely not the case, and we all loved and respected each other. Sure, we had squabbles and minor battles like any siblings, but we mostly managed to limit the extent of the damage to the end of the battle. Battles and squabbles are won and lost and then left there.

I am located in the front row in the second position between Richard and Aloise. I am pictured with a bowed elbow. This happened in an unfortunate minor accident. More on this later. We didn't carry grudges. We played every game we could think of. We had no TV and not a lot of movies. We all gathered on the floor and couched near the Philco radio. I remember the good old radio programs, like the *Lone Ranger, Captain Midnight, the Great Gilder Sleeve, Gunsmoke, This Is the FBI, Enter Sanctum,* and *Henry Aldridge* to mention a few. We never missed *Hit Parade*. I particularly liked the orchestration of the "William Tell Overture." We all went to Mass on Sundays. It was celebrated in Latin. As altar boys, we responded to the priests for the congregation.

My father was strict and quite a character. When things would get Dad upset, he would express his anger and then, about an hour later, we would hear him singing or yodeling from a distance. Richard was the only one in the family who could yodel. I never heard Dad swear, but I did hear him, at times, speaking and shouting in his native tongue in terms that you could probably guess. I remember him saying, *"Dunder, watter, blatta, bleece"* (Thundering weather, lightning strikes). Dad never said the n-word, the four-letter word, or the b-word, and I never heard him swear. He watched his mouth around the kids.

Dad was a talker, and he liked to tell a good joke. He would repeat jokes that we all heard of before, but he would still laugh. One of his other favorite expressions was *"Du furekta nundi stantz blausy kibb"* (You crazy fool standing and behaving like a stupid mule). Of course, we all would say that same tripe in our corrupt Swiss.

We all loved our parents, and people liked our dad very much. Richard was much like Dad in many respects—except for dad's beer drinking. Richard had polio when he it was about twelve years old, which left him with a slight limp that never handicapped him. All the siblings were very sad; he was the first sibling to die at the age of seventy-eight. Richard left his wonderful legacy as a God-fearing husband, father, high school teacher, principal, and head of adult education in Tulare, California. In addition, Richard was the president of Tulare's city council for many years until his demise from complications of heart surgery. Everyone misses brother Richard. Dad sure would have been very proud to know that Richard left a wonderful legacy in the city of Tulare, California.

Minorities

Dad hired all kinds of people to work on the farm. He hired relatives, relatives' friends, blacks, Hispanic, poor people, people in bad need for a job during the Depression, and so on. During cotton and potato season, Dad would hire anybody and everybody who was willing to work. During the severe Depression days, Mom would feed anybody who would traverse the farm.

Dad even allowed families to squat on the farm under a large grove of trees near the big water pump. Mr. Barker and his family made camp in that oasis for many years. Dad hired him to do all kinds of farm labor. He almost became part of the family. The family would treat the Barker family like any other family. This is the Christian way.

Family Sports and Bonding

We were left to our own devices to play games and get into mischief. We played a lot of softball, football, kick the ball, hide-and-seek, marbles, hopscotch, basketball, and other games. Looking back, I think that all of this togetherness and family sports playing—with Mom, Dad, and some of the neighbors watching on the sidelines—resulted in great family bonding. This bonding lasted as long as most of my siblings were alive.

Sports and Family Mischief

Since I couldn't participate in sports in high school because of my heart murmur, I set up hurdles, high jump, and pole vault pits, and I practiced jumping and running those makeshift barriers at home. We would make fishing poles to practice casting in the large storage barn. We would plan our own parades and march along for the dogs to watch.

Weasel's Antics

We called my older brother Aloise, Weasel, after his uncle by the same name. We liked to play a game where someone would be blindfold, put into a large Red Flyer wagon, and hauled off somewhere. Once at our destination, we were then asked to guess where they were. This was great fun until Aloise devised a scheme to haul me off to the big manure pile and park me. Then he had the mitigated gall to guess where I was. I didn't have to guess. I could smell. I was lucky it wasn't the fresh or overly moist kind of manure. We all got a big laugh out of it. No grudges. There was another time when Aloise playfully dragged me along the side of a declining pit that was used to load trucks. That prank backfired. I dislocated my elbow in the short fall. Aloise was punished enough by shaming himself for having done that. The Weasel struck again. No retaliation.

Cow calf being fed (public domain)

Richard and I would get into a little mischief now and then. Dad would take us to see rodeos. So Rich and I would go the calf barn and try our stint at being cowboys. I would hold the calf so Rich could mount the calf and rodeo around the pen. Boy, were we smart. We were cowboys. The problem was that the pen was too small to safely maneuver around all the trees and tree stumps. Rich got bucked off one time and center punctured a tree. Rich survived with a few bumps and bruises. That calf made us both smarter in a hurry. We soon left for bigger and safer ground to play on.

My Little Red Flyer

My brother always liked a good joke. Joe just loved to tell everybody about my stuttering joke. I was driving my little Red Flyer wagon. You could put one knee in the wagon and the other leg was stuck outside the wagon to motor around. I forget what the situation was, but for some reason, I asked Joe to push, but when I got to the word "push," I began to stutter badly. I could never get the word out. Finally, I gave up.

Still in my Red Flyer, I returned to my motoring position and drove away—varoom, varoom, varoom. Joe has told this story many times, and he would always laugh—almost to the point of tears. I didn't mind. It brought a little attention to me, which was very welcome as a middle brother of five. I am the fourth sibling in a family of eight. Since I stuttered, it made the matter worse.

We all made it as a family. Mary, my oldest sister, was very wise and observant. She also was there for me and understood my situation very well. We always washed the dishes together. A wonderful experience. We had many conversations about life, girls, boys, and sisterly advice.

Brother Joe's Horse, Sugar, and Aloise (Family Photo)

My Older Brothers Were My Mentors

My older brothers Joe and Aloise would always look out for me, and they tried to keep me out of trouble. They taught me how to swim and surf, drive a car, drive a tractor, and do many other farm duties. They also taught me how to play all kinds of innocent card games, including poker. Joe taught me how to ride his horse.

Joe always let us ride the horse as a family resource. Sugar was pretty independent. No matter where you were on the farm, if you would give her the rein, Sugar would beeline her way to the stable. She had a one-track mind. She was hard to rein back in when she galloped back to the stable.

My Wild Horse Ride

On occasion, I would ride Sugar to do what was called "checking the water." We had a variety of alfalfa fields that needed irrigation. Checking the water meant observing how far along the water traveled between the small levies. When the water would get very close to the end of the row, we knew when to change the water.

I liked to ride Sugar, and it was an opportunity to go bareback as fast as I could. I always rode without a saddle. The saddle was very expensive, and Joe's pride possession was only to be used for special occasions. I started at one end of the field and gave Sugar a free rein to gallop as fast as she could. Luckily, the alfalfa field was almost grown before the next cutting. It took about five weeks to mature. Going absolutely full speed, Sugar detected something in the alfalfa that unexpectedly spooked her. She made a perfect left turn, and I went straight over the side of Sugar's shoulder and head. I went straight as an arrow in a swan dive.

The alfalfa growth was long enough to break my fall. I hit the ground and wondered what had happened. By that time, Sugar was halfway to the horse barn. I had to complete my errand on foot and walked home. I told everybody about my mishap. Richard usually spoke his mind by saying, "What the hell, Fritz? You could have busted your ass." That got a big chuckle and laughs from the family members. Sugar and I were still friends. It was all part of growing up on a dairy farm.

Chapter 3

How My Parents Came to America

I am getting a little ahead in my story, but it would be very appropriate to tell my parents' Swiss story. Why and how did they come to America? I had the wonderful occasion to ask Mom and Dad to go to the 1962 World's Fair. I knew it would be a special treat, particularly for my dad. As a young unmarried man, he went to the 1915 San Francisco World's Fair, less than ten years after the devastating earthquake struck the growing vibrant city. I was going on a business trip in Seattle to attend a SHARE conference, a national group that utilized IBM large-scale scientific computers. This was a conglomeration of all the top computer software experts in the nation.

I visited many relatives and Swiss friends on the trip. I took some extra vacation time so my parents could visit many Swiss friends and relatives in Seattle and the greater Seattle area. Numerous relative visits, scenic vistas, and overnight stops highlighted our journey in Dad's 1960 Buick. We visited one's of Dad's sisters, Bertha, in Gilroy, California. We made other stops at the Swiss Hall in Modesto.

In Tillamook, Oregon, and Francis, Washington, we visited relatives and friends. In addition, we visited various beautiful scenic locations along the California and Oregon coasts. Early along the way, it was reported that Marilyn Monroe had died of unexplained causes. Mom followed some of the celebrities and was somewhat saddened by the loss of Marilyn so tragically.

On the trip, I read President Richard Nixon's *Six Crises*. I was in my early thirties when I made this trip with my parents. It was filled with many memories. Unbeknown at the time, my dad was in the early stages of cancer. He passed away approximately a year later at the age of seventy-one. Mom lived to be eighty-five years of age and died of cancer in 1982. I felt blessed that I was able to take my dad and mom on their last vacation trip before my father's demise.

Visiting Seattle

I attended a SHARE working group conference in Seattle during the 1962 World's Fair. The state of Washington has special memories to both my mom and my dad. They were married in Chehalis, Washington, in August 1922. Mom's destination was Washington when she came to America. I also had two uncles and an aunt living in the greater Seattle area. When I told my mom that I was going to Seattle on business, I asked if they would like to tag along. They both jumped at the chance. They both were very excited about going since it had been quite a while since they had been on a vacation trip to visit their relatives and Swiss friends in the state of Washington.

the 1962 Seattle World's Fair

The Swiss Chalet Restaurant

All three of us were strolling around, and I spotted a Swiss restaurant. Dad spotted it after I mentioned it to him. He was excited for two reasons, namely the word *Swiss*, and probably more importantly, the thought of good old Swiss beer got Dad's extreme attention. Mom went along for the ride. Ordering lunch, the restaurant was rather quiet. I called the waiter over and told him, in my very poor Swiss dialect, "*Mi fatter and mutter bischt ein switzer.*"

He said in Swiss, "You mean, a real *switzer* from Canton *Schwyz*?"

I responded by saying in Swiss, "Ya yaw," which translated very close to "You're damn right."

The waiter immediately went over to the Swiss band and whispered something in the bandleader's ear. He told all the guests, "We have a Swiss family visiting us today. Let's give them a *switzer velcomen.*"

All of a sudden, they played a very popular spirited Swiss folk song for the occasion.

Dad raised his stein and chugalugged some beer, and then he gave a broad smile to say thank you.

We finished our bratwurst, and Dad and I had a couple more brews. We left with applause and smiles that lasted the rest of the day.

Many potential customers decided to enter the chalet. We brought in many new happy customers. The restaurant did not give me a bill and thanked us for visiting their chalet. Dad enjoyed the Swiss music, and he enjoyed the Swiss beer—as much if not more. What a fantastic day.

Mom had a glass of a nice Swiss white wine. She enjoyed the music and wine, and she was getting into the spirit of this wonderful and jumpy atmosphere. Then we enjoyed many other exhibits and entertainment venues. One of the venues was a burlesque show. We did not attend the show, but a couple of burlesque queens who were dancing at the entrance got my attention. Mom encouraged us to scurry by, but Dad and I took our time observing the sights.

As we left the area, Dad looked back to get one last look. Mom joking said, "You sindabucks," which was a euphemism for "shame on you." I stayed a few nights with Mom and Dad at the motel.

In order to tease Mom, I would jokingly tell dad in my corrupt Swiss, "Hey, Dad, after Mom goes to sleep, why don't you and I go back to the fair and take in the burlesque show." I said it loud enough for Mom to hear my clandestine plan. Both of my parents laughed about it.

Mom reminded me, "You are a good boy. You would not do that."

"Yes, Mother dear."

This is a further indication of how the family was raised. Thank God.

Wandering around the Fair

The other story is not a story—but more of a rare coincidence. About ten days before, I was having a meeting in my office at Edwards AFB with some IBM personnel. I told them that I planned to take my mom and dad to the world's fair next week. They responded by hoping that my folks would have a great time. "You have a great trip and enjoy the fair."

That day, I took a little time to roam about the fair by myself. Would you believe it that the same two IBM guys were walking down the main strip? I spotted them. This was totally unplanned. Those IBM marketers traveled all around the United States. They decided to go to the Seattle World's Fair almost on a whim. There I was, and they were there. I decided to walk by them and surprise them with a casual, kind hello.

They said hello back without looking. Dale Edwards who was the account representative for IBM for Edwards AFB was a very good friend. He was the nephew of the very famous Glen Edwards, and Edwards AFB was named in his honor. When he recognized my voice, he said, "Wait a minute. Is that you, Fritz?"

I said, "The one and only."

We marveled at the timely coincidence. We conversed for quite a while—until I had to meet up with my parents. They gave me pointers about what to see. I told Dale that I would see him when I returned. We had some business to talk about. End of coincidence.

Ferry Ride to British Columbia

Mom particularly wanted to see the Butchart Gardens near Victoria, British Columbia, and then go up to Nanaimo and over to British Columbia to see the famous Stanley Park in Vancouver. So we took a large ferry boat from Seattle to Victoria. The Buick was transported in the underbelly of the ferry. We also rented a stateroom so Mom could rest and freshen up.

We had a few hours, so Dad and I spent some time at the bar. It had been a while since I had a private sit-down with my father with a cold beer or two. Dad never spoke much about his youth and about living in Switzerland. When I got about halfway through my second can of Olympia beer, I posed the $64,000-dollar question to him, which was made popular by the television program title by the same name.

Dad in Switzerland (Family Photo)

Dad played in a Swiss band that featured much brass. Dad is holding his trumpet in the back row in the middle. Dad was very musically inclined. He would hum and sing by himself, making up words and short lyrics. I remember him making up lyrics to "My Country Tis of Thee."

My country tis of thee
Sweet land of liberty, my name is Fritz;
Bring in the sauerkraut, don't leave the weenies out:
And bring in a barrel of beer, and we'll all say here.

Why Did Dad Come to America?

I asked my dad, "Whatever bit you in the ass to come to America?"

Dad had some well-known gestures, and he would raise his right hand and arc his hand over the top of his head to scratch the left side of his head, next to his left ear, for inspiration. After very little scratching, he simply responded that there was no future for him in Switzerland. There was very little land left for agricultural unless you could farm vertically. The Swiss custom was to will the parents' estate to the oldest son.

Dad was born in the middle of ten siblings. He had two sisters who had previously moved to America. Margarethe sponsored Dad to come to America. My dad's younger brother John immigrated to America after my dad made it successfully.

Why did Mom come to America? (Family Photo)

Mom is the oldest sibling standing behind her father. Mom's father died at a young age, and Mom went to work to help support the family. Three of her brothers came to America. One sister, Anna, came to America and lived in my hometown of Wasco. The other sister, Kathrine, settled in New Zealand and raised a large family. Two brothers, Rupert and Joseph, lived in the state of Washington. Mom's brother, Aloise, lived in Wasco and milked cows for my dad. Mom came to America sponsored by her brother Joe.

Mom came to America at the request of a Swiss suitor. Her brothers did not want her to marry this suitor, and they hid her out in a small town called Chehalis, Washington. Mom was employed in another Swiss family's home as a housekeeper. As fate would have it, my dad found out about my mom being in America. Dad's family knew the Miller family because they lived on the other side of the mountain in a small community called Kussnacht, Canton, Schwyz. The families belonged to the same Catholic church. Dad was about five years older than Mom, and Dad came to America when he was about eighteen years old, which meant that he hadn't seen Mom for at least ten years. Dad was off to the races.

Quick Courtship

Dad was about thirty years old at the time and found out that Mom (Marie Marti) had come to America. They went on a whirlwind courtship in the state of Washington that lasted about three weeks. Mom and Dad got married in August 1922, and the newly married couple returned to the small town of Wasco.

Dad had a partnership with another Swiss friend by the name of Joe Strieff. They owned a very fertile piece of dairy farm property. It was very successful. They worked long and strenuous hours, farming and milking cows daily. Joe Strieff got married as well and began a family at about the same time as my parents. My sister Mary and brother Joe were born in the farmhouse near Pond, California which was five miles north of Wasco.

Return to Switzerland

In 1927, my dad sold his property along with his partner, and they both returned to Switzerland with their families. Through hard work, persistence, and daily dedication, they were able to amass suitable estates and enough money to travel back to their home country with their families. They had sufficient funds to purchase another farm and begin a larger dairy farm just south east of Wasco.

My brother Aloise was born in Switzerland and possessed dual citizenship. Dad built a new home on the dairy farm, and I was born in the master bedroom. A total of eight siblings were raised on the dairy farm. It was immigrants like my dad who made this country great. The growth and expansion of agriculture in the nineteenth and twentieth centuries was absolutely phenomenal. I am very proud to be the son of a Swiss immigrant. In addition, I am proud to be an American despite its many problems and self-made troubles.

Return to Switzerland in 1948 (Family Photos)

I was a senior in high school when Mom, Dad, and Aloise went to Switzerland for another visit. It had been more than twenty years since their previous visit. Aloise was in Europe, which left many of duties on the farm to be accomplished by the rest of the family and other part-time help.

Mom overlooking hometown (Family Photos)

Aloise, Dad's sister Ida, Mom, and Dad in the Alps

Chapter 4

Milking Cows

During the middle of World War II, my uncle Aloise, who was one of the two dairymen milking cows on the farm, suffered from acute appendicitis and couldn't work for a few months. It was very difficult to get dairymen, particularly during wartime. My brother Aloise and I were pressed into service at fourteen and seventeen years of age. This was a very difficult and arduous 24/7 job. I remember our uncle telling us about a teacher's tour of our dad's dairy farm. They all were very interested in their first visit to a cow barn. One said, "I would like to see a buttermilk cow."

Milking Cows at a Very Early Age

We would arise at two o'clock every morning, rain or shine. We began the day and finished about eight, and then we repeated the process at two in the afternoon and finished at eight at night, making it a twelve-hour day—seven days a week. Needless to say, this was a long day. I would get some sleep between the morning and afternoon shifts.

We would attend Mass on Sundays. I don't remember much of the preaching, but we never missed Mass. I remember that my brother Joe was in the navy and was home on furlough. On some nights, he would get home about the time that Aloise and I had to get up to milk cows. He would say good morning to us, and we would say good night to him. The work was long and tiring. We had to spray the milk house to get rid of the blackened ceiling covered with flies, scoop up the dead flies, and clean the kitchen. This was very important to keep the bacteria count low. It was periodically inspected by the county. Then we would get all of the machine equipment ready for milking the cows.

Cows to the Barn

We would herd in the cows, twenty at a time and arrange each cow in a stall. We washed the cows and fed the cows beet bulp which is made from sugar beets. My dad manufactured corn silage made out of corn that was raised on the farm. We feed this silage to the cows along with the beet bulp to enhance milk production.

Big Silo Cutting and Storing Corn Silage (Family Photo)

The corn was raised on the farm. This corn was harvested with a corn binder, which bundled about a dozen corn stocks. These bundled stocks would be transported to the corn cutter and offloaded into the corn-cutting machine. The huge tractor would be coupled with the corn cutter to drive the attached blower to deposit the silage about thirty feet for storage in the huge silo. As I got a little older, I would perform most of the chores to make silage. Silage was a staple food for milk cows to enrich milk nutrients.

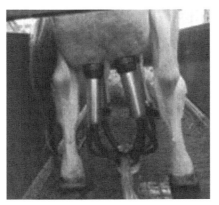

Milking cows by machine and by hand.
Then we would begin milking cows by machine.

Montz would strip milk the cows by hand.

Milk Refrigeration

We had to lug the milk into the milk house in ten-gallon cans and lift the can over our heads into a large cooler. The milk would trickle down over a refrigeration unit and into very sturdy ten-gallon aluminum can and stored for pickup and delivery to and by the Wasco Creamery. Then we would have to repeat the process four additional times and go at it. So, while the next group of twenty cows would be processed in, I would go near the silo and fall sleep on the hard ground for a few minutes. It sure felt good. Some of the cows did not like to be machine milked. They had to be milked by hand, which added to the labors. This was accomplished at the end of the shift. I got experience in milking cows by hand as well as by machines. Those cows were very stubborn.

Farm home, yard, barns, and milk house right next to refrigeration tower (Family Photo)

Beware of the Cow Kickers

Talking about being stubborn and ornery, three cows were kickers. My older brother made up names for them. The Holstein was Hitler. Holstein Friesians are a breed of dairy cattle originating from the Dutch provinces of north Holland and Friesland and Schleswig-Holstein in northern Germany and Jutland. They are known as the world's highest-production dairy animals. The guernsey was Mussolini. The Guernsey is a breed of dairy cattle from the island of Guernsey in the Channel Islands. It is fawn or red and white in color and is hardy and docile. Its milk is rich in flavor, high in fat and protein, and has a golden-yellow tinge due to its high beta-carotene content. This cow is not a good characterization of Mussolini, but it will have to do. The Jersey was Tojo. The Jersey is a British breed of small dairy cattle from the Channel Islands. It is one of three Channel Island cattle breeds (Wikipedia). Tojo was the Japanese general of the army and was rather rotund. See the resemblance?

Dad was an equal-opportunity employer. He had cows from all over the world, namely Germany, England, and Holland. Naming Hitler after a Holstein cow was appropriate because the cow was the biggest, strongest, and stupidest ornery cuss that gave the most milk and the most trouble. He had a good back-right punch that came from nowhere. I had to learn my lesson.

Old Montz wanted us to get all the experience we could. He never told us which cows were the kickers. We had to fend for ourselves. My brother and I got kicked around a bit—accompanied by a loud, throaty laugh from Montz. He knew that we would not get seriously hurt. He didn't take into account our feelings. I got kicked unexpectedly about a half a dozen times. Most of the time, I got cow dung all over my face from the blow. I tumbled in cow manure—the really moist kind. The dirtier we looked, the louder he laughed. I chalked this up as another realistic experience in milking cows. This reinforced my decision that I never wanted to milk cows again. *For that matter, I am going to college. Thank you, cows, particularly you bad kickers.*

Lessons Learned

My milking days were a great lesson in life. *College, here I come. My milking days are over.* I learned to work hard early in my life. Despite the fact that I had a heart murmur at the time, milking cows was good for me. My restriction was not to engage in long, strenuous sports activities that would overtax my heart. The cow experience was the right medicine and therapy, and it gave me a very strong incentive to go to college. In addition, all the farm chores and lifting all that milk over my head made me muscular and very athletic. I was lean and mean, as the saying goes. I did not flaunt it or walk around acting macho Camacho, but I did like to jackknife and swan dive in the swimming pool to entertain the girls.

Chapter 5

Airplanes, Rockets, Jets, and German V-2s

My teenage interest in airplanes began as a boy out on the farm. I watched numerous T-6 training aircraft being flown by military cadet pilots assigned at Minter Field, near Bakersfield, California. I would be standing out in the fields, driving a tractor, or driving around the farm, and I could see all these T-6s whirling around and doing practice rolls, minor stunts, and playful war gaming. I was most impressed and took great interest in flying. What a marvelous scene! I must have seen those flying cadets tooling around hundreds of times. If Dad did not own a dairy farm or build that silo, I never would have had the great experience of watching airplanes flying. The silo provided a very visible landmark for new aviators to maintain their locations. How do they fly! Did I really want to fly? I found out in future years employed at Edwards AFB.

Ryan Aircraft T-6 Trainers

These student pilots would practice all kinds of maneuvers in the sky near the Miller farm. Dad had built a very large silo in 1935 that was needed to store silage hay for feeding milk cows. Evidently, the silo was big enough to be used as a large ground reference point for those cadets. There would be more than a dozen of those T-6s flying near the farm at any given time of the day. This training activity went on for most of the war. Airplanes became an extreme interest of mine. I would draw pictures of all the airplanes. I made some airplanes out of model kits. The B-19 aircraft was never produced, but it was fun to draw. It was the largest bomber designed at that time. I liked the beautiful picture of the P-38.

Needless to say, watching airplanes fly and drawing airplanes etched an indelible nameplate in my mind. Ryan Aircraft was the same aircraft manufacturer that built the *Spirit of St. Louis*, which was made famous in 1927 by Mr. Lindbergh. This was the same year that my parents returned to Switzerland with my oldest sister Mary and my oldest brother, Joe. My brother Aloise was born in Switzerland prior to the family's return to America. I was born three years later. Aloise is the only sibling to possess dual citizenship.

NACA (NASA) X Series Research Vehicles

The NACA was engaged in all kinds of research testing and exploring the unknown with all of the X series vehicles.

Exceeding the Speed of Sound

Captain Chuck Yeager broke the sound barrier (Mach 1), flying the X-1A, on October 14, 1947.

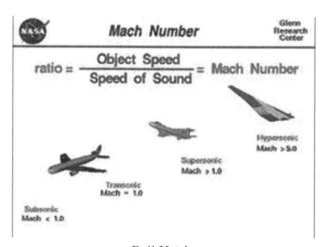

Bell X-1A.

Chuck Yeager and Glamorous Glennis.

X-1 in flight.

Life Magazine Article

In the high school library, I read about Chuck Yeager and his historical achievement. He was featured in a very impressive *Time* magazine article, including a fabulous picture of the X-1 landing on the Rogers dry lake bed. I thought to myself, *Way to go, Yeager.* I went about my senior year not thinking much more about it. Later in my career, I had the privilege of meeting him a number of times.

Lockheed F-80 Shooting Star

Then jets came along. In 1946, the Wasco Airport had a dedication ceremony. The event included a surprise flyover of three F-80 Shooting Stars flying about a hundred feet off the ground. That really rang my ears.

What an impression! I saw the sight and heard the deafening roaring sound of jets flying by in a flash. It left a lasting impression and a desire for jet aircraft.

My Lockheed Bridge Player Friend

When I retired, I was playing bridge with my usual partner against a couple of other bridge club members. Mac McDougal was a wonderful guy. He was a test pilot for Lockheed and a very accomplished flight test engineer for the Lockheed Skunk Works. He worked on many classified programs, including the SR-71. This heightened my interest. I told him about the first time I ever saw a jet fly at the dedication ceremonies for the airport in my hometown of Wasco. To my amazement, he informed me that he was one of the Lockheed pilots who flew the F-80 Shooting Star at the dedication. What a coincidence—and what a small world! We became good friends after that conversation. We shared many stories.

Confinement

When he was confined to a long-time full-time care facility, I visited him a few times. It was a very sad sight to see him fiddle with the TV remote. He was such an accomplished and dedicated man in his profession, and he was very successful at designing, building, flying, and testing all kinds of Lockheed aircraft. The only thing he could do was to control his TV remote or press the call button for an attendant to help him. It was absolutely unmerciful.

God did show him mercy, and he died a short time later. I must say that Mac McDougal left a great Lockheed legacy and cherished memories for all members of his family. Now, he is sporting angel wings rather than eagle wings and is maneuvering in absolute formation with the angels in heaven. He probably will teach them a few rapid rollovers and split S's that not every test pilot can perform. It was like trying to perform a triple on a trapeze high wire—blindfolded.

German Rockets

Toward the end of World War II, Germany developed drones and V-2 rockets that terrorized England and the Allies. German scientists brought the technology to America with varying amounts of controversy.

V-2 German launch site.
German scientists brought to the United States
to work on rocket technology.

Article authored by history.com

In a move that stirs up some controversy, the United States ships 88 German scientists to America to assist the nation in its production of rocket technology. Most of these men had served under the Nazi regime and critics in the United States questioned the morality of placing them in the service of America. Nevertheless, the U.S. government, desperate to acquire the scientific know-how that had produced the terrifying and destructive V-1 and V-2 rockets for Germany during WWII, and fearful that the Russians were also utilizing captured German scientists for the same end, welcomed the men with open arms. Realizing that the importation of scientists who had so recently worked for the Nazi regime so hated by Americans was a delicate public relations situation, the U.S. military cloaked the operation in secrecy. In announcing the plan, a military spokesman merely indicated that some German scientists who had worked on rocket development had "volunteered" to come to the United States and work for a "very moderate salary." The voluntary nature of the scheme was somewhat undercut by the admission that the scientists were in "protective custody." Upon their arrival in the United States on November 16, newsmen and photographers were not allowed to interview or photograph the newcomers. A few days later, a source in Sweden claimed that the scientists were members of the Nazi team at Peenemunde where the V-weapons had been produced. The U.S. government continued to remain somewhat vague about the situation, stating only that "certain outstanding German scientists and technicians" were being imported in order to "take full advantage of these significant developments, which are deemed vital to our national security." The situation pointed out one of the many ironies connected with the Cold War. The United States and the Soviet Union, once *allies against Germany and the Nazi regime during World War II, were now in a fierce contest to acquire the best and brightest scientists who had helped arm the German forces in order to construct weapons systems to threaten each other.*

My Historical Perceptions and Reflections

Little did I know what was in store for me as a bashful, stuttering boy. I would transition from milking cows, driving farm horses, tractors, and performing other farm chores. I have always said that milking cows was a 24/7 difficult experience that convinced me to go to college. In addition, in my early teenage years, I had the experience of observing, reading, and watching all kinds of technological advancements during World War II. That broadened my interest in airplanes, rockets, and space, which inspired me even more to achieve an advanced education. God put me in the right place at the right time. God guided Dorothy and me through our joint travels. Going from cows to space and raising eight children, God certainly had to be our copilots. I certainly could not have done it alone.

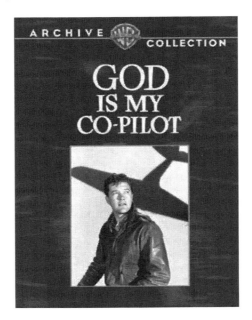

Chapter 6

High School Sports and Activities

I wanted to join high school sports. When I was about eleven years old, the doctors informed my parents that I had a heart murmur. This heart condition prevented me from participating in any strenuous sports activities. The only way for me to get involved in sports activities was to volunteer. As a freshman, I volunteered to perform as a water boy at football games.

The next year, I became a member of chain gang at local football games. In later years, I became an assistant equipment and supplies manager for all sports. For my senior year, I performed duties as the school's top equipment manager. These volunteer duties allowed me to participate and attend all football, basketball, and track activities for Wasco High School. I became friends with all the coaches and many of the students involved in sports.

Many Ethnic Students

Wasco had many different ethnic groups and students from poor families who came to Wasco from the Midwest to find agriculture work. There was a government housing camp located in Wasco. I didn't know or pay attention to who or where the students were from. Since I went to Saint John's Grammar School, I didn't know many of the students initially. There were two very large Hispanic and African Americans living in communities in Wasco. The Wasco High student body was very multicultural. I was friends with all ethnic groups. Hoffman Won, a very bright Asian student, was in my algebra and other mathematics classes. We became the best of friends.

Making Friends

Since I was a rather shy person going into high school and still had a little bit of my childhood stuttering habit, I was still able to converse one-on-one with the coaches and students. As water boy, the football players were glad to see me as I trotted on the field with cold water. Of course, they wanted water, but I was the one who fetched water for them. Sometimes, I would be given a thank you, and I would respond, "Go! Go! Go!"

I was able to attend all of the away games, which kept me quite busy with packing up all the equipment for transit and distributing the equipment prior to the game and then gathering up all of the dirty football gear for the return trip to Wasco. I would unload all the equipment in the evening. Some of the players were very kind and assisted me. This was hard work at times. I enjoyed it. I didn't mind the periodic hard work. After all, I got a bird's-eye view of all the games. All that work was nothing compared to milking cows 24/7.

Makeshift Sports

Even though I was not permitted to perform long-term strenuous activities, I built a pole vault pit, a high jump pit, and set up a makeshift array of hurdles at home on the farm. My brother Aloise held the high school record in the seventy-yard high hurdles. I wanted to get good at running hurdles like my brother, but I couldn't participate in formal track events. I would have given him some competition. I was in pretty good shape because of all the physical activity that I was engaged in on the farm. I used to lug milk in ten-gallon aluminum cans and dump the can full of milk above my head into a large container to cool off the milk that trickled down an array of refrigerant cylinders for storage. This hard physical labor put me in excellent shape.

My senior year, I was allowed to participate in sports that did not require an extended strenuous effort. I participated and lettered in three track events: pole vault, high jump, and the long jump. I participated in the annual Tulare High School Relays. Mr. Bob Matthias participated in these relays since he lived in Tulare and went to Tulare High School. About a month later, Bob Mathias won the 1948 Olympic Decathlon Championship at the Olympic Games in Rome, Italy. During the Tulare Relays, Bob Matthias participated in all the track events that I entered and many more. As usual, the custom was that a person a non-running event could begin his competition at any height desired. In all three events that I participated in, I fouled out before Bob Matthias began his competition. He won all three events—and all the other events he entered. He was a very remarkable athlete.

Rome 1948 Decathlon

Bob Matthias won the 1948 decathlon about a month later. When I heard that he won the decathlon championship, I realized that I had lost to absolutely the very best. He was the youngest person ever to win a gold medal in the Olympics, and he repeated his decathlon championship in Helsinki, Finland, four years later.

My brother Richard became principal of Tulare High School. In addition, Dr. Matthias, Bob Matthias's father, was Richard's medical doctor and became acquainted with Bob Matthias. Richard told me that Bob Matthias, as a youngster, was in ill health. His father remarkably restored his health to become one of the most famous athletes who has ever competed in world events.

Richard and Dr. Matthias were good friends. Richard was undergoing his annual physical. One of the procedures was for the doctor to perform a prostate exam. The doctor jokingly asked, "Do you want a second opinion?"

Richard was a little alarmed at such a request. Richard asked quite seriously, "Do I need one?"

The doctor informed him that he would gladly give Richard a second opinion. "Next time, I will use two fingers."

Richard realized that the doctor was joking. Richard said, "No, Doc. One poke, one joke, and one opinion is sufficient."

I said, "Richard, boy, that was really funny." I tried to better that joke when I told him about a comedian on a cruise ship. He compared a doctor's prostate exam to jamming his finger up the patient's butt and then making a long-distance call using a ring-dial phone.

Richard laughed and said, "Exactly. He got that right."

Skiing Escapades

My older siblings made a great looking ski surfboard, called Hitler, which was much better than the one shown below. They sure had a lot of fun—until Hitler decided to land ski. While driving and pulling the surfboard with a skier onboard, it was under the pickup driver's control as he maneuvered down the road next to the canal. The canal had a few quick turns and more gradual turns. This was very sporty, particularly when you negotiated the turns. The skier would swing out in an arc to follow the contours of the canal.

One time, the pickup driver sped too fast as he entered a turn. This added speed and pulled the skier toward the bank and through the tules rather than in a graceful arc around the curve, as intended. Hitler wasn't designed to transition from water through tules and canal banks. Hitler crashed, and as it scrambled through the tules and stumbled and cartwheeled its way down the road, it broke into pieces. Nobody got hurt. The skier was aware of his doom and bailed before the surfboard ran into the canal bank. This was a good omen for the prediction of Hitler's Nazi defeat.

Hitler Surfboard Got Behind the Power Curve

It was like flying an aircraft and applying power when the pilot was behind the power curve. This phenomenon was sadly demonstrated when a pilot out of George AFB, located nearby, attempted to make an emergency landing at Edwards AFB. As he approached the 15,000-foot runway, flying a new F-100, the pilot was having a problem controlling his aircraft. He wobbled in as he approached and wavered down the runway. He tried to execute a go-round by applying maximum power, which was the worst thing to do. Being behind the power curve, as it wobbled, his aircraft was not in proper angle or position to use the added thrust to recover. The added burst of power propelled his aircraft sideways, and the pilot fatally crashed in a massive fireball. It was a pitiful sight. The crash was recorded on one of the takeoff and landing towers near the end of the runway on high-quality 35 mm cameras. The film was a major source of documented evidence for the accident investigation. This tragic accident has been shown many times in the media and movies.

Hitler Crashed

Hitler met its death, not so much as being behind the power curve, but Hitler was being pulled with too much power, which prevented the surfer from making a safe arc around the curve. The surfboard and the surfer were pulled over the riverbank. At the time, a popular song was "Right in the Fuhrer's Face" by Spike Jones.

When der führer's says we is de master race
We heil right in der führer's face
Not to love der x is a great disgrace
So we heil right in der führer's face
When Herr Goebbels says we own the world and space
We heil right in Herr Goebbels's face
When Herr Goring says they'll never bomb dis place
We heil right in Herr Goring's face

My Skiing Escapades

As I got older, I did the same thing with my friends. The advice from my experienced brothers was: "Don't speed up too fast approaching those turns." I carefully followed their advice and judgment. I wouldn't let my cousin Frankie drive the pickup because he was too much of a daredevil. I couldn't trust him. When the other students at the high school found out at that we were waterskiing, they wanted to join in all the fun. I didn't want to take on the responsibility for the other high school rowdies.

One Tough-Looking Football Tackle

One underclassman, a big football jock who played tackle and weighed about 240 pounds, politely asked if he could ski with some of his friends. I was the one who told him very reluctantly no. That infuriated him. "How dare you say no to me?" Every time he saw me, he would clench his fist and try to scare me. "I am going to beat the hell out of you." He came across as serious. He was a popular guy who acted very macho and was known for his pranks. I didn't want to get into that kind of nonsense. He repeated his boast at many locations, occasions, and among his so-called friends. He would get even get madder when I ignored him. I could sense over a period of time that he was making somewhat of a fool of himself. I could hear him as I walked away on more than a few occasions. I continued to ignore him. He would say, "Someday I am going to kick his ass around the block. Why make somebody else's problem your problem?"

He tried to harass me many times. I think he finally decided he wasn't doing himself any good. About a year later, we apologized to each other. I explained why I turned him down. I didn't want to accept the responsibility for him and his mischievous buddies. He seemed to accept my explanation. He finally agreed with me, and we became friends again. I turned the other cheek at my expense. I won the battle peacefully rather than forcibly or stupidly. He realized that he had acted like a bully. I thought to myself, *Right on.*

Chapter 7

My Early Dating Years

On a bright beautiful day in the fall 1945, just after the end of World War II, I began my sophomore year at Wasco High School. I was a very shy redheaded kid who lived on the farm with eight siblings. I was starting my sophomore year and getting my books to begin the first day of class for the fall semester when a pretty freshman brunette with beautiful brown eyes knelt beside me as I stooped to get into my locker. As a freshman, she had her locker directly below me. I don't remember whether we spoke or not, but she was very pretty. I was my shy self. I recall that we did exchange smiles. We did not meet at the water cooler or playing spin the bottle. We met at the book lockers. Her name was Dorothy Alice Worley. Little did I know that years later I would change her name.

Teenage Boys and Girls

As a kid, I stuttered. I wasn't big on making conversation. As the semester rolled on, Dorothy and I would meet at the lockers to exchange our books. I admit that I would go to the lockers to see if she was there. This went on for her whole freshman year and my sophomore year. In my junior year, Dorothy got my sophomore locker, and I graduated to the next level above my old locker. Here we go again. To this day, I don't know if she had it fixed or if the school was following a planned procedure. Then it happened again my senior year, and my locker mate returned. As shy as I was, it took a long time for me to take advantage of the situation.

My Dates with Dorothy

In my senior year, I decided to ask her out for a date. We went out a few times to movies, football games, and dances. I got enough courage, after our fifth date, to drive out near the Wasco Airport, which was somewhat quiet and peaceful. I figured I had a good chance to pitch a little romance. My intentions were admirable as far as I was concerned. All I wanted was a little kissy face.

When Dorothy realized what I had in mind, she turned the auto ignition key to start the car. It was her way of telling me no thank you. Like a bashful gentleman, I started the car and drove her home. It was very obvious that she wasn't interested in me or romance. I summed it all up by saying that she had a bad hair day. With here long bundled hair, she certainly had many opportunities to have bad hair days.

Dorothy in high school (Family Photo)

One More Date

I decided to take her out one last time. We had a nice evening at the high school dance. After about half a dozen dates over a three-month time, I thought to myself, *Boy, tonight is the night to get my first kiss.* Dorothy was absolutely beautiful. I escorted her to the door, and I very romantically tried to kiss her good night. She discouraged me once again. That was it. I gave up. I didn't date her again until later in college. She told me much later that she had an abusive stepfather. She had to be careful about who she dated. He had a tendency to run off her other dates. She didn't want that to happen to me. Unbeknownst to Dorothy, my dad knew her stepfather because they met by chance. He knew my dad was a successful dairy farmer in Wasco. Dad occasionally went to the saloon where Dorothy's stepfather worked as a bartender when heavy-equipment operators jobs were scarce or not available. I met Dorothy's stepfather later. We got along just fine. He liked my dad. He would talk my ear off.

Junior-Senior Banquet

We had met socially again at the junior-senior banquet. I looked into her beautiful brown eyes. "Hi. Good to see you. How have you been?"

We exchanged pleasantries, and I realized that she was going to sit next to me. I thought to myself, *Serendipity*.

She told me very nicely that she had arranged the seating when she was on the planning committee. I really enjoyed her company, but what was this all about? Maybe she did care for me after all. For some unexplained reason, I did not follow up and ask her out on a date that summer or during Dorothy's following two semesters of her senior year. No doubt, I was as stupid as a post.

Other Girls and Anticipating College

Meanwhile, I was dating other girls—but nothing serious. I graduated from Wasco High and was accepted to attend Bakersfield Junior College in the fall of 1948 as a business major. I worked every day but one Sunday that summer. I was anticipating my entry into college. I was completely focused on college.

During my second semester, I was stressed out by an incident that took place in my psychology class. I was in no frame of mind to date. I lost contact with Dorothy that summer. It was a very busy summer for me and my other siblings.

Bakersfield Junior College Renegades, here I come.

Chapter 8

Joe Miller and Sons and Miller Brothers

My two older brothers, Joe and Aloise, were the farmers in the family along with our dad. They became Joe Miller and Sons. Dad formed this partnership after it was apparent that I didn't like to milk cows and that farming was not my interest. He knew I wanted to go to college, which he supported wholeheartedly with encouragement and finances. In fact, he was very proud of the fact that I was going to the university.

I remember the time he drove me up to Berkeley to look for a residence. We stopped at a Shell gas station in Fresno. In those days, the gas attendants would fill her up for you. Dad would stand there and talk to the attendant to inform him that we were on our way to Berkeley. "My son is going to the big university."

In my embarrassment, I walked around to the other side of the car. I was a very shy lad. Despite the fact that there was now Joe Miller and Sons rather than just the Miller farm, it didn't matter. All the siblings worked the farm as a team and did everything to help each other navigate the farm.

Billy the Workhorse

My job was to maneuver Billy to go back and forth and pull the Jackson fork filled with hay. It was rotated into the proper place by a huge derrick to build a uniform haystack. Billy was my specialty, the Jackson fork was Aloise's responsibility, and Joe would be the haystack builder. I remember the time we had a whole series of haystacks that were visible enough to form another landmark.

Billy was a worn-out horse that did a great job pulling a cable back and forth. Billy was dressed in a special harness that allowed him to handle a double tree that was connected to a cable that was attached to a huge derrick structure about thirty feet tall.

Derrick (Prior to 1923)

The derrick had a swivel arm that rotated from side to side. The other end of the cable would be attached to a Jackson fork, which was used to scoop up a large bundle of hay to be offloaded as the derrick was rotated in place to form a large haystack. The following pictures show how the fork was used and how the derrick was used to unload the hay.

Jackson Fork (Family Photos)
Clemons Strieff, a farmworker, with me on the left looking down with my brother Aloise standing next to me. In addition, my younger brother Richard is irrigating the large cotton field in the background.

Hay being offloaded to the hay stack

Joe stacking hay
My oldest brother, Joe, on the receiving end of shocking hay, which is the triggering end that dumps the hay to form a haystack. In the background is shown a number of milk cows next to another hay stack that is partially visible.

When we were finished for the day, I would take worn-out Billy back to the horse barn. One time, I decided to ride him back instead. I jumped on his back. In the process, my foot and leg got caught up between the strap that was part of his harness and Billy's back. This spooked him and scared me, and he started to buck rather violently. He kept bucking.

I lost control and ended up on the belly side of the horse—holding on for dear life and upside down. I thought I had it. Thank God I wasn't trampled. He was tired enough from working, and he was completely worn out trying to buck me off. Billy eventually calmed down out of mere exhaustion, and I carefully unleashed myself from the predicament. I never tried that again. Billy and I stayed good friends.

Sequoia drive through tree (Family Photo).

Mom and the wash house (Family Photo).

Sequoia Vacation

When I was about sixteen years old, my dad and my three older siblings took off on a short vacation. I can visualize Mom washing all of the family laundry using very primitive means. Mom was with her cat, the laundry, garbage cans, and a makeshift stone stove for heating water to clean dirty clothes. A laundry bag and other items were littered on the ground. A large washtub was used for heating the water and cleaning the laundry.

She would have to rinse out the clothes as best she could. Then she would use a large hand-turn roller to squeeze out the water prior to hanging up the laundry on the clothesline. We all would chip in to help her with some of the tasks we could do without getting in her way. Then she would have to hang all those clothes up on the clothesline. Mom had an old worn-out mechanical washing machine that was used for the tender stuff. This was a long, arduous task, but this was necessary because inexpensive labor-saving devices weren't available on the market.

We had a large GE refrigerator that we called the icebox. The big coils on the top rattled and rolled in the dead of night. Life was not easy in those days. Just imagine how many clothes would have to be washed, cleaned, dried, and stored away for a family of eight kids, which included five filthy working and mischievous boys. Mom hardly ever complained.

My Opportunity to Manage the Miller Ranch

I took on the responsibility of managing the farm. There wasn't a lot of managing to do, but it felt really good being in charge. I would get in the best pickup truck and survey the farm with my left arm hanging out of the driver side of the truck. That's what farmers did, of course. When I loaded hay, I didn't just throw the hay on the wagon. I made sure that it was loaded neatly and squared off. It really didn't matter because we would just shove the hay off the wagon as we passed along the lengthy cow-feeding troughs alongside the cow-holding corrals. I just had the feeling that I wanted to do the work exactly right. That work ethic served me well as I took on more and more responsibility at Edwards AFB.

Miller Brothers' Partnership

A conflict arose within the Joe Miller and Sons partnership. My brothers wanted to mechanize cotton picking. Big cotton-picking machines were available on the market. Joe and Aloise had seen a few other farmers using them. They wanted Joe Miller and Sons to purchase one. "The future is upon us. Let's join the parade." They did it on their own.

Mechanical cotton pickers (International Harvester)

Dad did not want to spend that kind of money. The brothers decided to form Miller Brothers to engage in the mechanical cotton-picking business. This turned out to be a good move, but it was a lot of work. They picked their own cotton—and a lot of cotton owned by many of the surrounding farmers in the Wasco area. Dad eventually had to admit that it was very worthwhile enterprise. The Joe Miller and Sons Partnership remained amicable. Good for those Miller brothers. Joe and the Weasel struck pay dirt.

Picking, Loading, and Transporting Cotton

I would watch them pick cotton in the fields, dump the hay into a large trailer, and transport the trailer with a Minneapolis Moline Z rubber-tire tractor two miles to the cotton gin near the railroad underpass by the outskirts of downtown Wasco. Aloise's job was to mount the cotton picker's storage container to tramp down the cotton. In addition, he had to repeat this procedure as the brothers would offload the cotton from the picker's container to a large trailer. This would provide more storage space for transporting cotton to the cotton gin.

Aloise was showing off one day as we watched him jump inside the wagon, which was about eight feet tall. He hit an uneven soft spot of cotton and went ass over tea kettle and tumbled flat on his wallet sprawled on the other end of the wagon. He only hurt his pride. We all roared laughing at his mishap laying foolishly on the other end of the flatbed trailer. We all experienced vicissitudes of the dangers and mistakes of working on a dairy farm. We were all in good physical shape, and a little misfortune now and then was all part of farm life. In retrospect, living a farm life as relatively short as I experienced as a young teenager and a very young adult was a life I will cherish and never forget. God is good.

Summers on the Farm

No more milking cows, thank goodness, however I still liked to drink milk. During the summer months, when I wasn't in college or the university, Dorothy went back to her regular routine duties helping her mother with her younger siblings. I returned and enjoyed seeing the family and performing the many summer farm duties. There were many chores to be accomplished: mowing hay, pitching hay, storing hay, irrigating, picking cotton, plowing the fields for new crops, and chopping weeds. In addition, chopping indestructible Johnson grass, which seemed to flare up all over the farm, fertilize crops, work at another small grape farm about two miles west of the main farm that Dad owned, and general maintenance and cleanup tasks. These tasks seemed to never end. We did have some time for recreation. The brothers and some older neighbor kids went swimming a lot in the farm reservoir and the neighbor's reservoir, which was very close to our home. When I rose at five o'clock one morning to quick-start crop irrigation, I noticed the neighbor's reservoir spilling over its broad and high banks. I immediately shut down the neighbor's big water well pump and quickly started shoveling dirt onto the top of the banks that were gradually spilling over. Another twenty minutes, with all of my family sleeping, we would have woken up to a reenactment of the sinking of the *Titanic*. God watched out for us. God is good.

Joe and Richard tending a young heifer (Family Photos)

Brother Joe on a tractor

Aloise in the cotton field

Dad Aloise, Joe, and Richard

Me and Aloise

Back of home, backyard, and barns
Cooling tower in the background to the left of the milk house

Rose sitting on a tractor

Chapter 9

Sisters, Fun, Music, and Mary

There is lot more to talk about than male sports and macho stuff. I had an older sister, Mary, and two younger sisters, Rose and Theresa.

Mom, Rose, Mary, and Theresa

Mary was selected as the rodeo queen for the biggest event of the year in the town of Wasco. She got to ride in the parade and participate in all the events and festivities. Years later, Rose repeated the same honor. Of course, that made the whole family very proud. I think that the two Miller sisters were the only pair of sisters to be recognized for this great honor.

My sisters provided the music in the family. Mary liked to sing, Rose played the piano, and Theresa as a young girl would hang right in there.

Beer Barrel Polka

During World War II, the Beer Barrel Polka was extremely popular. You could hear it played everywhere. When my mom and dad would take us to Pismo Beach, the fun house played it constantly. We all sang it at home a lot.

Theresa graduated from Holy Names College in Oakland, California. She became an accomplished soprano. She would sing at all kinds of family functions. In later years, Theresa joined a very accomplished musical theatrical group in Bakersfield, and she performed leading roles in a number of popular musical productions. We would all go Bakersfield to see our baby sister perform. I remember Rich saying, after one of her performances, "Theresa put tears in my eyes." I didn't admit it, but I suffered from the same sentimental malady. One of Theresa's favorite stunts was running like hell toward me or Rich, and then she would jump, expecting us to catch her from falling down. We always caught her with a big laugh. We were macho.

All of us kids eventually destroyed the family Zither by pounding on it like a piano. You can say that we had a lot of music in the home. My brother Aloise had a large collection of popular records that he allowed to be used at high school dances. I was a beginner piano player. I took piano lessons at Saint John's Catholic Grammar School instead of getting involved in sports due to my heart murmur. Richard, Mary, and I liked to sing and joined the church choir. Eventually, Rose played the church organ.

Sheet Music

I bought modern sheet music that Mary and Rose played on the home piano. I was too bashful to sing at home, but I could sing to the animals, tractors, and crops while driving the tractor—and for the birds. I thought I could sing. Bing Crosby, Perry Como and Frank Sinatra were my favorites. I played a lot of piano. Since I couldn't sight-read very well, I learned a bunch of harmony chords limited to a single key. I could play a lot of modern tunes by ear. My sisters were much better at it than I was, and they could sight-read very well. My sisters were special. I was around Mary a lot more than my younger siblings. They were young when I went away to college, and then I went off to the university and got married. I missed most of their teenage years.

Mary and Fritz (Family Photo)

This picture was taken when we were on our way to Mass at Saint John's Church. Mary and I washed a lot of dishes. She would talk a lot about many things. She dated quite a bit. Mary could handle herself very well. Mary and a bunch of her friends would go to Minter Field, halfway between Wasco and Bakersfield. They would dance with the cadets at special dances on various occasions. She worked at the local malt shop. She knew practically everybody in town. She could mix with the guys just as well as her many other friends. Mary had many boyfriends.

Boys Like to Tease

Rich and I would tease Mary terribly about a special friend she knew and liked. His name was Johnny Coyne. Richard and I would tease Mary almost unmercifully. She would get even with us. As we would leave from taking a bath from the single bathroom in the house, she would run after us and try to pull our towels off to embarrass Richard and me by making us barefoot all over. She never caught us as we scampered out of her reach. I asked Mary one day what she would do if she ever caught us. She said, "Nothing." She knew that we could outrun her, but she sure had fun acting like she would really rip off our towels. Mary said that she knew our stuff by saying, "Hell, I changed your diapers many times. I don't have to catch you. I have seen all I needed to see before."

Sometime later, Rich was sporting a bruise. I asked him what happened. He responded, "I said a little too much Johnny Coyne."

Mary would go out with bother Joe, his friends, including Johnny Coyne, and they would have a lot of good, wholesome, active fun. The farm was located next to a very large land company that owned a lot of fallow land. There were big levees with trails all over the place. They made a sled, attached it to the pickup truck, and pulled the sled up and down those levees. Mary participated and joined in all the fun. Mary was not a tomboy, and she was very secure in her own skin. Everybody loved Mary, and she was a great sport. Very sadly, after becoming an officer as a pilot in the Army Air Corps, Captain John Coyne lost his life during World War II in the crash of a B-17 bomber.

B-17 flying fortress (US Army Air Corps Photo)

Chapter 10

Hunting, Fishing, Pearl Harbor, and the Wasco Rifle Club

Richard and I liked to go hunting with Dad, who loved to go hunting. His idea was to travel around in the pickup truck and look for doves that were resting on the telephone wires on the dairy farm and the neighboring farms. Dad would hunt the easy way. Instead of being sporty about bagging doves, he would open the door of the truck, rest the double-barrel shotgun between the door and the truck frame, and go pow—sometimes with both barrels simultaneously. He could do a lot of damage with a double-barrel shotgun. Richard and I would hear the loud gun blast as well as the shock wave in the cab of the truck. One time, Dad got three doves in one double blast. In any case, Dad's hunting ability really impressed Richard and me as seven and nine-year-olds hunting with our dad. That loud blast would scare off the other doves in the area. Richard got all excited and asked Dad to go hunt for more doves.

Game Warden

We were driving around looking for more birds on the farm and other farms nearby. I don't know if Dad always hunted in season or not. Dad was a good talker and was very friendly with neighboring farmers. As he was driving around, a nice gentleman acted like he wanted to talk to Dad.

He might have been a new farmer in the area, so Dad stopped to see what he wanted. Dad wasn't sure who he was, but he wasn't going to take any chances. He might be a game warden. Dad rolled down the window, and they began small talk. Richard couldn't keep his mouth shut. He was so proud of Dad that he blurted out that Dad got three doves with one shot. Dad immediately tried to shut Richard up. Richard was more determined to spill the beans and embellished the feat. He blurted out again that Dad got three birds with one shot. Dad wasn't sure where this guy was coming from. As it turned out, it was a game warden. He got a big kick out of Richard's honesty, enthusiasm, and how much pride that he showed for his dad. All the while, I just sat there taking it all in. The game warden laughed as Dad got a serious look on his face. The game warden didn't have the guts to pinch Dad—even if he broke the gaming rules and laws—in front of his two sons with Richard being so enthusiastic. The warden sternly reminded Dad not to hunt during the offseason. Dad thanked him for being considerate, happily started the car, and drove home. Dad didn't scold Richard because he knew that he was guilty and that Richard didn't know any better. This was a good lesson for Dad to stay within the rules. No more hunting until next dove season. Richard and I cleaned the dove, Mom cooked, and Dad declined to eat dove. Richard and I really enjoyed the way Mom cooked dove.

Dove Hunting with My Older Brothers

My older brothers would like to go dove hunting within season. I had my own twenty-gauge shotgun. I would tag along with Joe and Aloise. They were true sportsman and hunted dove out in the open where birds would gather for food and water. They knew where the doves were more plentiful in the southern San Joaquin Valley. We would hunt in the foothills of Ducor, which was about fifty miles from Wasco. We were very sporty the way we would hunt, and we would wait in their habitats to fly over or near our strategically located spots. When the doves would arrive and get within range, each of us would stand up, point our shotgun, and go bang, bang, and bang. My two older brothers were pretty good shots. I wasn't bad on occasion, but I tried to be helpful and be the retriever. My brother Joe shot one that spiraled into the ground in tall grass sixty or so yards away. I said, "Joe don't worry. I kept my eye on it, and I will fetch it." I took off like a rabbit and kept a bead on the location of the dead dove. I ran full speed into a knee-high barbed-wire fence. I immediately disappeared from sight in the tall grass. I fell ass over teakettle. Sorry, folks, but that is the way we spoke on the farm. The brothers couldn't see me. They wondered if I fell in a hole or broke my leg or my neck. I survived, uninjured, got up, reoriented myself, and found the dead dove after all. I proudly returned, and they were relieved that I didn't bust my ass and laughed like hell. I didn't think it was that funny. I had a torn pant leg. We were very successful that day, and we all bagged our limits. We got thirty doves among us. I shot two. I only had a twenty-gauge shotgun compared to their automatic twelve-gauge shotguns. I beat them in one category. I retrieved a lot more doves than they did. We had a very successful outing.

Upon our return home, we cleaned the doves. Mom prepared a special feast. The two doves I shot had fewer and smaller buckshot from my small twenty-gauge shotgun. I went dove hunting with my brothers for many seasons as a teenager. I have many cherished memories, particularly my disappearing act.

Dad's Favorite Fishing Hole

Quite often, we would go fishing with Pop. We would go about twenty miles west of Wasco on Highway 46 near the Lost Hills Junction, which is now the 5 Freeway. Jerry Slew made a nice secluded fishing canal to capture the flood irrigation water that overflowed from the crops. This canal would run almost every day. It wasn't large enough to be called a river, but it was about twenty-five feet in width and meandered and was alive with catfish, carp, bottom fish, and crawdads. Not many people knew about this canal, and Dad did not advertise it either.

My dad and two or three of my brothers would go fishing after Sunday Mass. Dad prided himself on being a good fisherman. About every mile, there would dams that made good crossover roads for farmers. Large pipes were embedded in the dams, which allowed the water to tunnel under the road. Dad always liked to fish on the side where the outlet made a large swirling motion, which provided a rather large and deep fishing hole. This was our dad's favorite spot, but he didn't catch many fish to brag about this particular day.

My Favorite Fishing Spot

I decided that I would fish on the other side at the entrance to the dam. The water was still, almost like a lake, and the water collected and flowed freely through the pipe. I liked the still waters, and Dad liked the large swirling bowl of deep water. He always liked to catch big catfish, but he would settle for a less desirable carp. Despite the fact that he would catch his share of fish, he hardly ever caught the big ones. Every once in a while, he would show us his fish as he went to the cooler for another Acme or Dutch Lunch beer.

I was on the other side, patiently fishing, when all of a sudden, I tagged onto a big catfish, probably larger than anyone else has ever caught or seen in the canal. I immediately showed Dad my big catfish. It had a very large mouth. Dad said that I got a good one and was a little chagrinned that his eleven-year-old son got the biggest fish that day—or, for that matter, for quite a while.

Pearl Harbor

That was a big event for me that day, but it was totally and completely overshadowed by the greatest event in the twentieth century. Almost immediately after I caught that big fish, we were told by a rancher driving by in his pickup, with a radio, that Pearl Harbor had been attacked by the Japanese.

December 8, 1941 President Roosevelt Addresses Congress

December 7, 1941 is a date that will live in infamy. The United States of America was suddenly and deliberately attacked by naval and air forces from the empire of Japan. Despite the fact that the public did not know that he was severely handicapped, his voice was stern, steady, loud, and clear. It conveyed calmness and a sincere resolve that the United States of America, without any doubt, would prevail. I am sure that many of us who are old enough will remember some of the songs that were written to enhance our patriotism, including "Remember Pearl Harbor" and "Praise the Lord and Pass the Ammunition." I remember singing these songs at home with some of my brothers and sisters. Even Dad would hang in there. Needless to say, this dastardly attack on Pearl Harbor, as Roosevelt forcefully told Congress the next day, ended our fishing trip. We all sadly got into our dad's pickup and drove home.

Lifestyle Changes

The effects of World War II were felt immediately. I remember the real concern about the possibility that the West Coast being attacked. We had to put shades over all of the windows in the home during scheduled blackouts. Gas, meat, war-essential products, and materials became scarce. No new cars were made for the consumer. My older siblings would perform spotter duty, which meant that they were used as miniature federal aviation trackers (my definition). They would go to the outskirts of Wasco at night to watch for airplanes and report the location and direction of flight activity in an assigned area. My older brother would tag along. I was too young to participate. All of this defense activity was a continuous reminder of the war extending all the way to our homeland. Everyone was very patriotic, which was reflected in popular songs and music at the time.

Patriotism
Remember Pearl Harbor
Abstract
Quin Barkley

History in ev'ry century records an act that lives forevermore
We'll recall, as into line we fall, the thing that happened on Hawaii's shore

Let's remember Pearl Harbor
As we go to meet the foe
Let's remember Pearl Harbor
As we did the Alamo
We will always remember how they died for liberty
Let's remember Pearl Harbor
And go on to victory

Honoring the American Flag

Dad would honor the flag no matter where he was. If there was an American flag in a movie, he would clap his hands. If he saw a flag on the street, he would remove his hat. Dad was so proud to be an American citizen. He found his dream when he came to America during 1910 as an eighteen-year-old.

The Wasco Rifle Club

Joe and Aloise were members of the Wasco rifle team. This team was very active and competed with special twenty-two caliber target rifles. We had competition matches with many city teams within a hundred-mile area. The Wasco rifle team did very well with three Miller brothers competing. Dad always liked to brag about his boys. We didn't have to because Dad bragged enough. Of course, I had to follow my brothers and joined the rifle club's sport shooting activities. I was able to purchase a Remington model 36 that was specifically designed for sports competition. My brothers had similar sporting guns that they used for competition as well. The rifle above is the latest national competitions would allow four positions: prone, sitting, kneeling, and standing. We would use the official fifty-foot rifle target. A one hundred score was the best score. Each bull's-eye would be recorded as a ten and so on. Ten shots would complete a round per position. The brothers and I could deliver a one hundred score prone. We almost always scored a one hundred sitting. A score of ninety-nine kneeling would be considered outstanding, and a score of ninety-six would be extremely good for the standing position. All competitions would be established using three different positions. You needed a steady hand to shoot those scores in competition. There was always the need to practice to stay sharp. In addition, the yips could set in any time.

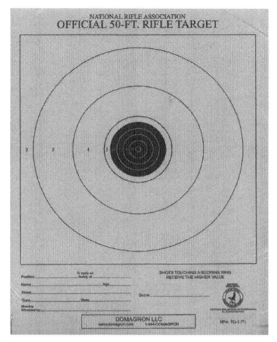

Small-Bore Official Fifty-Foot Rifle Target

The fifty-foot rifle target does not include a very big bull's-eye. It is smaller than a fly. The Miller brothers had great time competing with other rifle clubs within about a seventy-five-mile radius as well as competing among ourselves. My two older brothers were a little better at sporting events than me. That changed when I joined the university rifle team since I had performed more practice and participated in more competitive events. The club had a big fund-raising affair, and one of the club members had recently been on an African safari. He took all kinds of pictures of his adventures and hunting successes. This turned out to be a great fund-raiser. We managed to raise enough money to fix up the old Wasco shooting range. We increased our membership in the club. I remember the time when there was an elderly gentleman who came in with his rifle and wanted to join the club. He looked at all the guns the other club members were using, and he remarked, "Boy, you guys are shooting cannons." He hadn't realized that you needed special twenty-two target rifles for a sport competition. He left and was somewhat disappointed. I remember the days when my brothers and I would take our sporting guns on the school bus to practice with our volunteer trainer. The shooting practice range was near the high school—absolutely unheard of today.

Aloise, Richard, and his BB gun

Richard wasn't left out. He settled for dragonflies and homemade targets that he set up. He also would shoot bottles, beer cans, tree leaves, and anything else that he could shoot at for his own amusement. Richard's stance lets you know who is in charge. I have my artillery to back me up.

Chapter 11

Finally, College

I was ready to go to college, which was a big deal for me. Having the experience of milking more than one hundred cows twice a day, at the age of fifteen, with my older brother, Aloise, and another nice Swiss gentleman, Montz, for over three months, was enough of an education to motivate me to go to college. I was undecided in what to study. The only reason I took business was the results of a battery of tests that I took in my senior year of high school. One semester of accounting and all the other stuff I was taking as a business major didn't appeal to me.

God's Intervention

Out of the blue, I was inspired—I look at it as God's intervention in my life—to change my major about halfway through my ham sandwich. I went to the dean's office to tell him that I wanted to change my major to mathematics. I told him I had a mentor in high school, Mr. Clifford Harrington, as my math teacher. He said that he knew Mr. Harrington. Math was my best subject, where I got most of my A's. I was impressed by that great big slide rule mounted above the wall in his mathematics classes.

Mr. Clifford Harrington, my high school math teacher, had a very large slide rule that extended above the blackboard from one end to the other. I was absolutely amazed how he nonchalantly slipped that slide rule in performing multiplications and divisions. In addition, this advanced slide rule had a log/log scale to use logarithmic numbers. I was absolutely impressed. I decided to go with my strengths. Dad was always good with numbers. Mathematics became my major—a decision I never regretted. I got my first slide rule in high school. My many thanks to Mr. Harrington for inspiring me. I purchased a small pocket slide rule (shown below).

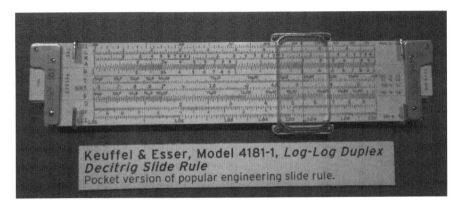

Keuffel & Esser, Model 4181-1, *Log-Log Duplex Decitrig Slide Rule*
Pocket version of popular engineering slide rule.

My Psychology Class

I was in my second semester at Bakersfield College, taking all of the required courses as a mathematics major. One of the classes was psychology. A course, I found interesting, but I took with some trepidation. I had minor bouts with depression as a teenager. All of a sudden, the person right in front of me in my psychology class hit the floor with a loud bang. His sudden disappearance right in front of my eyes, hearing this load flop as he hit the floor, and the way he looked scared the daylights out of me. I dashed out of the room. I came back in time see him revived and explaining to the teacher that merely mentioning the word *optic nerve* frightened him and made him pass out. The teacher dismissed the class. I was still a very sensitive and impressionable kid. That really affected me.

Clinical Depression

Depression, a major depressive disorder, is a common and serious illness that negatively affects how you feel, the way you think, and how you act. Following this trauma, coupled with the stress of starting a new, difficult major, I went into a depression that I kept to myself. I didn't know what was happening to me. I wondered if I was going crazy. I struggled for the rest of the semester but finished my courses and managed to complete my first semester as a mathematics major. Depression is a very debilitating condition. It constantly nags at you, except when you are able to get some sleep. The mornings are the worst because you just know that feeling will last for the rest of the day. The best way to describe my depression is doom. You have the horrible feeling that you are never going to feel any better—almost to the point of total despair. I certainly understand the reason for young and old people that might contemplate suicide as being the only way out. I remember that a nun told us in class that God will only test us no more than we are able to handle. I never forgot that quote. I forced myself to act and behave like there was nothing wrong at home or in college. I didn't curtail any of my activities. I went to class and studied and went home to do some work, time permitting. When I reflect on this traumatic experience, particularly not telling anybody about my depression, I was almost as foolish about almost losing Dorothy. How many young people today struggle with doubts about life in general, living with some form of depression, in a society without God? I am most thankful that I grew up in a household with faith in God. In my family home, there wasn't a great big slide rule hanging above the dinner table. It was Father God, Jesus, and his mother Mary displayed in beautiful art form.

God's inspiration and my trust in God (Public domain)

I don't know if I could have struggled through my depression without a strong faith in God. Illegal drugs is not the answer. There were proper drugs for depression in my time, but I didn't have enough sense to realize that. Back in those days, seeing a psychiatrist was taboo. I struggled alone with God. I survived. God is good.

Living with depression (Public domain)

I dogged my way through the remainder of the semester. I went back to my farm duties full-time. I began a little research on depression, but I couldn't find much. I did read that depression was quite common. I also read about how one feels during depression. It felt better to realize that I was not the only flute in a brass band. The article or the book I was reading described my symptoms almost to a tee. What a revelation that was. It put a little smile on my face. Still, I tried as best I could to behave as if nothing was wrong.

At the dinner table, Mary, the inquisitive one, looked at me and said, "What is wrong with my little brother?"

I told the family that I didn't feel well.

That didn't satisfy Mary. She pressed me for a better answer.

I told them that I experienced a little incident while in class at the college. I tried to downplay it, which seemed to satisfy everybody except Mary. She said she observed that something was wrong for quite a while.

I wanted to tell her to shut up, but I told her that I would explain a little more when we washed dishes. She was very happy with my answer. I had the problem of deciding what I should tell Mary. Mary liked to gossip some. *What to tell and what not to tell?* I told her the most important aspects of my psychology class encounter. She was very kind, listening, and was very sympathetic. What a great sister! I found out depression was somewhat common. Knowing the symptoms, I was finally able to talk about my feelings in more detail to Mary. It was much better than taking depression pills, which I never took. Spilling the beans and learning more about depression was the best medicine and the best therapy. I felt better and better as the summer wound down. I even had a couple of dates with some very nice girls from school. Despite my lingering feelings for Dorothy, I didn't date her. I was rejected enough. I went back to college for my second year.

Clinical Depression Again

I suffered from a second serious depression after I turned thirty-one. I had become a branch chief; Dorothy was having gallbladder attacks almost daily. She was pregnant with Keith. Dorothy's mother and two kids, Pam and Stan, had moved in with us, including two Siamese cats. I was selected to attend a six-week executive development program at the University of Oklahoma in Norman. The stress of the extended seminar along with being away from Dorothy, in her condition, and family was just too much to bear. I came down with a severe case of free-floating anxiety with a depression component (my family doctor's diagnosis). He prescribed medications to better cope with my anxiety and depression. My bosses were very considerate. I returned to work about two months later.

The Holy Eucharist

When I returned to work, we installed the latest modern computer on the market: the IBM 704 electronic computer. After I fully recovered and was back on my feet, I continued to study my Catholic faith. I was moved to attend Mass at least three or four times a week. I would get up early in the morning and attend Mass before work. I continued this regimen for the rest of my career and retirement. I didn't suffer from a serious depression for the next forty-six years. This definitely assured me that God remained with and within me and was with me as my copilot. During special days that I was dealing with unusual problems, I would pray to God for additional help. This gives credence to the fact that, prior to the receiving the Eucharist at Mass, the priest would announce the final doxology through him, with him, and in him. Undeniably, the Bible says, "He who eats My Flesh and drinks My Blood will have Life Everlasting" (John 6:54). Amen.

Father Gerald Osuagwu, the associate pastor of Sacred Heart Parish located in Lancaster, California, presenting the Sacred Host during Consecration.

Chapter 12

Dorothy Enters College, Relationships, and Courtship

Since I was going to college, I was not subject to the Korean War draft. I started my second year of college, still trying to overcome my depression. I got on the college bus that transported college students from Wasco to Bakersfield. As I got on the bus, book locker memories appeared again before my eyes. Dorothy was sitting in the bus—on her way to her first year in college.

Renewed Acquaintance

The seat in front of her was open, so I sat down. We exchanged smiles, greeted each other, and talked about college, her major, her senior year in high school, and what she did in the year and a half since we dated. She was to pursue her studies as an occupational therapist. We had a very pleasant conversation. It was more than a year since I had seen her working as a car hop at a drive-in in Wasco. She was absolutely beautiful—just as I remembered her.

Sweet Sixteen

I was taken back as I noticed that she was wearing a golden shoe that was given to her by an upperclassman who was a big track star. Erroneously, I thought she was wearing an engagement ring on her left hand. She appeared happy to see me after more than a year and a half since we dated in high school.

As I got on the bus day after day, I looked forward to seeing her on the bus. Actually, Dorothy was not engaged. She told her boyfriend that she was not ready to marry. I would guess that Dorothy kept her options open. Dorothy was to pursue her studies as an occupational therapist. We had wonderful conversations day after day both on and off the bus. As I got on the bus, I noticed that she would look to see if I was there too. She later told me that she had an engagement ring but did not wear it.

Revived Relationship

One day, on the bus, while we were greeting each other and involved in our usual banter and pleasant conversation, she asked, "When are you going to ask me for a date?" Boy, that was all I needed. I wised up this time. God saved her for me. I wasn't going with any other girl at the time. I asked her when. She said, "How about this Saturday?"

Saturday came, and I got the old pickup truck we used on the farm. It was loaded with shovels, dirt, old pipes, and grease guns, and it looked very messy. I cleaned out the cab as best I could, and I picked her up and went to the movies. She told me much later that she asked me because I was spinning my wheels.

First College Date

Dorothy was living in her grandfather's home when I picked her up for our first college date. She was living with her mother, stepfather, and five younger siblings. Stan, the youngest, our ring bearer, was still in diapers and scooting around on the floor. Pamela, our flower girl, was about two years old. Sitting in a chair, she was probably wondering who I was. I met Dorothy's mother when I would walk home from school and pass her house on F Street. She remembered me, and we would talk a bit while she was watering the lawn and flowers. Dorothy's mother was very outgoing and was willing to talk to almost anybody. Everybody liked her. I met her again when I picked up Dorothy, and she was very pleasant.

Overcoming Depression

I never told Dorothy about my depression. As I dated and engaged in developing my relationship with Dorothy, I gradually felt better and returned to my old self. I never told her that she greatly helped me overcome my depression. I thanked God many times for that. Depression is horrible—but curable. It would have been much easier with a doctor's consultation and help. For anyone wondering, it is a sickness like anything else. Get help immediately upon the onset of depression. I wish I had been honest with my parents. Maybe it was God's way of testing my faith. This time of God supposedly not intervening in my life helped me become a stronger person, which increased my faith in God. I was in a much better mental condition to accept a minor setback in our relationship.

I decided to date another girl about that time. I dated another very nice girl from Dorothy's class. We went out on a Halloween night and had a great time going to the movies and driving around Wasco. We retrieved onions left in the field after harvest time and threw smelly onions at some friends. We didn't hit anybody. I acted much out of character as I got caught up in the Halloween spirit. We had a great time acting like foolish teenagers getting into innocent mischief.

Dorothy returned his ring

Later, I don't know how, but Dorothy found out about it. Wasco is a small town. Not too long after that, Dorothy told me she returned her track star's engagement ring and gave the ring to his mother. He joined the air force. Coincidence or not, I never asked why she returned his ring. He joined the air force. I wasn't playing hardball. I was playing with fire. I was desperately in love. I did a lot of fishing with my dad, but this magnificent catch was the most wonderful and greatest catch of my life.

Dorothy in College

Our courtship reminds me of a great song by Stephen Sondheim. "Send in the clowns" is a great love song about a breakup. Dorothy and I never broke up. In high school, we didn't date each other very often. I was a shy kid. Where were the clowns when I needed them? "Send in the clowns" was an expression used in theater by a director when a rehearsal didn't proceed very well. The director would shout, "Send in the clowns!" to shake up the cast. God intervened and clowned around his way for Dorothy and me to realize that he made us for each other to live our lives together in celebrating married life. God is always near and everywhere. God is good.

Castor Beans

Raising castor beans was one of Dad's ways of contributing to the war effort. Our adjoining neighbor contributed to the war effort by raising guayule, a plant to make rubber synthetically due its scarcity during World War II. All kinds of oil and rubber were needed to support the war effort. The castor bean oil was not necessarily used for gasoline but for all kinds of other uses as grease and oil for all types of war equipment and vehicles. Castor beans grew to become very large—almost the size of God's mustard tree. We had two fields of castor beans that grew large enough to make some of the roads on the farm look like tunnels.

Praying the Rosary

My older brothers were courting their future wives, and Dorothy and I would get in on the act. On some Saturday nights, we all would compete for the best spots to park on the farm on the roads among the castor beans. The two older brothers had dibs on the spots farthest from the home. Dorothy and I would have been satisfied to park at a leftover location. Dad would jokingly refer to our parking escapades as out praying the rosary. Rest assured that there wasn't much praying going on, but as far as Dorothy and I were concerned, no commandments were broken. This was to be the case throughout all of our courtship. Back in my early days, this kind of behavior was more of God's way than today's so-called modern way. Today's decaying morals have eroded to the point that almost nothing is taboo. Anything goes. This has led to far-reaching dysfunctional and warped attitudes among the populace, particularly the young and immature. I am absolutely convinced that living God's way has greatly contributed to our success in married life. We have been immensely blessed with eight lovely children and a job opportunity to provide for all of our needs. God has been our copilot from the beginning of our courtship to our twilight years. Living God's way certainly is the best way and the right way. I want to strongly advocate that these principles have served our long and sometimes difficult life together as evidence that God's way is the only way. Amen.

Chapter 13

Dorothy Alice Worley

Who is Dorothy Alice Worley? Despite her young age, she has quite a story to tell. She and her brother Pat were born—as I was—during the beginning of the Great Depression. Her father was an alcoholic and left the family destitute when Dorothy was two years old and Pat was less than one. They moved in with Dorothy's grandparents. Her grandparent, lovingly cared for them. Dorothy loved her grandparents very much. They epitomized the very hardworking California pioneers who made this country great. Dorothy often spoke very kindly about her mother and grandparents.

Dorothy's Grandfather: John Rogers

During our courtship, when I would visit Dorothy and have dinner and listen to Jack Benny, and lounge around, I would have wonderful conversations with Dorothy's grandfather. He moved in with the Trew family upon the death of Dorothy's grandmother, Lura. He would tell me a variety of stories and events that happened in his life. He told me about people wearing "hog legs," pistols. He drove the first balloon motor tire in California, which is partially true. The real truth would be that he drove the first make of car that had balloon tires. He referred to cars as *motors*. He would tell me about building the famous Ridge Route, early farming days in San Fernando Valley, his construction days building the

Grapevine Highway, and cattle ranching on Cooks Ranch, which is now called Vandenberg Air Force Base. In addition, he would happily relate many other life stories.

Don't forget your roots (Lincoln Park AFB)

Dorothy has deep California roots. I am proud to tell anybody who will listen that my kids are fourth-generation Californians, which makes our grandkids and great-grandkids fifth- and sixth-generation Californians and counting. The roots extend all the way to Switzerland.

Dorothy's Mother: Alice Rogers Trew

When Dorothy's mother, Alice, got remarried, that brought the Worley family back together. They moved many times since her stepfather worked as a heavy-equipment operator, building roads all over Kern County. They lived in Thousand Oaks for a while. Her stepfather had to find work wherever he could find it. They eventually settled in Wasco, California.

Dorothy's Stepfather Franklin Trew

Shell Oil Company Oil Exploration

During the late 1930s, Shell Oil Company was doing some deep ground sonic testing in search for oil. The dirt road from the Miller farm to the main Central Valley Highway was about a mile. This oil exploration was being done on a neighbor's ranch alongside the dirt road. Dad and I were on our way to town. Dad was very curious as to what was going on. He noticed a gentleman along the side of the dirt road. Dad stopped to talk to him. Dad introduced himself as the owner of the dairy farm nearby. The gentleman responded that his name was Frank Trew. Dad asked him what was going on. Mr. Trew proudly responded that he was doing oil exploration work for Shell Oil Company. Dad became very interested. The Shell Oil Company, understandably so, was very secretive about their sonic testing, but Dad heard the loud explosions less than a mile away on the farm. That perked my dad's ears. Dad became very interested. Mr. Trew was very pleased to brag and impress a well-known dairyman. Sometime later, dad got a reserve lease contract from Texaco Oil Company for 160 acres of prime land for $25 per acre each year to do oil exploration on the Miller farm. Dorothy would have been about seven years old at the time, a year younger than me. Later, as the earth-moving business turned sour, Mr. Trew was employed doing other jobs, including being a bartender at a saloon on Main Street in downtown Wasco.

Dad Enjoyed His Beer

Dad liked his beer, and on his trips to town, he would visit this saloon. He would have a couple of beers and talk to Mr. Trew. He liked my dad because he knew that Dad was a dairy farmer, and he remembered meeting Dad previously. On occasion, Dorothy's mother would visit the bar to be with her husband. No doubt that Dad met Dorothy's mother as well. They both were very talkative. Mr. Trew, knowing my dad, very kindly accepted me when I dated Dorothy many years later.

Dorothy's Date

Dorothy had a date with a popular football player. He was a smooth talker and was impressed with himself. He was a disk jockey for a radio station about a mile from the ranch. He had a music program called "High

Teen Tune Time." He was quite glib on the radio. Later, he got a TV newscaster job at a station in Bakersfield. One time, I was sitting there with Dorothy's stepfather, watching the news. All of a sudden, he came on the TV to report the news. Mr. Trew proudly remarked, "I kicked that SOB out of the house." I told him good job and thanked him. He didn't elaborate as to why. I assume that he didn't like that pompous ass. He was in my class at Wasco High, and I knew him very well. I was surprised that Dorothy dated him. She has a very good sense about sizing up people. I think that he dated every girl in his class—as well as some of the girls in the other classes. He became a security officer in the air force. When he left the service, he joined the air force reserves. As a military reserve officer, Lieutenant Colonel Orval Brown was assigned for a two-week tour at Edwards AFB as the commander of all the security forces. We met a couple of times and had lunch together and talked about our days at Wasco High and his career in the air force. He wasn't that interested in what I did at Edwards, but he was interested in telling me about his career. He was a big guy and made quite a presence in his blues with scrambled eggs on the front of his hat, designating that he was a commander. What a show-off!

Dorothy and her mother (Family Photo)

Dorothy's Formative Years

Dorothy's formative years were full of many life experiences both good and bad. She read the Bible cover to cover in grammar school and was baptized as a young teenager. I am convinced that her time spent during her very young years with her grandparents was very positive for her character development. Furthermore, despite Dorothy's mother's abusive marriage with her second husband, she remained a positive role model for Dorothy. Dorothy was a wonderful role model for her siblings.

More Dorothy

When I met Dorothy, she was very mature for her age, both emotionally and physically. Despite the fact that she dressed very modestly, she really looked good wearing a sweater. I could tell that she had a wonderful figure as she gracefully walked from class to class. She was absolutely charming. She never missed a day of school all the way through grammar school, high school, and probably college as well. When I first met her, she had a large bundle of hair that was always braided. Despite her exceptionally good looks, some of the boys didn't like her bundled hair. She wore her hair the same way throughout her high school years until the first semester at Bakersfield College.

Dorothy's long hair (Family Photo)

Her hair didn't bother me. It was an asset as far as I was concerned. It kept some of the jocks away. She had good reason for keeping her hair long—even though it took about an hour a day to fix and manage. When she went to college, she cut her hair short. She said it took too long to fix.

Dorothy's Sensible Outlook on Life

I remember the day she got on the bus with short hair. What a shock! How beautiful! She was the same person of course. Very intelligent. She had a very sensible outlook on life, and she witnessed two bad choices made by her mother regarding her first two marriages. Even though Dorothy's mother made a very poor decision on marrying her first husband, Dorothy and her brother were wonderful offspring. God is great. Sour lemons make great lemonade. Dorothy vowed to herself not to make wrong choices in her life as her mother did.

She also witnessed some of her friends and acquaintances making wrong decisions and becoming young single parents. She stood by her firm belief to make reasonable and sound decisions. That's one reason I refer her as being very smart and intelligent. She wasn't about to make a decision to marry until she was absolutely convinced that the one for her was dependable, motivated, and responsible for a good and proper marriage. Not knowing her life's history at that time, I understand why she behaved hard to get. Dating is a means of becoming more acquainted to determine if your partner is the right person to enter into a lifelong marriage relationship. Dating must be viewed as the remote preparation for marriage. Our on-and-off relationship did look very remote at the time. I stayed around—but not totally out of sight. I kidded her about being hard to get and that she kept running away until she caught me.

Final Realization

As we both grew older, we became better acquainted. When I went to college and the university, she realized that I could possibly be her one and only. When I asked her to marry me, she responded immediately, "Yes." She told me later that the reason she gave up her jock boyfriend, who treated her very nicely, was his lifestyle and career. He was going sideways and lived a little bit on his laurels as a past athlete. Evidently, Dorothy decided that I met all of her dreams. Thank God.

She had exceptional role models in her grandparents and her loving mother, whom she loved dearly. Dorothy's mother married three different men. First was Dorothy's father, an alcoholic, who left her mother and two kids at the very beginning of the Depression. She married Frank Trew, who was a domineering husband and a stepfather who Dorothy didn't particularly care for. He was abusive to her mother both verbally and physically. As far as I know, Dorothy was verbally abused, and she might have been knocked around a bit as well. Dorothy said that she would just stay away. When the atmosphere became vulnerable, Dorothy kept her distance.

Dorothy's mother ended up divorcing her second husband, and she married a very nice person who treated her with love and respect. Her mother's second marriage resulted in the addition of two half sisters, Carol and Pamela, and two stepbrothers, Howard, called Ellis, and Stan Lee, called Stan. Dorothy would tell me about her stepsister, a brother, two half sisters, and two half brothers. It was confusing to me. I finally figured it all out. Dorothy was the oldest and assisted her mother in raising her siblings. She did a lot of babysitting both at home and for many other family friends and acquaintances.

In the eighth grade, Dorothy was given the great honor by being selected as a Job's daughter, an award for young people. She had a very large eighth grade class. Thomas Jefferson was the only upper-grade grammar school in Wasco, California, at the time. An outstanding honor given to a young girl from a poor and dysfunctional family is particularly noteworthy. Dorothy excelled from an early age on. God has blessed Dorothy. God is good.

I did not know her then, but she was recognized by her peers as someone special. In high school, she was scholastically at the top of her class. All the jocks wanted her homework papers. She was the class valedictorian upon graduation. She was always low-key. She never reveled in fanfare. She is modest and always does the right thing. She is solid. She has the stamina and perseverance to make a wonderful wife for a lifelong commitment. She is beautiful on the outside and on the inside. She is definitely a keeper.

Chapter 14

John Rogers's Pioneer Family

Dorothy's grandparents were John and Lura Rogers. Dorothy's grandfather is in the first row on the right and her grandmother is standing behind her grandpa. Dorothy's mother is in middle of the back row. Next to Dorothy's mother on the top row far left is Helen Rogers, the daughter of Joe Rogers.

Grandma Lura Rogers

I knew Dorothy's grandfather very well. I never met Dorothy's grandmother, Lura, who passed away about the time I started dating

Dorothy in college. Her grandmother came to California in a covered wagon when she was only ten years old. Her grandfather was born in Monrovia Ranch, which is now called the city of Monrovia. He was born about three years after the Civil War in 1868. He was an honest-to-goodness California pioneer and a proud cowboy.

Grandpa John Rogers

When I was dating Dorothy, she lived on her grandpa's ranch just a mile or so west of the Miller dairy farm. Then later, the Trew family moved into a two-story home on F Street near downtown Wasco. Grandpa was in his eighties and moved in with the Trew family. While he lived there, I had the opportunity to talk to Grandpa about many old times. Her grandpa raised cattle on what was known as Cooks Ranch, which is now called Vandenberg AFB. He also farmed in the middle of San Fernando Valley, where all the palm trees could be seen as you drove south down the San Diego Freeway years ago.

Grandpa John Rogers pioneering adventures.
Ariel view of San Fernando Valley in 1946.

San Fernando farming in the early years.

Photograph of farmers and ranch hands seeding five thousand acres of wheat on the southeasterly portion of the Lankersham Ranch in the San Fernando Valley. Here, the outfit is stopping for noon lunch in the fields. One hundred horses were used in this field for plowing. Five tall trees are visible in the distance. A mountain range rises in the distance (circa 1898/1900). Photo courtesy of USC.

An Agricultural Hinterland

Grandpa Rogers farmed in San Fernando Valley in the early years. If it were a separate city, the San Fernando Valley would be the fifth largest in the nation. With more than 1.7 million inhabitants, it is one of California's largest suburban areas and epitomizes suburbia in the public imagination. However, for much of its early history, the region was a sparsely populated agricultural hinterland, just over the hill from Los Angeles. Even as LA's urban spaces expanded through the late nineteenth and early twentieth centuries, the valley remained largely rural and did not experience its full transformation into an immense suburban area until the latter half of the twentieth century. In the decades following America's conquest of California, remnants of the valley's early rancho days remained. Owned largely by Pio Pico, California's last governor under Mexican rule, the valley was well known for its cattle and sheep. A severe drought in 1862–63, however, hastened the disappearance of daily cattle roundups in the area, and ranchos, including Rancho Encino, turned their focus to sheep shearing.

San Fernando Valley Farming

While farming in the San Fernando Valley, he told me the story about working out in the fields. There were no paved roads. Many of the dirt roads were made by farmers as they planted their crops. When all connected, it resulted in a passageway through the valley. Not many cars could be seen driving by. This one day, a man and his wife drove close by his ranch. They stopped for a chat and some water for themselves and their new car. They were very happy for the visit, but they were more eager to tell someone about their great achievement. They excitedly told him that they left Los Angeles about six o'clock in the morning and drove like a bat out of hell until they arrived five hours later by averaging almost ten miles per hour, including stops. Grandpa told him that he couldn't do that with his horse in a million years. They enjoyed a little picnic and lively conversation and then left. The couple was so proud and happy to share their travels as they chugalugged off in a cloud of dust.

Construction of the Ridge Route (Prior to 1923)

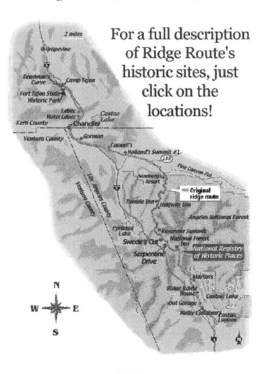

Placing ⅝" Sq. reinforcing rods in 20'x4" Concrete Pavement 8-7-19

In the early part of the twentieth century, Grandpa Rogers helped build the famous route with earthmovers pulled by a large team of horses and paving equipment. This was a very hot, arduous task that employed many construction personnel in hazardous locations and situations. Living conditions were not the best. It was very difficult to get construction equipment and supplies. It took about four years to complete the Ridge Route, including paving the entire route. Despite the difficult construction task, it was performed with pride, knowing that everyone was involved as pioneers in developing Southern California and uniting the northern part of the state of California. Grandpa was very proud of his efforts, and he would not hesitate to talk about his accomplishments.

Butterfield Stage (Prior to 1923)

Two Butterfield Overland Stagecoaches pause at the 5,534-foot Guadalupe Pass

The Butterfield Stage Line—and later the Southern Pacific Railroad into Los Angeles—displays an inscription that states: The Ridge Route is an engineering marvel.

Harrison Scott discovered the Ridge Route in 1955 (Credits)

Mr. Harrison Scott was an amateur historian. When he was eighteen, he was out freewheeling in a new Ford he'd bought with a loan from his parents. His sinuous route, an engineering marvel that tamed the San Gabriel Mountains through the highway corridor that is now known as the Grapevine, was already a relic. Scott liked the abandoned motorway but did not return to the route until exploring it again in 1991. Harrison Scott discovered the Ridge Route in 1955, but this time, he took his son on this road trip, spurred by his son's interest, and retired from a long career with Pacific Telephone.

Hollywood celebrities (More credits)

He learned that it had once been dotted with gas stations, diners, nightclubs, and hotels that hosted gangsters and Hollywood stars. Clark Gable, Jean Harlow, and Bugsy Siegel visited places such as Kelly's Halfway Inn, set dead center in the twelve-hour automobile journey between Bakersfield and Los Angeles, and Sandberg's Summit Hotel, which had a sign by the front door that said, "No Dogs or Truck Drivers Allowed." The Ridge Route was born after engineering crews operating horse-drawn scrapers carved a narrow two-lane passage between Castaic and Grapevine. The new road included 697 curves and climbed to more than 4,000 feet above sea level. Fully paved by 1919, it was considered a construction triumph. Though it featured dangerous curves and a speed limit of only fifteen miles per hour, the route was soon home to commercial enterprise.

Van Norman Dam (Public domain)

Grandpa Rogers helped build the Van Norman Dam just north of San Fernando Valley. This dam was built with many teams of workhorses and primitive moving equipment. The question remains whether it is wise to live below a dam when millions of acre feet of water are stored. It is usually rather low on people's lists of daily worries. Most dams are constructed and built for eternity. However, when you live in earthquake country, you might want to give the question a second thought. More than once, dams have failed or were severely damaged by the shaking of large earthquakes with devastating consequences for the people living downstream. Forty-eight years ago, the possibility of such a sudden dam burst was the hair-raising fear in the chaos and devastation following the magnitude 6.7 earthquake that struck the San Fernando Valley north of Los Angeles. We all felt the quake in Lancaster, particularly in a two-story house, which took place at six o'clock in the morning under the town of Sylmar. It caused hospitals and schools to collapse, brought down sections of elevated freeways, and cost sixty-four people their lives. It was the first strong quake to hit the area since the 1893 Pico Canyon quake—with an epicenter several miles west of Sylmar.

LA County Fire Relief Association

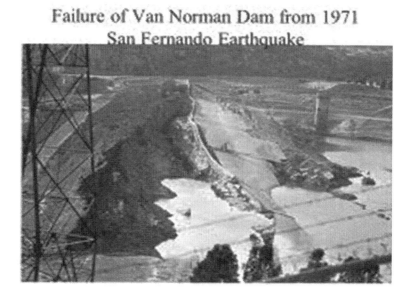

After the partial collapse of the Van Norman Dam, the water came dangerously to overtopping the dam. Once the shaking was over and rescuers started to assess the damage, the imminent fear of a new catastrophe arose. The Van Norman Dam, just northwest of the town of San Fernando, where 3.6 billion gallons of drinking water were stored, was severely damaged. This earthen dam had partially liquefied and the top thirty feet of the edifice had crumbled. More chunks of earth collapsed with each new aftershock, reducing the height of the crown and bringing the water table dangerously close to the top of the dam. As the dam might collapse further and then be breached by the enormous pressure of the water behind it, authorities decided to evacuate an area of ten square miles along the San Diego Freeway. Dorothy's sister Pam lived very close downstream. They were evacuated. In addition, Pam's mother-in law was in the Sylmar Hospital, very close by the toppled a hospital wing, which left her with a complete open view of the valley. They immediately rushed over to the hospital to carry her down four flights of stairs. Violet Boyle was very handicapped at the time. She told us about this horrendous experience many times. More than eighty thousand people living downstream had to leave their homes for four days while engineers frantically shored up the dam and lowered the water level. In the end, the dam was saved, and the evacuees were allowed to return to their homes. Later, scientists at UCLA estimated that flooding following the collapse of the dam could have killed between 70,000 and 120,000 people.

Violent Shaking

When seismologists checked their records, they were utterly surprised. In some areas of the epicenter region, the ground had shaken so violently that seismic sensors recorded accelerations of more than 1.25 g, where g is the standard gravitational acceleration at the earth's surface. Objects under such forces would have been weightless for a few seconds, like astronauts in space. Never had such a strong acceleration been recorded in an earthquake. Even more surprising was the location of the focus of the quake, which later came to be known as the San Fernando earthquake. Geologists had known for a long time that the San Gabriel Mountains above the San Fernando Valley were riddled with faults, but it was generally accepted that none of the demarcation lines between two separate geologic units were active, meaning that they had not produced any earthquakes recently. But when seismologists checked the epicenter, they realized that for about six miles, a fault along the foothills of the San Gabriels had broken through the surface during the quake. In some areas, it was offset more than five feet. The two geologists, Carl Wentworth and Robert Yerkes, from the US Geological Survey in Pasadena later wrote that the San Fernando Fault was discovered to be active only when it ruptured the ground surface on February 9, 1971. It was evident that there were more blind faults in the area.

San Fernando Quake in January 1994

How right they were. It was demonstrated twenty-three years later when almost the same areas of the San Fernando Valley were again struck by a damaging earthquake. I felt that quake in Lancaster, which was about thirty miles from the epicenter. During the Northridge earthquake in January 1994, more than fifty people died, and it caused damage worth $35 billion. It also occurred on an unknown fault, albeit a different one from the San Fernando Fault. Such faults, which are unknown but can produce devastating quakes, are called blind thrust faults. Following these two earthquakes, geologists are now sure that many more of these hidden faults crisscross deep beneath the San Fernando Valley. But even now, after further detailed studies, they are not sure whether they have identified all blind faults in the area or if the valley's inhabitants are in for more surprises. Following these two earthquakes, geologists are now sure that many more of these hidden faults crisscross deep beneath the San Fernando Valley. But even now, after further detailed studies, they are not sure whether they have identified all blind faults in the area or if the valley's inhabitants are in for more surprises.

Construction of the Grapevine Highway

Upon completion of the original ridge route, Dorothy's grandfather helped build the Grapevine Highway. Grapevine is an unincorporated community in Kern County, California, at the southern end of the San Joaquin Valley. The village consists mainly of roadside services. At an elevation of 1,499 feet, the community is located at the foot of a grade known as the Grapevine, which starts at the mouth of Grapevine Canyon, immediately south of the community, and ascends the canyon to the Tejon Pass in the Tehachapi Mountains via Interstate 5 (formerly US Route 99). The village and grade are named, not for the once-winding road known as the Grapevine that used to climb the steep mountain canyon but for the canyon it passed through with its wild grapes that still grow along the original road. Its Spanish name was la Cañada de las Uvas (Grapevine Ravine).

Early Construction Days

Before the road was straightened and widened during 1933–1934 by the three-lane Ridge Route alternate (US 99), the Grapevine was infamous for its high accident rate. There are escape ramps branching off both sides of the downward part of the road for heavy trucks whose brakes fail on this five-mile-long, 6 percent grade, 1600-foot descent grade. I remember Dorothy's stepfather telling me as a truck driver that he had to be very careful fully loaded coming down that grade. It was comforting to know that he had a long stretch of a sand off-ramp to break an uncontrolled flight down the winding road. Occasionally the road is still closed due to heavy snowfall during winter storms. It has also been closed for fires and mudslides. The Grapevine is the major route between Central and Southern California, and any closure is a major disruption to traffic along the West Coast. At various times, when Dorothy's mother would drive to the LA area from Wasco, her father would proudly comment on the construction of the Grapevine. He was very proud of his involvement in its early construction.

Current view (Public domain)

Chapter 15

Grandpa John Rogers's Sons Were Also Pioneers

Uncle Joe started his career in the Taft oil fields and then moved on to South America doing oil exploration working for Shell Oil Corporation. He later moved to Long Beach where he began working on Signal Hill for Shell Oil. He was involved in utilizing new techniques in oil exploration that employed direction drilling and logging. I remember him telling me that they would whip stock, which was another name for directional drilling. Logging had to do with water saturation.

Uncle Joe Rogers Signal Hill oil exploration
American Gas and Oil Historical Society

History of Signal Hill Exploration (Credits)

Signal hill has a rich and colorful history. Most famous for the discovery of oil in 1921, and commonly known as an oil town, the city is now a diverse community with an oil history and a bright future. In the 1500s, the Puva Indians used the hilltop to signal other native tribes on Santa Catalina Island, twenty-six miles offshore. Because of its use as a signaling point, Spanish settlers called the hill Loma Sental, which translates to Signal Hill. Signal Hill's first owner of record was Manuel Nieto, who received the land in 1784 as a grant from King Carlos III of Spain. Nieto later divided the land into six cattle and horse ranchos, two of which encompassed Signal Hill: Rancho Los Alamitos and Rancho Los Cerritos. Later purchased by New Englanders, the ranchos were used mostly for grazing and agriculture in the 1800s. A harsh winter in 1862, drought, and other financial hardships resulted in the sale of the ranchos to the Bixby clan, who used the land to raise sheep. By the turn of the twentieth century, stately mansions dotted the hilltop, and the value of the panoramic view became evident. However, by 1917, the prospect of striking oil on the hilltop surpassed the value of the view, and the Union Oil Company drilled the first oil well in the area. The well failed to produce any oil, and it was abandoned. Further exploration was suspended until the Royal Dutch Shell Oil Company resumed exploration and hit pay dirt on June 23, 1921. That first gusher, at Alamitos well number 1, marked a turning point in Signal Hill's history and put the city on the map.

Uncle Howard Rogers

Uncle Howard spent a few years in the rodeo circuit after he got married. He was in assigned to the Twenty-Sixth Cavalry Regiment, which was the only regiment in existence in World War II. He worked as a cowboy on Santa Rosa Island and helped raise and fatten up beef cattle on the island about forty miles off the coast of Central California.

Cattle offloaded from the Vaquero II, Santa Rosa Island (Prior to 1923)

Cattle were placed on Santa Rosa Island as early as September 1844 when Alpheus B. Thompson took 270 head of cattle to the island. The cattle belonged to island owner, Don Carlos Carrillo, and had the Rocking Horse brand on them. Cattle remained on the island for 155 years, through every change of ownership, until 1999 when Vail & Vickers were required to remove their herds by the National Park Service. The Vail & Vickers cattle boat, *Vaquero*, was taken from them for service in World War II. Ranching continued, but cattle had to be barged off the island and landed in Ventura, California.

Herding Cattle on Santa Rosa Island

From Cows to Space With God as My Copilot

Granite Station, California 1970s (Family Photo)

Uncle Howard

Uncle Howard lived in a small house just to the left of the main station. Granite Station is a former stage stop, which is located in the mountains about forty miles northeast of Bakersfield, California. For many years, Uncle Howard was the lone resident. His responsibility was to ride and check and fix fences of this very large cattle ranch—a job he took very seriously. He was a good friend of James Rogers, the son of the famous Will Rogers.

Uncle Howard and Jimmy Rogers (Family Photo)

Uncle Howard was well known and respected in many small communities in the area. On at least one occasion, he would be the grand marshal for the town of Woodie's annual rodeo and grand parade. He had to have an appendectomy, which kept him from riding the range for only two days. He was a very tough and determined and a tough old buzzard who did his job no matter what. Despite the fact, he was a very tough old codger, he saw all four of our daughters for the first time: Melissa, Natalie, Jennifer, and Meribeth. As tough as he was, he demonstrated his sentimentality and his depth, and he cried seeing his niece Dorothy with four beautiful daughters. Howard was something else. God love him.

Birthday Celebrations

Since Dorothy's mother and Uncle Howard have the same birthdays, many birthday picnics were celebrated at Granite Station and on the benches close by. Dorothy's family and some of my siblings and friends would celebrate their birthdays. The station was surrounded by open country and foothills. All of our young kids and other youngsters would run and roam the foothills. At picnic time, we needed a long tablecloth to cover the tables. Uncle Howard improvised, went into the barn, and brought out a couple of canvas tarps. One of the tarps had blood on it. Of course, the blood was an old dried-up bloodstain. He said, "No problem—a little blood won't hurt anybody." This to him was no different than drinking his very strong cowboy coffee. This coffee is made by just adding more fresh coffee to the pot and boiling it. When there were too many coffee grounds in the pot, he would empty the coffeepot and start over. This is the cowboy way. I drank a little of that stuff, just one time, and it almost took the top of my head off.

He also worked on a large ranch in Carrizo Plains. One day, as a good ranch hand, he was cleaning up the ranch and lit a fire to burn all the debris. The fire got out of control and started a forest fire. He was charged with a federal crime. Uncle Howard wasn't afraid of anything. This charge really got his attention. He dreaded appearing before a federal judge. He couldn't afford a lawyer, so he decided to go it alone—except for Dorothy's mother. Alice, Howard's only sister, is quite a lady and gave his brother excellent advice. Dorothy's mother had a personality that blended well with

Uncle Howard. The San Andreas Fault located not too far from the ranch, was a shaking reminder of what he was up against.

San Andreas escarpment (Public domain)

Dorothy's mother went to his preliminary hearing. She gave him good advice: "Howard just be yourself and be honest with the judge. Just talk as you normally do. For Pete's sake, Howard, watch your mouth and don't cuss."

Upon entry to the courtroom in downtown Los Angeles, the judge looked at this old cowboy, who did not have a lawyer, and was taken in by his presence. He liked his demeanor and the way that this frail-looking cowboy was dressed up in a suit with a cowboy hat and boots. The judge put him at ease with a little small talk. The judge then asked him what he had to say about the case. He brashly said, "Doggone it, Judge, have you ever raked leaves in your own backyard?"

The judge played along with him and said yes.

Uncle Howard Rogers said, "Hell, Judge, that's all I was doing. I was scraping up all the crap that was accumulated over many blue moons. I didn't mean to start a forest fire. I am very sorry that the fire spread and got out of control. You know, Judge, that was awful stupid of me. I am just an innocent cowboy who was in the Twenty-Sixth Cavalry Regiment in World War II. Since then, I have been cowboy ranching all my days, cowpunching to make things meet. I have always taken my work seriously. When I saw that this old ranch was a cluttered mess, I decided to clean it up. I am damn sorry for screwing up. I am most sorry. Please forgive me for this awful blunder. I beg for your forgiveness."

Twenty-Sixth Cavalry Regiment during World War I and World War II

The federal court judge was moved by his straightforward, salty, remorseful explanation and sincerity. He followed up with a few questions and dismissed the case. Later, Uncle Howard told the judge that there was good hunting on the Carrizo Ranch and invited him to come to the ranch for a hunting trip. Sometime later, the judge followed up on his invitation and enjoyed his noteworthy hunting trip. Case definitely closed.

Jack Rogers

Jack Rogers is Dorothy's cousin and is the oldest son of Marion Rogers, who was killed in an auto accident when Jack was very young. In addition, there was another brother, Bill, who was in my graduating class at Wasco High School. Jack was an upperclassman. Jack's wife, Donna, was in Dorothy's graduation class. Donna also attended the University of California, Berkeley, the same years as I did. Jack got along very well with his uncles. Jack and Bill both were a popular presence at Wasco High. Dorothy's two cousins also lived with her grandma and grandpa for a while before they could be reestablished in Aunt Ruth's home between Wasco and Shafter, where they grew up on the prosperous Lohr Ranch. Jack was quite a character. He didn't get involved in any athletics that I remember. Even though Jack was not a jock, his personality carried the day. He was liked and respected by everyone. He had a peculiar sense of humor. I remember him greeting one of his old friends at a major high school reunion. He said, "If I knew that you were coming, I would have brought my double-barreled shotgun." That was Jack. Everybody laughed. He was a fiery redhead. After he came back from the Korean War, he went to college at Cal Poly, San Luis Obispo, and graduated with a bachelor of science degree in agricultural science. Jack never forgot his roots. He considered himself a cowboy despite having various jobs as well as being a rancher and farmer. He particularly liked his Uncle Howard. Jack would always look after his favorite uncle. He took special care of him in his final days.

Granite Station

After Uncle Howard's death, Jack purchased the Granite Station. The previous owner left everything undisturbed and in place. The station was the area's post office and country store. A huge number of open bins were installed that provided as mailboxes for grocery bills that were owed by customers. All of the furniture, kitchen stoves, furnishing, old pictures, bedroom furniture, and many other items were there and in place. You might say that this station was left in original and pristine condition. He moved into his pride and joy: a rustic old picturesque ranch home. After about ten years of ownership, Jack and Donna were not at the station, unfortunately, and it burned down from unknown causes. Jack and Donna were totally devastated. Jack had a very difficult time recovering emotionally from his treasured loss. Jack always considered himself to be a cowboy as he was influenced by his grandpa and Uncle Howard. He joined a very expensive exclusive riding club called Los Rancheros Visitadores. Yes, Jack was definitely a cowboy.

Celebrating Horsemanship on the Santa Ynez Trail

Rancheros Visitadores was the brainchild of a small group of prominent Santa Barbarians who were horse lovers and wished to commemorate the important role horsemanship and ranching had played in the history of the South Coast. Cowboy artist and enthusiast Ed Borein suggested to his friend Elmer Awl that they gather some buddies together for a few days of riding and camping in the Santa Ynez Valley. Borein had spent a good part of his youth as a working cowboy in California and Mexico. Today, he is considered one of the finest artists to portray the range life of the American West. The rancheros' first official trek began May 9, 1930, and lasted four days. A group of ninety men rode from Dwight Murphy's Los Prietos Ranch in the Santa Ynez Valley to Nojoqui Falls. Among the participants were, in addition to those already mentioned, some of the most prominent citizens of the South Coast: county supervisor Sam Stanwood, newspaper publishers Reginald Fernald and Thomas Storke, and philanthropist and yachtsman Max Fleischmann. During the next few years, the organization solidified, and membership grew to include riders from all over the state. In the late 1930s, Walt Disney took part aboard his horse, Minnie Mouse. Clark Gable rode in 1939. Ronald Reagan would ride in the 1970s. Los Rancheros Visitadores numbers almost seven hundred members today and is international in scope. Selected members sit on the board of Los Adobes de Los Rancheros, a separate charitable organization. And every spring, the rancheros mount up for their traditional trek through the Santa Ynez Valley.

Dorothy's California Heritage

    Dorothy has deep California roots. I am very proud to be associated with the John Rogers's pioneering family. They were significantly involved in the early settlement of the greater Southern California empire. They were pioneers in the finest tradition. What a story. I thank God for the many historical accomplishments achieved by the remarkable and noteworthy John Rogers pioneering family.

Chapter 16

Dorothy's Return to College and Studies

I had enough units to graduate with an associate's degree from Bakersfield College in June 1950. I only had a little more than one year taking courses as a math major. With Dorothy beginning her second year in college and me being able to take all the courses I needed to advance my curriculum in mathematics, going to Bakersfield College for a third year was a no-brainer. I did well with my studies the third year. Dorothy continued to excel in college. She was studying to become an occupational therapist. She had to take a lot of those bacteriology, biology, physiology, and psychology courses. We both studied in the college library. We could be seen going from class to class. Everybody knew we were sweethearts. It was much more enjoyable to go to college with your sweetheart not attached to another boyfriend. My third year in college was a stable year where I grew in confidence and comfortable in my major.

Texas Tech University

One of my major concerns was what area of mathematics I should concentrate on. With a math degree, should I teach? What else could I do with a mathematics degree? God took care of me and had a ready-made answer, which in large part is my story.

The Wasco Creamery

The old Wasco Creamery that processed and sold milk commercially finally closed. Dad had sold the dairy cows and then only farmed. Very few dairy farms remained in the Wasco area. The creamery was ideal for a company that needed all kinds of vats, tanks, and other storage facilities. A bio firm company bought out the facility to locate a yeast factory and manufacture other products for vitamins.

My Brother Robert, Production Manager

Then brother Bobby came along to work at the research facility. By then, a major Swiss company called Sandoz had bought the facility. Bobby's industrial engineering degree from Fresno State served him well as the production manager. Bobby ran the stickiest place in town. You could smell it driving on Poso Street when leaving downtown Wasco. For years, Bobby left his mark—or should I say stench.

Need for Lab Assistant

A couple PhD bacteriologists began their research in Wasco. They needed a lab assistant. They went to Bakersfield College to look for their best student in bacteriology. The professor in her bacteriology class chose Dorothy as her best student. Who other than Dorothy? She lived in Wasco about a mile away on the same street where the plant was located. She studied hard and tried to do her best, proving again that those qualities excel. The job included odd hours. The products the lab was dealing with had to be cared for and nurtured. She filled in with my help in and between dates, and we had to go over to the plant and check on the progress of the smelly mixtures in making yeast. She was paid a modest salary. She was broadening her resume, which went beyond babysitting, potato picking, cotton picking, working in fruit sheds, and serving as a carhop. She could multitask, which is a most-needed capability to raise a batch of kids.

Color-Blind

Dorothy and I were studying in the library when her bacteriology professor came dashing into the room acting like he was on a mission. He was halfway panicked looking for someone who was color-blind to use as a guinea pig to demonstrate color-blindness. After exhausting his chances on others in the library, he noticed Dorothy—after all, she was in his class—and he came over to talk to her. She found out what he wanted, and Dorothy told him, in her own oblique way, test me out. "He has trouble with colors." She got the instructor excited. He showed me a whole bunch of pictures with all kinds of colors on it. He asked me what I saw. I said the number twenty-three. Wrong number, but it was the right number he was looking for. He proceeded to test me by showing all kinds of pictures. Every answer I gave created a crescendo of excitement. He told me I was color-blind. Dorothy was amused. My initial response was no surprise because I would get into arguments with my friends regarding the colors of things. I thought to myself, *Well, I'll be darned. I am color-blind. Imagine that.*

Dorothy's Class

I reluctantly contemplated the teacher's request to go to his class that day. After much encouragement from Dorothy, I decided to go. Dorothy was in the front row. The teacher introduced me. I was asked to perform some tasks. I had to select the ribbons of the same color from a display of ribbons on a large table. I was asked to separate them into different piles. The instructor also had a "don't know pile" for me to deposit rejects. Before I was done, I had the class in stitches. I would pick up one color, look at it, and put it back in the same large pile. I got most of the blues and yellows properly located in the right pile. I was able to pile many in the "don't know pile." It was a challenging and embarrassing set of tasks trying to figure out the proper colors. I was playing what I call dirty pool.

The instructor realized he had punished me enough. Witnessing Dorothy's laughter, he came to my rescue and asked a final telling question: "What color dress is Dorothy wearing?"

I thought about it for a bit. I realized I failed again with my response.

The instructor turned to Dorothy and said, "It doesn't matter what color clothes you wear. Fritz won't be able to appreciate them." This brought applause. The instructor was happy, Dorothy still liked me color-blind or not, and she got an A in class. I was relieved to find out I was not dumb about colors—just color-blind. I couldn't blame my mother for passing on ancestral color-blindness. It is all God's fault for giving me such a gift. One of my sons is color-blind—and so are some of my grandkids. The DNA and genes go on and on. Finally, I was happy to leave the class on a high note, holding hands with my sweetheart and being a little wiser.

Dating, Dancing, and Chewing Gum

We continued our next year at Bakersfield College, riding the bus back and forth from Wasco each day. We would continue dating by going to football games, college dances, movies, family functions, and other outings. I remember the time I took Dorothy to one of the dances. I was chewing gum while we were dancing. As we twirled around on the dance floor, her hair removed the Dentine from my mouth with the speed of light and dangled the gum right in front of her eyes. She immediately screamed bloody murder, thinking it was a large spider. The couples dancing around us were as startled as I was. One or two couples gave me a strange look as if I had gotten carried away. I quickly recovered and explained what had happened to those within earshot. We all laughed at this comical incident. I joined the laugh to neutralize my embarrassment.

College Sweethearts

Since Dorothy and I were known as sweethearts, we were asked to pose for pictures to be used as advertisement in the 1952 Bakersfield College annual. We had an enjoyable year together. Dorothy graduated with honors.

Goodbye, Bakersfield College—and off to the universities to begin our upper-division studies in our majors.

Chapter 17

Shake, Rattle, and Roll

The big Tehachapi earthquake (All quake pictures were obtained from Bakersfield. com)

I was sound asleep in the predawn hours of July 20, 1952, and I was nearly shaken out of bed. I looked at the ceiling, heard all kinds of cracking, and finally realized an earthquake was happening. I rubbed my eyes to see if I was dreaming. It seemed to never stop shaking. It scared me. I looked out the window from my bedroom and saw the cotton moving and rattling around between the farmhouse and Joe's place, about 150 yards across the cotton field.

What really caught my eye was watching the downtown Wasco streetlights swaying. They were only about mile and a half away. It was still very dark as I watched the city of Wasco jumping up and down to the rolling frequency of the quake. I thought to myself, *Holy cow, gee whiz, holy smokes, things are going to get very dicey around here.* I got up, put on my Levi's, put on my slippers as fast as I could, and managed to get through a den area and down a utility hall. I had to negotiate the old noisy GE refrigerator, with a large cooler on top, which was wobbling in front of me as I dashed out the front door.

When I finally got outside, I looked south toward Bakersfield, and I witnessed a great explosion that lit up the sky. Bakersfield was about twenty-five miles away. I immediately thought it was an atomic blast. The big flash was a power station that lit up.

Our neighbor Clara came across the cotton field from her house and approached me. She was carrying a crucifix and a rosary. "Did you feel that?"

I felt like laughing, but I didn't because I didn't want to offend her.

Don't Cuss

By that time, the rest of the family had gotten out of the house. Richard told me later that he heard Pop state, "Don't cuss." Dad was known to fly off the handle. I think that order was meant for himself rather than the kids. Later, we teased my dad in a casual manner that reminded him to clean up his language, particularly when he got upset. Wasco had minor damage but rattled nerves. This was a 7.3 earthquake, with the epicenter located about fifty miles distant, the way the crow flies. Only superficial damage was done to the city of Wasco. Even the brick Catholic church survived the tremor. People lost some sleep and were shaken up and somewhat terrified by all the shaking. I heard that a gentleman in the housing area of downtown Wasco ran out of his house without anything on. His wife told him to go into the house and put some clothes on. He returned a very short time later—with only his hat on.

Downtown Tehachapi

Aftershocks

Following the earthquake, there were aftershocks, and some resulted in a fair amount of shaking. Richard and I, as pranksters, would play tricks on Mom and poor Clara. The family kitchen was built over the cellar, which meant that you could shake the kitchen a little bit by stomping on the floor. A couple of times, we would shake the kitchen while Mom was cooking. Mom would say, "There goes another quake." We would say, "We didn't feel anything." Then she realized we were playing a little dirty pool and laughed it off. Mom got wise to us, but a small aftershock rattled the kitchen while we were sitting at the kitchen table with Mom. Mom thought we were up to our old tricks and was about to scold us until she realized the kitchen kept shaking. She stopped what she was doing for a minute and then went about her kitchen duties. We all laughed. Another time, I said, "Rich let's go over and shake Clara's house." We tried, unsuccessfully, but Clara got wise to what we were doing. She forcedly ran us off and said, "Don't you have anything else better to do?"

Year of the Earthquakes

The year of 1952 is now known as the year of the earthquakes. Dorothy and I got married a couple of months later. When asked, "When were you married?" I would jokingly respond during the year of the earthquakes.

During the earthquake, Dorothy was living on F Street in Wasco in a two-story home with her mother and the Trew family. Dorothy slept upstairs along with her very young sister, Pamela, and her younger brother, Stan. During an earthquake, hibernating upstairs, one feels a little more shaking—enough to send them outside to sleep at nights. Dorothy and her young siblings slept outside; Dorothy, Pamela, Stan, and Ellis slept outside the next evening and for weeks following the big quake. I would occasionally join them, a night or two, to accompany them. The kids were all excited, and Howard Ellis wouldn't keep his mouth shut. Dorothy told him many times to keep his mouth shut. Dorothy was becoming a little exasperated. "Howard Ellis Trew, you better keep your mouth shut—or I will slug you a good one." He immediately responded "You just heard it." I began to laugh very loudly, and Dorothy got a little angrier, which turned into a big laugh and giggle. Everybody settled down after that exchange, and we all finally got some sleep. No more aftershocks.

Off to San Jose to Buy the Wedding Rings

I had arranged to take Mom on a trip to San Francisco for visiting friends. I took the occasion to stop in San Jose to pick up our wedding rings. One of Dorothy's roommates was employed at a jewelry store in downtown San Jose. I was offered a sweetheart deal. Walking across the street to enter the store, my mother noticed a very slight shake. I didn't feel anything. My mind was on the rings. The family at home knew that we would be there before a given time in case of an emergency. As we entered the jewelry store, Dorothy's friend informed us that someone called and wanted to talk to Mom. It was Dorothy's mother to inform us that Mary, my oldest sister, just had twin girls at Mercy Hospital in Bakersfield. She told Mom to call Mary at the hospital ASAP. Mom called and spoke to Mary. The twins came earlier than expected. Everybody was just fine.

Dorothy's mother has many friends, and Dr. Mary Hendricks was her primary doctor. Dr. Mary was my sister Mary's doctor as well. Upon going to see Dr. Mary on a routine pregnancy visit, Dr. Mary decided there was an emergency need to go to the hospital. The hospital in Wasco was limited, so her doctor said that she must go to more experienced staff of pregnancy doctors to care for her emergency delivery. Dr. Mary tried unsuccessfully to contact her husband. So she told Dorothy's mother to rush Mary to the hospital in Bakersfield. Dorothy's mother was rather leadfooted. She said, "Okay, no problem." As fate would have it, the deadly earth quake that hit Bakersfield on August 22, 1952, occurred during the delivery.

Bakersfield College library

Department store

Bakersfield historic clock tower

When Mom talked to Mary, she did not say anything about the earthquake. She was probably under a sedative. After the delivery, she wasn't thinking about earthquakes, understandably so. If Mom had called about ten minutes later, she would not have been able to get through for three days due to the earthquake.

Off to San Francisco

On the way to San Francisco, Mom had some concerns about having an earthquake in San Francisco. After the Tehachapi 7.3 earthquake, which severely shook, shocked, and jolted almost all of Kern County, just a month prior on July 20, 1952, we were all getting very quake conscious. By the time we were on the freeway headed, it was all over the news on the radio. We kept getting updates piecemeal as we traveled. It was reported that there were five deaths in downtown Bakersfield. Three were killed in Lerner's Dress Shop, and a couple more died at the San Joaquin Farm Equipment Center.

San Juaquin Farm Equipment Center

In addition, the famous Bakersfield historic clock tower landmark was heavily damaged and downtown stores and buildings were severely damaged as well. The clock tower had to be torn down and replaced. Bakersfield was not the same for quite a while. Dorothy and I had to get our marriage license at a temporary location downtown, and we shopped at some of other major stores set up in temporary buildings. Less than a month later, Dorothy and I got married.

Chapter 18

The Wedding

We decided to get married, and Dorothy decided not to return her senior year at San Jose State College. After more than three years of courtship, we both wanted to get married. Dorothy, with her mother, decided a good date would be the September 14, 1952, which was the weekend before I had to return to the University of California for my senior year. The Catholic wedding was a large affair. My dad was a very well-known dairy farmer in the greater Wasco area. Dorothy's mother, Alice, was well known in Wasco for all of her charitable and volunteer work efforts. Dorothy was not Catholic, but she was baptized in the local Congregational church. The cutest part of the wedding ceremony was Dorothy's very young sister Pamela as the flower girl, and her brother Stan Lee as the ring bearer. Nicely dressed, they made a great impression.

Wedding Party with Pam and Stan (Family Album)

I made a serious faux pas. I forget the wedding rings. I left them on my dresser at home. I pressed my younger brother Richard to go home and pick up the rings, in crisis mode, and asked him to return as fast as he could. This he did in spectacular fashion. As Richard entered the church in time, he didn't have to miss a step when he got in line along with the other brothers as they all marched toward the altar together. Richard saved me from immense embarrassment, and I thank God and Richard for saving the day.

Our wedding vows (Family Album)
Reception line (Family Album)

Dorothy and I exchanged our vows, and shortly thereafter, we greeted all the people as they left the church, and then proceeded over to the church hall for the reception.

The celebration began. All kinds of finger foods, snacks, and other dishes were provided by Dorothy's mom and other friends. Dad bought sufficient and different kinds of liquor, including Swiss schnapps, in addition to all of the refreshments for all the kids. Dorothy and I did not drink since we planned to travel about one hundred miles to Paso Robles for our honeymoon.

Dorothy and I at the wedding reception (Family Album)

Adult beverages (Public domain)

Most of the other adults drank the booze, including Dorothy's mother, Alice, who drank enough to be a little tipsy. She was tipsy enough to let my brother Richard wear her fancy large-brimmed hat. Richard had enough to drink to parade around the dance floor wearing her hat. Richard has the special talent to be funny without making a fool of himself. Everybody enjoyed the show. Richard was celebrating our wedding and his great ring-retrieval expedition.

Clemens Strieff (Montz)

Montz, a wonderful Swiss gentleman, was one of the milk hands for many years on Dad's dairy farm. He now works 24/7 on my uncle John's dairy farm. He knew he had to get up the next morning very early. He doesn't get very many nights or days off except for vacations now and then. He was sitting among a number of a Swiss friends. He was drinking Swiss schnapps. As he sat there, another friend of his walked up to greet him. Montz, the gentleman that he was, began to stand up to shake his hand, and he fell back into the arms of another friend. He wasn't hurt. We all laughed at his throaty laugh. He had to leave early because of his early morning commitment to milk cows. Richard escorted wobbly Montz, still wearing Alice's fancy hat, to board his old Ford sedan, which was built like a German tank.

Ford Model T (Public domain)

Montz never drove a car. He just milked cows and raised four children. His wife, Lena, got behind the steering wheel, and Richard helped him into the car. Richard jokingly told him to safely drive Lennie home. That got a special schnapps laugh from him. He would throw his head back and belch out a very loud laugh.

Bound for San Francisco

Later in the evening, Richard and Rose boarded the *Midnight Streamliner* to return to San Francisco. Rose was going to St. Mary's Nursing School, and Richard was going to the University of San Francisco. Knowing Richard, he probably still partied on the booze that he previously consumed at the reception until about halfway to San Francisco—and then the other half was probably more unpleasant.

Honeymoon

That evening, Dorothy and I left to go to Paso Robles for our honeymoon. Earlene Borjon, Dorothy's childhood friend, and a few others greatly modified the appearance of our 1948 Chevrolet two-door sedan. A bunch of beer and soda cans were wired on the bumper that was very difficult to remove. They mounted baby shoes that dangled on the inside of our windshield, along with a display of diapers. They chased us a long way out of town, and I stopped and removed the cans—but not before I burned one of my hands twisting off all that wire. The trip over to Paso Robles was long, and we snuggled the way there. We had a late snack at the Paso Robles Inn, and Dorothy proceeded to spill rice all over the floor. We stayed at the Clifton Motel, which was an above-average motel.

Unbeknownst to us, at the time, it was where Joe DiMaggio and Marilyn Monroe spent their honeymoon. I am sure that we didn't have the same room. I am proud to say that we both consummated our marriage vows after marriage. I am convinced that the Lord has blessed us for living his way before and after marriage. The next day, we left for Berkeley and arrived at our single-bedroom apartment on the north side of the campus. The apartment had a separate small kitchen and a single cot in the kitchen area. This apartment was about five blocks from the campus. Our first home together. How sweet it is—as Jackie Gleason would expound.

Yosemite National Park

The next day I registered for my senior year at the University of California at Berkeley. The university had it organized, and I was able to complete registration by noon. Dorothy had a lunch all prepared, and we left on a honeymoon trip to Yosemite National Park. We stayed at Camp Curry. Of course, we saw all of the fantastic views. The most spectacular was the night Fire Fall and the lovely song "Indian Love Call." The following is reproduced from the official Yosemite Park website.

"Let the Fire Fall!" (Credits)

For decades those words ushered in one of the most famous spectacles: the Yosemite Firefall. Each evening in the summer, a roaring bonfire was built at the edge of g, which towers 3,200 feet above Yosemite Valley. By sundown hundreds of spectators had gathered in Curry Village below. At 9:00 p.m. sharp, a master of ceremonies in Curry Village shouted out, let the fire fall! and the bonfire's glowing embers were pushed over the edge of Glacier Point, creating a glittering waterfall of fire.

The Yosemite fire fall was inadvertently started in 1872 by James McCauley, owner of the Glacier Point Mountain House Hotel. Each night in the summer, McCauley built a campfire at the edge of Glacier Point to entertain his guests. He then put out the fire by kicking the smoldering embers over the edge of the cliff. As the glowing embers tumbled thousands of feet through the air, they were spotted by visitors below in Yosemite Valley. Before long, people began requesting to see the firefall. Sensing a business opportunity, McCauley's sons began asking visitors in Yosemite Valley for donations. They then hauled extra wood to Glacier Point to build bigger campfires, resulting in more dramatic Yosemite firefalls.

In 1897 McCauley was evicted from Glacier Point, and after twenty-five years the nightly Yosemite firefall came to an abrupt halt. Several years later, Yosemite Valley Hotel owner David Curry heard his guests reminiscing about the firefall, and he took it upon himself to reinstate the spectacle for special occasions. He also added a few dramatic flourishes of his own. After his employees had built a roaring fire at Glacier Point, Curry would call out in a booming voice, "Hello, Glacier Point!" After receiving a loud "Hello" in response, Curry would thunder out, "Let 'er go, Gallagher!" at which point the burning embers were pushed over the edge.

In 1913 the National Park Service banned the Yosemite firefall (possibly as punishment over a leasing dispute with David Curry), but it was reinstated in 1917. Within a few years, the firefall had adopted the following ritual: at nine o'clock sharp, a master of ceremonies in Camp Curry would bellow out the following exchange with a fire master at Glacier Point:

Hello, Glacier Point! Hello, Camp Curry! Is the fire ready?

The fire is ready! (Public domain)

Chapter 19

Senior Year at the University

The next day, we left for Berkeley and arrived at our single-bedroom apartment on the north side of the campus. The apartment had a separate small kitchen and a single cot in the kitchen area. As it turned out, my sister Rose made good use of that cot as a reprieve from her nursing studies. When Roque Borjon returned from Korea, we picked up Earlene Borjon at the Berkeley train station to stay with us for a couple of days, so she could be reunited with her husband. Roque had just returned from Korea on a troop ship. We all met him and waved to him as he came down the ramp of the ship, and we brought him to Treasure Island to muster out. He got off about midnight, and I picked him up and brought him to our apartment—and they honeymooned again. I brought Roque back to Treasure Island to make roll call a few hours later. Dorothy and I slept on the cot. It proved once again that it is single cot. Neither of us weighed nearly as much as we do now. No problem. They had gotten married shortly before Roque went to Korea. They didn't have much time together before he departed. We were great friends. We were very happy in our new home in Berkeley. No more trips to San Jose! I didn't join the rifle team my senior year. Dorothy bought her first Christmas tree for five dollars. The Christmas tree had to spend time alone as we went to Wasco for the holidays.

Pregnancy

We were practicing what was called Vatican Roulette after we got married. This lasted a couple of months, and then Dorothy became pregnant with Melissa. It wasn't long before Dorothy suffered morning sickness that seemed to last most of the day—for at least three or four months. What a miserable way to start a marriage! The Lord rewarded our sacrifice with Melissa, our first of four marvelous daughters. Tomato soup was about the only thing Dorothy could eat without getting sick. I had to go out a few times in the middle of the night to find a market that sold Campbell's soup at odd hours. As my senior year progressed, Dorothy got to feeling better. I studied hard. I did very well my senior year. I had an interest in mathematical statistics and included mathematical statistics as my minor. This was very fortunate because I was introduced to computers in one of my probability classes.

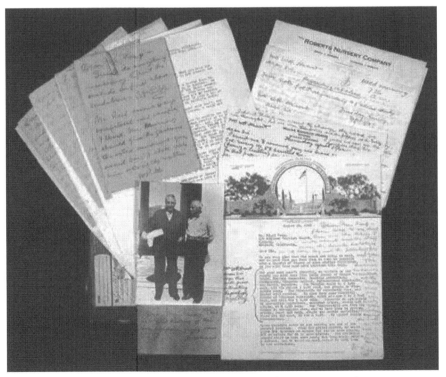

Mr. Nigel Keep, Horticulturist (Prior to 1923)

William Randolph Hearst

Hearst Castle (Public domain)

I worked for a nice old gentleman by the name of Nigel Keep. He had a very interesting career and worked directly for William Randolph Hearst as his private horticulturist. He landscaped all of the surroundings of Hearst Castle in the early construction days. He told me all kinds of personal stories about Mr. Hearst. He first met Mr. Hearst at a large nursery where Mr. Keep was employed. Mr. Hearst wanted to buy three hundred trees. Mr. Keep asked him what for. When he responded, he told Mr. Hearst not to buy the trees. Mr. Hearst did not buy trees that day, but a day later, he came back and offered him a job.

Part-Time Jobs

When I met and worked for Mr. Keep, he was a ninety-year-old cigar-smoking gentleman. We became friends, and I worked in his yard and cleaned his home in the Berkeley Hills. He would follow me around, on occasion, and want to talk because he was a lonely elderly gentleman. He gave me shoes. He would sneak them out, so his wife wouldn't see him, and then hide the shoes in the bushes and tell me where to look. He was featured in the Hearst Museum, which is located near the passenger entrance for tourists waiting for the bus ride to Hearst Castle.

President Dwight Eisenhower's Election

I worked in Oakland on Election Day when President Eisenhower was elected. Once you get selected for one of those election assignments, you were put on the list for other elections. I served in another local election. I worked at a number of other odd jobs to help pay expenses. I continued my last semester as a senior and was eager to move on and get a permanent job to support my family.

Socialization

More of the same grinding away. Very little socializing. Dorothy spent a good part of my senior year with morning sickness. Four upper-division mathematics courses kept me out of the pool halls. We had good neighbors living across the hall from us. They had a TV and invited us over to watch the wrestling matches and other programs. Those wrestling matches are about as fake as some politicians, but they enjoyed them. Dorothy spent quite a bit of time visiting and talking with her. She was a very pleasant lady.

Our neighbors from across the hall came down to visit us once when we were living at Edwards AFB. He said that he never saw a mathematician at work before. I gave him a tour of our computer and the flight line. All that computer stuff and all those different aircraft really overwhelmed him. We had a visit from Dorothy's cousin, Jack Rogers, who was visiting his fiancée, Donna Giddings, one of Dorothy's classmates at Wasco High. He recently returned from the army serving in the Korean War. He didn't have a car, so they used our faithful Dodge. In addition, I had other high school classmates who attended the university. Mr. Charles Harrington—the son of Mr. Clifford Harrington, my math teacher mentor in high school—also attended. Charles later got a law degree from Berkeley and became a judge in Alameda County in the Bay Area.

Mr. Clifford Harrington was a great inspiration for me. I marveled the way he worked the gigantic slide he had on display in his class. He always referred to the University of California at Berkeley in his class. When I went off to university, Berkeley was my one and only choice. I was able to get into the university my junior year. At the time, being accepted was not a problem. I was not an A student, but my grades were adequate. On one occasion, I was taking a planned trip to Berkeley. He had reason to visit his son Charles and needed a ride. I offered him a ride with my dad. We had a nice travel companion and visited with my former mathematics teacher in high school. During World War II, Dad had difficulty obtaining cotton pickers to harvest cotton. Arrangements were made to have high school students pick cotton on specified afternoons during the week. Mr. Harrington was there in his overalls, and a few other teachers picked cotton as well. Dad arranged to allow German prisoners to pick cotton. Since Dad could speak fluent German, he liked to communicate with them. The guards didn't mind, and it was motivation for the prisoners. I would pick cotton in the same fields separated from them. The prisoners would look at and mention something in German that I did not understand. By the time I was growing up, the teachers at school advised my parents to speak English, so I never could converse in Swiss except with some short phrases. Dad was known to cuss a little bit in Swiss. He watched his language in English. So I got to know a few choice words and exclamations in Swiss. We never heard Dad speak the four-letter word. We did not either.

Ready to Start My Career

After three years at Bakersfield College and two years at the University of California—and with Dorothy pregnant—I was eager and ready to begin a career. Edwards Air Force Base, here I come. As a former farm boy going to the hot confines of the Mojave Desert, I did not know what to expect. I worried and wondered if I would be able to do the job as a mathematician. I wondered if everybody else in my position would feel the same way. I had to convince myself that I was capable. That was when I prayed to God. Help me! Ever since, I felt that God assisted me many times and in many ways unbeknown to me. God was and is my copilot. I hopped on the bandwagon and went on a terrific journey toward outer space.

Chapter 20

The Right Place at the Right Time

    I graduated from the University of California, Berkeley with a BS degree in mathematics and mathematical statistics. Two days later, I was at Edwards Air Force Base in the Mojave Desert ready to begin my career. I did not attend my graduation ceremonies.

    Dorothy and I arrived at Edwards Air Force Base on June 25, 1953, on the second anniversary of the establishment of Edwards AFB. We made a right turn east of Mojave, California, near the famous Ma Green's store, located just outside the north gate entrance to Edwards Air Force Base. This was our first visit. Dorothy was seven months pregnant with our first child, Melissa. It was very hot in the afternoon with temperatures above one hundred degrees. We didn't have to say it, but I'm sure we both thought it: *What the hell are we doing here?* I was fulfilling a dream of working with airplanes, and I didn't care how hot it got. Dorothy never complained. It was a beginning of a long journey that Dorothy and I would experience together. Traveling as partners through life, I was employed at Edwards for more than thirty-eight years, including my years as a consultant.

Government Housing

The United States government permitted a few civilians to live in base housing. Since I had special skills as a mathematician, we were allowed accommodations in base housing. We got settled in a rented two-quadraplex, two-bedroom apartment that was perfectly adequate for Dorothy and me. I started working at Edwards Air Force Base as a lowly GS-5, making about $260 a month. Rent on the quadraplex was $60 a month and included all the utilities. A good deal indeed! We shopped at the base commissary by taking benefit of very low food prices.

On my first day of employment, I was impressed when I arrived at personnel. I was offered three different positions at Edwards Air Force Base. I could either work up at the rocket lab on Lehman Ridge, the track branch south of the base, or the Data Reduction Branch, which was located on the flight line. When I was at Berkeley, one my mathematical statistics classes utilized an IBM calculating punch computer. My professor was involved in developing sampling techniques for polling that was used during the general election polling process leading up to the election of President Dwight D. Eisenhower. This statistics class involved probability theory, expectations, computer-sampling techniques, and solving many other applicable statistics problems. We were asked to solve a problem to determine how many names would have to be drawn from a random sample taken from the Berkeley phone book to locate two individuals with the same birthday. The answer is an average of twenty-three. We were all surprised at such a low number. I enthusiastically chose the data-reduction branch that had a computer and very close to the aircraft flight line. I was set up with a consultation meeting with the civilian director of flight test located in the main aircraft hangar on the flight line.

Orientation with My Flight Test Director

Mr. Paul Bikle had a nice nameplate as director of flight tests. He was the top engineering manager at Edwards AFB. I later found out that he was the famous Paul Bikle who won and owned the world's gliding record, reaching an altitude of 43,000 feet, without a space suit of any kind. He held that record for many years.

Mr. Paul Bikle Record Holder (AF Photo)

Sitting in his office, I remained silent for a short time. I just sat there while he was writing. I was patiently desk facing him when I realized that he was writing my job description. I read the job description and was quite amazed at how well he could write about my job, which was so low in the directorate of flight testing. He was very kind and wished me a wonderful and successful career at the flight test center. I was directed and shown my workplace, which was located in an old World War II duplex near the flight line. It didn't look like much from the outside, but it contained all kinds of IBM equipment, including a card-programed calculator (CPC). This was IBM's first attempt at getting into the scientific computer field. As modest as it was, IBM was the United States premier computer business corporation in existence at the time.

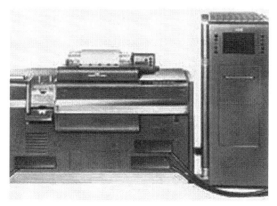

The IBM card programmed calculator (IBM picture)

Major Test Programs and Other Aircraft Testing

YF-100A Supersonic Sabre

The North American YF-100A made its maiden flight about one month prior to my arrival at Edwards. The F-86 series of aircraft were becoming outdated. The YF-100A was the first American fighter jet capable of supersonic speed in level flight. The F-100 was conceived in 1949 and developed in the 1950s during some of the hottest years of the cold war. The famous F-86 Sabre jet fighter was the aircraft on which the YF-100A was loosely based. It was one of the first American aircraft to incorporate significant amounts of titanium. The structure of the F-100 was much more than a redesigned F-86.

The F-100 began as an unsolicited proposal from North American Aviation for a supersonic fighter for the United States Air Force. North American's mock-up of the design was inspected on July 7, 1951. After numerous modifications, the new aircraft was accepted as the YF-100A on November 30, 1951. On January 3, 1952, the United States Air Force ordered two prototypes of the YF-100A to be followed by numerous production buys. The YF-100A was first flown in May 1953. The YF-100 prototype performed so well that the F-100 went into reproduction just five months later.

XB-52A Long-Range Stratofortress (AF Photo)

When I started working at Edwards Air Force Base, Boeing Aircraft and the air force began planning and testing of the prototype XB-52A Long-Range Stratofortress. This new bomber was designed to replace the bombers used during World War II. This flight test program was the biggest game in town. I would have a front-row seat in aviation and space development. What a ride!

Computers and Flight Testing

The little experience I got with computers in my statistics class at the university opened my eyes that computers were the way to go. I had a love relationship with airplanes *and* computers. I had no desire to become a pilot, but I certainly wanted to get involved with airplanes. The good Lord provided me the great opportunity to engage in my two technical passions: involvement in flight testing of all the latest aircraft in development and the opportunity to explore my strong interest in the utilization of scientific computers. What more could I ask for?

There were all kinds of test activities going on at Edwards Air Force Base when I arrived. This included all the models of the F-86: A, B, C, D, E, F, and H.

North American F-86E Sabre (All AF photos)

The F-86 is by far the best known of the first generation of American jet fighters. Work on the F-86 began in 1945 and resulted in the first prototype in August 1947. The Sabre was the first swept-wing jet fighter to enter service—and the first to be able to exceed Mach 1 in a dive. The Sabre made its name during the Korean War against the Soviet-designed MiG-15. The F-86E is the improved version of the F-86 day fighter. The Sabre was used extensively around the world—with twenty-five countries flying the aircraft. The sabers were also licensed in Australia, Canada, and Japan. Maximum speed for the F-86E was 599 miles per hour—with service ceiling of 48,000 feet and a range of more than a thousand miles!

The F-86H Sabre Hawk

The F-89 Scorpion

One of my flight test engineer friends, Bill Borkowitz, was killed along with the test pilot attempting to fly Mach 1 in a nosedive.

The Mammoth B36 Long-Range Peacemaker

The C-97 Globefreighter

The C-97 was the first airplane I ever flew in. That was about two weeks after Melissa was born. A couple of new mathematicians, flight test engineers, and summer aides were hired that year. They were given the opportunity to fly as passengers in this very large double-decker cargo aircraft.

C-130 Hercules aircraft assigned to the Blue Angels, flies over western Montana by official US Navy imagery.

All those aircraft parked near the flight line—as well as those stored in two gigantic hangars—were a spectacular sight indeed. What a computations nightmare the flight test engineers had with only the use of a slide rule! A new computer arrived at Edwards before I did. Needless to say, Edwards was in desperate need of mathematicians. I answered an Edwards AFB recruitment call made by USAF Lieutenant Griesedieck of Griesedieck Brothers Beer fame. I filled out an application. Thankfully, this job, as a mathematician, provided Dorothy and me a long, wonderful journey. God gave us eight great kids—four girls and then four boys. Being a mathematician, I figured out that it was two to the eighth power chance of our kids being born in that sequential order, which is 1 out of 128. Dorothy encouraged me day by day as we pursued my career every step of way. I could have never made it without her lifelong support advancing my career spanning from cows to space.

Chapter 21

All You Need to Know about Edwards Air Force Base

Note: This information was taken from the official website files of AFFTC.

Edwards Air Force Base was established in 1951. Edwards is a United States Air Force installation located in Kern County in Southern California about thirty miles northeast of Lancaster, California, and fifteen miles east of Rosamond, California. It is the home of the Air Force Test Center, previously named the Air Force Flight Test Center (AFFTC), USAF Test Pilot School, and NASA's Armstrong Flight Research Center. It is the Air Force Materiel Command Center for conducting and supporting research and development of flight as well as testing and evaluating aerospace systems from concept to combat. It is also host for many activities conducted by America's commercial passenger jet industry for certain tests. Throughout my career, I have witnessed many commercial aircraft doing takeoff and landing refusal tests, using the Edwards AFB runway for FA certifications. Edwards Air Force Base covers 308,000 acres and spans three counties. It is twelve square miles larger than Los Angeles. Kern County, which covers the major portion of the base, is larger than Rhode Island. It features twenty-two runways, four of which are paved. Edwards AFB is surrounded by flight test areas, the largest of which is the R-2508 complex.

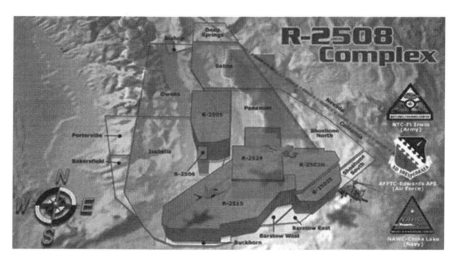

The R-2508 complex includes all the airspace and associated land used by the three principal military testing activities in the Upper Mojave Desert region. Namely, the Naval Air Weapons Station at China Lake located near Inyokern, the National Training Center at Fort Irwin located near Barstow, and the Air Force Flight Test Center, which collectively use this gigantic area. The R-2508 Complex is composed of internal restricted areas, military operations areas, and other special use airspace. Use of these areas includes bombing ranges, supersonic corridors, low-altitude and high-speed maneuvers, radar-intercept areas, and refueling areas. The airspace is used for precisely measured and surveyed for the establishment of speed courses. Many aircraft speed records were set and certified.

Captain Glen Edwards (Air Force Photo)

Edwards AFB was named in honor of Captain Glen Edwards, who lost his life flying the YB-49A, known as the Flying Wing, during a test mission flown on June 5, 1948. I was a senior at Wasco High School.

The Flying Wing (AF Photo)

The Flying Wing silhouetted strange shapes in the sky before UFOs became a mystery. I met and worked with his nephew, Dale Edwards, a great friend, who was IBM's sales representative for this area. Later, when I became chief of the Data Reduction Branch, we rented all kinds of IBM computer equipment from Dale as the IBM sales representative. We made Edwards AFB's entry into the modern computer age.

Air Force and NACA joint flight test agreement (AF document)

The Air Force Flight Test Center, in the early days, established a joint flight test agreement with NACA. The air force was heavily involved in NACA research, which included all the famous X-series research aircraft. The air force provided all the airspace and most of the base facilities. Test pilots flew with and for NASA in support of almost all NACA research programs, including the X-Series research vehicles. In addition, the air force provided technical support for programs that needed flight test engineering, computer programming, or other computing services.

Flight testing is a branch of aeronautical engineering that develops and gathers data during flight of an aircraft and then analyzes the data to evaluate the aerodynamic flight characteristics of the vehicle in order to validate the design, including safety aspects. The flight test phase accomplishes two major tasks: finding and fixing any design problems and then verifying and documenting the vehicle capabilities for government certification or customer acceptance. The flight test phase can range from the test of a single new system for an existing vehicle to the complete development and certification of a new aircraft launch vehicle or reusable spacecraft. Therefore, the duration of a flight test program can vary from a few weeks to many years. Flight testing of military aircraft is often conducted at military flight test facilities.

My Early Involvement in Flight Testing

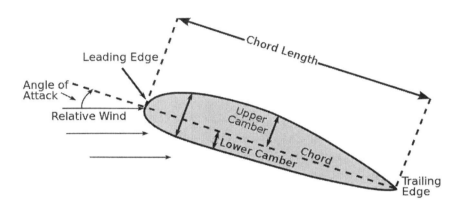

When I first began working at Edwards AFB, my assignments were working with and for flight test engineers in accomplishing the Edwards flight test mission. The flight test engineers were kings in my eyes. It was their responsibility to make sure everything was accomplished and the test reports were prepared. Approved, signed of course, we couldn't accomplish anything without the test pilots. Test pilots are extremely confident and capable of doing their jobs. I know quite a few who paid the ultimate price. Test pilots are brave souls to do what they're doing. When I first started to work at Edwards, most of the famous test pilots would buy and drive the oldest jalopies they could find. It was their badge of courage and honor to sport themselves around the base in those old clunkers. The test pilots got the glory, and the flight test engineers and all other technical support people got the work. I agree that they were made of the right stuff, but the right stuff included a lot more stuff that was provided by all the support of highly trained aeronautical engineer and technical support personnel working behind the scenes.

My story unfolds as a mathematician, computer programmer, and general supervisory engineer managing a plethora of vital key organizations, including the manager of the Edwards Flight Test Range (EFTR). I was technically involved in supporting virtually all the AFFTC test programs and NASA's X series of research aircraft. I had a front-row seat, and a bird's-eye view, working hand in hand with many organizations and personnel engaged in flight testing at Edwards. I marveled in awe when I witnessed aviation and space history in the making. My story, to a certain extent, is a behind-the-scenes look at what flight testing is about from my perspective. In addition, this is not only my story, but also, in certain ways, it is a flight test engineering story of those who provided the United States of America with the first line of DOD offensive and defensive weapons systems, keeping our country great and safe through many gut-wrenching times. You kept the United States number one in the world. My hat is off to all, and I salute you. God bless America.

Chapter 22

YF-100A Supersonic Sabre

The YF-100 ushered in the supersonic era for military vehicles in level flight and quick-started my career at the Air Force Flight Test Center at Edwards AFB. The YF-100A made its first flight on May 23, 1953.

I was assigned as the mathematician to work with Alfred D. Phillips, the chief aeronautical flight test engineer. He had the overall responsibility to plan, conduct, collect, and analyze test data and then prepare a final report that would be used to prepare Dash-2 manuals. These manuals were prepared by other air force experts but based on the results of the flight tests. These manuals provide the documentation needed for prime air force pilots to perform their combat missions. It contained all kinds of aircraft performance data. Needless to say, these Dash-2 manuals were considered bibles for aircraft flying operations under all flight conditions. I was flying my vehicle that I designated as the WS-100, which was the name I gave to my World War II GI desk. The WS stood for my workstation, and the 100 stood for the outside air temperature on a relatively mild day.

History in the Making

I was in the middle of all these historic events, but I didn't realize at the time that history was in the making. Back in the early days, there was no reference to the "right stuff." It wasn't until Tom Wolfe wrote *The Right Stuff*, which was turned into a movie. The movie was made at Edwards Air Force Base. I have to admit that I wasn't even close to having the right stuff. I was assigned to one of the most important test projects at Edwards, and the signature hadn't completely dried on my diploma. I certainly didn't have the right stuff in terms of flight testing. Berkeley prepared me well. Pilots have their talents, and I have my skills.

Mr. Alfred D. Phillips, the flight test engineer came to me to assist him in performing all the computations to reduce test data using the new IBM CPC computer. I stood there in awe and watched the daring test pilots fly those new vehicles at their own peril and risk. They had their stuff, and I had my stuff. Hopefully together we made the right stuff happen. The *Mercury* astronauts had the right stuff.

The Project Mercury astronauts (NASA Photo)

The Data-Reduction Process

A lot of work goes into the overall data-reduction process. All of the onboard flight test data needed to be recorded on photo panels and oscillographs. The photo film would have to be developed, and the oscillographs would have to be processed as well. With everything labeled and processed, they were given to the flight test engineer for further handling. The flight test engineer would forward the film to the Data Reduction Branch to read and record all the data on the film. This was a very laborious procedure. We had another section within the branch that provided these services. Thank God, that was not in my job description. After all the data was provided by the test engineer, the flight test data for a given flight would be sent to the Keypunch Section within the branch to prepare all the punch cards for entry that contained all the data for that flight. Then the software would be loaded and run with the test data to perform the computations.

Software Development

Prior to conducting any flight testing, Al Phillips and I worked hand-in-hand. He would give me all the aerodynamic equations needed to properly evaluate aircraft performance. There were three different computer programs, which are now referred to as *computer software*, to be developed. The largest software program I had to develop was entitled "Level Flight Performance." It's been over sixty years, but I do recall that there were about a hundred different parameters that needed to be recorded onboard the test vehicle—from one to ten times a second. One can imagine how much data this would amount to in an hour test flight. All that software would have to be prepared—up-front and ready to run—before flight testing could begin. Al Phillips did his homework, and he provided me with all of the necessary aerodynamic equations to evaluate the aircraft. I was absolutely amazed as to what was involved in the research, test, and evaluation of an aircraft.

New J-79 Jet Engine

The YF-100A was installed with a new General Electric J-79 jet engine. The J-79 is an axial-flow turbojet engine built for use in a variety of fighter and bomber aircraft and later in support of cruise missiles. The J-79 could perform afterburner thrust. The integration of a new aircraft with a new jet engine added to the challenge. I was armed with all those aerodynamics equations and left with the multiple tasks to develop computer software. When the computer software was prepared and checked out beforehand, the computer operators would process the software and run the punched card data that contained the flight data. Using the prepared software, the computer operator would run the software and the raw test data through the computer at sixty cards a minute. What a great slide rule!

Lt. Col. Pete Everest (AF Photo)

    The test pilot for the YF-100A was none other than Lieutenant Colonel Peter Everest. He was in charge of all of the test pilots at Edwards Air Force Base. This was a further indication of how important the YF-100A was to the United States Air Force. Later, Colonel Everest was to become known as Speedy Pete, the fastest man alive, a distinction he attained while flying the NACA X-2 research aircraft.

    Al Phillips, the flight test engineer for the YF-100A test program, had a disagreement with his test pilot. Occasionally, Lieutenant Colonel Pete Everest would do his own thing rather than follow the planned flight plan for a preplanned test flight. Al decided to go to the chief of flight test engineering to see what to do about it. WHILE explaining the situation to the engineering chief, he immediately called Lieutenant Col Everest the test pilot and told him what Al had just related to him. Al Phillips was a young engineer, and he felt like crawling underneath the chief's desk. The test pilot said, "Tell your boy that I will follow our test flight plans and established procedures." The engineering chief told Mr. Phillips to continue with his good work as a flight test engineer. Subsequently, during the planning of the next test flight, the test pilot never apologized, but he was very accommodating. Lieutenant Colonel Everest was an independent, firm, and outstanding test pilot. He certainly broadened the flight test envelope with his fearless dedication to his profession.

Mathematicians were excellent programmers and were referred to as computer programmers, which turned out to be a highly desirable profession. My mathematician friend, Donald Starr, was an excellent programmer. Later, he succumbed to the call from private industry. He jumped ship and transferred to rocketry. The scoundrel would send me copies of his pay stubs to entice me to join him. My job was great, but my pay was lousy. I decided to stay. Fortunately, I was able to get promotions as the years progressed. I never regretted my decision to remain at Edwards Air Force Base.

Computer programming in the early days was difficult. The computers had limitations. Basically, among other things, computers could only add, subtract, multiply, and divide. However, the computer was preprogrammed, or prewired, utilizing a large board that was wired like a telephone switch panel. This rat's nest provided all the instructions needed for programmers to write computer software. The software we wrote would be keypunched using a Hollerith IBM card, which was eighty columns wide. A software program could consist of hundreds of cards stacked and labeled as, for example, "F-100 level flight program." Then the debugging would start using input data provided by the flight test engineer. It was a happy day when I could duplicate his slide rule answers. Alfred Phillips had a smile on his face as well. This began a long-standing working relationship both on and off the job.

I was able to program all the software needed to support flight testing for the YF-100A on time. Three major software programs were needed to provide all the computations necessary to evaluate the performance, stability, and control of the YF-100A supersonic aircraft. The other two programs were an aircraft climbs program and an aircraft level acceleration program. The aircraft acceleration program was prepared to evaluate a new flight test procedure that had been recently developed by the flight research engineering branch. This new flight test technique was used to minimize flight test time in conducting aircraft climb tests. In simple terms, this computer software determined the amount of energy needed to accelerate during level flight. The computer software would translate that energy to simulate aircraft climb performance. This turned out to be very successful. The actual flight times were reduced. Certain climb flights would still have to be conducted to verify computer predictions and simulations. Other test programs used the same computer software I developed. We cranked out many test flights for the YF-100A program. We made the computer popular for assisting other flight test support engineers. This led to the use of computer operations for other flight test aircraft even though we were in the infancy stage of utilizing computers for flight testing. All this was happening when Melissa was an infant—and Dorothy and I were becoming adjusted to married life with a baby onboard.

Chapter 23

XB-52 Stratofortress Bomber

The next major program I was assigned to was the Boeing XB-52. I was assigned as one of the top mathematicians to support the highest-priority program in the air force. The XB-52 phase-2 test program was about to begin. By this time, our second daughter, Natalie, was born. Aircraft testing is conducted in multiple phases. Phase 1 is the contractor's airworthiness tests. In other words, can the airplane maneuver and fly safely? Phase-2 tests are the contractor's responsibility to demonstrate that the aircraft flight performance characteristics are in accordance with air force specifications. Phase 4 begins a long extensive test phase that is conducted by the air force with the aircraft manufacturer's support as required. Since most of the expensive ground support equipment required for testing was located at the Boeing plant, it was more practical and economical to conduct the air force phase-4 tests at Boeing. Some tests were conducted at Edwards AFB.

My Boss and the Boeing Computer Department

My immediate boss at the time was sent up to Boeing Aircraft to obtain information about the computer systems that Boeing used for their flight tests. His trip report stated that the Boeing company used the latest IBM 701 computer, which he did not know much about—and neither did I. The recently manufactured IBM 701 was the largest and fastest scientific computer available at the time. In addition, he stated in his report that the XB-52 is a big airplane, it makes a lot of noise, and the shipping docks are beautiful in the Seattle area. As it turned out, we could have gotten that same information from a telephone call.

Don Starr

Don Starr and I were sent up to Boeing in Seattle to begin the gigantic computer software programming tasks. We left on December 26, 1954. The twelve-to-sixteen-hour days covered the Christmas holidays, New Year's Eve, New Year's Day, and every day thereafter until we completed all of the software, operating procedures, documentation, and training for the Boeing Computer Department personnel to perform the vast computations involved to support the XB-52 phase-4 flight test program. As we entered the computer room, we just stood there in awe. We had to develop software for this new whizbang computer to support the accelerated XB52-A test program. We had to meet a February 1, 1955, start date, which appeared to be an unsurmountable task. The pressure was on since this program had the highest priority in the air force. The sweat started to run on a cold day in Seattle. They say that they had two weather seasons: rainy and wet.

IBM 701 and the advanced computer age (IBM Photo)

IBM 701 computer and Ronald Reagan (IBM Photo)

This picture shows Ronald Reagan, working for General Electric at the time, being briefed by the designer. The IBM 701 electronic data-processing machine, known as the defense calculator while in development, was IBM's first commercial scientific computer. Announced to the public on April 29, 1952, it was IBM's first large-scale computer. The 701 was designed for scientific work and research, which later led to the development of the high-level FORTRAN language. FORTRAN stands for formula translation. This new higher-level language was not developed at the time.

Software Development Begins

This was no small task, in and of itself, but it was necessary before programming any software computer programing could begin. We had to learn all about the 701 computer, department computer software tools, and procedures before we could even attempt software development. We were given top priority to learn all about their computer systems as well as computer time needed to develop, test, evaluate, and debug the computer software.

We had to program *assembly language* for the IBM 701. Only nineteen IBM 701 machines were built—a record volume for that era. Its internal memory contained 2,048 words of electrostatic memory and 8,192 words of magnetic drum memory. It had magnetic tapes for storage and was one of the first machines to use plastic-based magnetic tapes instead of metal tapes. This computer was well ahead of its time. It included microsecond circuits installed at critical locations to send electrical impulses from one unit to another at a speed faster than one-millionth of a second. Devised at Columbia University's Watson Lab, it rented for approximately $16,000 per month. What a fantastic leap in computer speed and technology! There was no comparison between a CPC card-programmed calculator and a new IBM 701. Computer technology had hit the electronic age. Comparing these two computers was like comparing the old jalopies that the test pilots would drive around the base and the F-100 Supersonic Sabre or jumping over the moon in one bound. The CPC card-programmed calculator measured in speed in terms of card cycles going through a keypunch machine at the rate of sixty cards a minute, which was much faster than a slide rule. The 701 computer could be measured in terms of microsecond circuitry that was clocked at speeds faster than one-millionth of a second. Need I say more? The 701 computer was by far the fastest supersonic computer in existence. It would be impossible to perform all the computer calculations needed to support the all-new XB-52 without an IBM 701 electronic computer. The volumes of data generated by a very large bomber with eight new J-79 jet engines and the need to record numerous sensory data throughout an extremely large aircraft platform created an instrumentation, data-collection, and computer-processing nightmare.

Onboard Instrumentation

The recording of all of the onboard data was just the beginning process. All the flight test data would have to be amassed and submitted for computer entry and subsequent computer processing. We had excellent support from the Boeing Aircraft Computer Department and the Boeing flight test organization. After all the software was completed and all the procedures were documented to run and operate the software, Boeing took over to turn the crank in handling and processing all the air force flight test data using the software that Don Starr and I developed. Remarkably, neither Don nor I had to return to the Boeing Company to assist with any glitches or software changes or updates.

Overtime and More Overtime

Don Starr and I worked countless hours of overtime. I did take time off to go to Catholic Mass on Sundays. During this time, I would phone home to see how the family was surviving, including Natalie, who I had not seen for more than half of her life. Toward the end of the assignment, I would tell Dorothy that I would be home in about a week. I would repeat that mantra more than once. It got down to two days, then one day, and then another day when I called Dorothy. I will absolutely come home the next day. That absolute day arrived, and I called Dorothy to inform her that I would come home the following day. She hung up on me in disgust. We had no control of the new demands for software changes.

Finally, we returned to LAX and were met by an Edwards AFB passenger aircraft just for our return. I was happy about that because the San Diego Freeway was not totally completed, and the 14 Freeway was not in existence at that time. It took about three hours each way to travel to and from Lancaster and LAX. Having very successfully completed our assignments over eight weeks, we felt very proud and important since we completed our software development tasks on time to begin the delayed XB-52 phase-4 testing. I felt a lot like Aloise and I did after milking cows for more than four months. Don Starr and I completed a horrendous task in a very short period of time. This certainly solidified my confidence as a mathematician and a worthwhile employee at Edwards AFB. The base sent a C-45 passenger aircraft to pick us up, and we both ended our assignments by figuratively thumping our chests. It was great to get home to be reunited with Dorothy, Melissa, and infant Natalie. Later, we were paid for all the overtime that we accumulated. This extra money greatly assisted a growing family. I found out many years later that Boeing Aircraft used the software that Don Starr and I developed for the XB-52 to test and evaluate the Boeing 704 commercial airliner.

Boeing aircraft commercial airliner (Boeing Photo)

That was Boeing's first entry into the commercial jet market. They got free software and all the latest aerodynamic equations and procedures used for air force testing and evaluation embedded in the software. They got a twofer. I assume that Boeing got approval from the air force to use air force software. In any case, we were both very proud of what we had accomplished in supporting the initial development of the B-52 program. As it turned out, Don Starr and I contributed indirectly to the development of Boeing's entry into the commercial jet passenger market. The Boeing B-52 is still in operation and has been a major workhorse for more than sixty years.

Chapter 24

New Computer and X-2 Computer Support

After I completed my assignment on the XB-52 project, I continued to work on a number of other projects involving the F-86 aircraft, F-84, F-89, C-123, and others for follow-up testing activity. In addition, I helped other new mathematicians who came onboard. I wasn't in a supervisory position at the time, but I was called upon to assist other mathematicians as best I could along with my other duties. After a couple of years utilizing the CPC calculator, it became obvious that we needed an upgrade. Since we were so successful in working with the IBM card program calculator, other computer programmers and I wanted to upgrade to the IBM 650 computer. This was a drum-driven machine that could actually execute instructions at 3600 RPM rather than being limited to 60 CPM on the CPC. What a fantastic increase in computer speed! I was not the chief of programming section at the time. Unfortunately, the section chief that preferred the Electrodata Datatron computer made by Burroughs Corporation.

Electrodata 204 Datatron computer (AF Photo)

The section chief wanted the Datatron computer. He advocated that the Electrodata 204 Datatron was superior to the IBM 650. He probably had a hidden agenda since he later resigned and went to work for Electrodata Corporation. Despite the superior success we had with the IBM CPC, he decided to purchase another corporation's first entry into the scientific computer field. We didn't particularly care for him. He came in as an outsider who wanted to do things his way. That led to my first major promotion as a section chief. I thank him for holding the position open until I was ready to take on a supervisory assignment. The Datatron computer was Electrodata's first entry into the scientific computer field using a decimal-vacuum tube technology. The Datatron computer got the job done, but it was a high-maintenance computer. Then came the software-conversion process. We had to rewrite all the software that was needed to support the computations for the growing needs of flight test data processing. We were all very pleased that the conversion process went well with minimum interruptions to the center's mission.

NACA Bell X-2 Computer Support

NACA did not have the computer capability to process X-2 trajectory data that would track the X-2 throughout its mission profile. Mr. Paul Bikle asked the Data Reduction Branch to assist NACA in computing range-trajectory data for the X-2 research aircraft. I was assigned the responsibility of preparing software and computer operations for NACA flight test engineers to assist in the testing and evaluation of the X-2 research testing. Mr. Bikle really motivated me again when he kindly invited me to attend the X-2 preflight activities. This meant that we had to get up in the wee hours of the morning to go out to the flight line to watch the installation of the X-2 under the wing of the B-50 launch aircraft.

(All AF photos)

The X-2 Mating Process with the B-50

I observed the test pilot crawling into the X-2 cockpit. When this was accomplished, Captain Fitzhugh Fulton, the B-50 pilot, cranked up all four engines. I was standing next to Mr. Bikle, and he said, "Let's go, Fitz." For a second, I thought he said "Fritz." The B-50 taxied down the runway, got into position, and lumbered off. It was great to watch this event and get paid for it. *It doesn't get any better than this—unless you're one of the pilots boring holes in the sky.*

Speedy Pete Everest

Lt. Colonel Pete Everest was the test pilot on this particular mission. He flew all the flight test missions for the YF-100A. Mr. Bikle invited me to attend the postflight briefing later the same day. I attended the postflight briefing in a conference room in one of the large hangars. I got there, and we waited and waited for the arrival of Colonel Everest. He arrived in his uniform with a scarf, plopped his feet up on the desk, and exclaimed "How fast did I go today"? He didn't say *we*—he said *I*. He knew that we didn't have the data processed yet because that was my job later in the day and the next day. I lost some respect for Speedy Pete after that encounter.

X-2 Post-Flight Briefing

It was really interesting to attend this postflight briefing where everything of importance was discussed from launch to landing. It was an understatement to say that I was motivated to a fever pitch. Fortunately, I had completed and checked out the trajectory software to run on the new 204 Datatron computer. All I needed was the input data from NACA to run the software program to compute trajectory data. Additional flights were conducted on the X-2 with other test pilots. Records were established on most flights. We successfully supported all the all missions, including the last fatal flight flown by Captain Mel Apt.

X-2 in Powered Flight (NASA Photo)

This in-flight photograph of the X-2 shows the twin set of shock diamonds—characteristic of supersonic conditions—in the exhaust plume from the two-chamber rocket engine. Credits: NASA photo

CHAPTER 25

Fatal X-2 Rocket Crash

Captain Mel Apt (Air Force Photo)

I was in the process of moving my office equipment from one building to another as I watched the X-2 streak high above Edwards Air Force Base. I knew it was the X-2 because it was on the schedule. About an hour or so later, I heard whispers going around that the X-2 had crashed. That information was considered classified. I was called into a meeting, and I was told that the X-2 had crashed and that I needed to get ready to process trajectory data in a crisis mode. Captain Mel Apt flew a perfect mission that carried him farther away from the lake bed than planned. The director of flight test, Colonel Horace Hanes, asked me point-blank when the trajectory data would be ready for analysis. It was about seven thirty on the evening of the crash. I told him, without hesitation, "Seven thirty tomorrow morning." Colonels like short straight answers. I put the pressure on myself.

Despite the fact that I did not have management control over the total process to do the job yet, I was expected to produce the results—as I had promised. NACA had to recover all of the onboard data possible, develop the film, and provide all that information to the Data Reduction Branch for film reading, data processing, and computer computations. I inserted myself as a one-time project manager to oversee all the steps necessary to complete the task by seven thirty the next morning. We all worked together, unified by the urgency and high-level interest in our task. All the personnel in the Data Reduction Branch were highly motivated to complete this urgent task on time. Kudos to all. We completed the task by seven o'clock in the morning. This gave me sufficient time to clean up my desk and be ready for the colonel as he arrived at our work area at seven thirty sharp. He immediately looked at the trajectory data and commented that the pilot had sufficient altitude in order to safely return his aircraft to Rogers dry lake bed.

Captain Apt did not know that he had enough altitude and speed to return safely. He flew a near-perfect flight profile, one that he practiced on the simulator many times, but it carried him farther than he anticipated. During his fateful mission, he was the first test pilot to fly over Mach 3—a major achievement in aviation history. He went Mach 3.3 at a speed of 2,178 miles per hour (36 miles a minute), which broke colonel Pete Everest's speed by more than 278 miles per hour. Colonel Everest owned the speed record until Captain Apt flew his final mission. In addition, Captain Apt set a new altitude record, at the time—over 70,000.

Thanks to the Data Reduction Branch

We all were thanked for a job well done. I was assured that I had provided everything necessary and was excused from duty and sent home to obtain some sleep. I was very pleased and still hyped up, but I was able to get enough sleep to go back to work the following day. It didn't take long to realize that, in the military, this kind of performance was considered standard. I recognized—and have not forgotten—that ten kudos could be wiped out by one crapola.

Appendix 1 includes an *Air Force* magazine article entitled "The Last Flight of the X-2," a 1957 article written by Clay Blair Jr. It is very interesting reading that explains the total flight and tragic crash in absolute detail.

Captain Apt Memorial in Hand (Air Force Photo)

I did not know Captain Apt, but I did know his wife, Faye. I played bridge with her at the Edwards Air Force Base officers' club. I met and played against a number of high-ranking officers as well as their wives. Fortunately, I played with very smart partners who were lieutenant officer graduates from Harvard, MIT, and other well-known universities who were assigned to me in the organization. The officers' bridge club didn't particularly like us to show up and play because we would win more than our share of the duplicate bridge games. The winner for the evening received a bottle of champagne, which we would consume and enjoy on various social occasions.

Chapter 26

Chief, Computer Programming Section

The Data Reduction Branch consisted of four sections: the Computer Programming Section, the Computer Operations Section, which included the vital Key Punch Unit, the Aircraft Photo Panel Reading Section, and the relatively new Data Processing and Handling Section. After about three or four years of providing computer services support for the Flight Test Engineering Division, the engineers began to realize that the Data Reduction Branch's support services were becoming more necessary and essential, particularly the Computer Programming and Computer Operation Sections. We were more closely relocated with the flight test engineers. When we upgraded the branch's computer capability, we were able to accomplish much more. With a recent move, we were relocated very close to all of the flight test engineers. The branch obtained a much more capable computer: an Electrodata 204 Datatron. As a result, the Data Reduction Branch was greatly challenged and had additional work cut out for it.

Promotion

In October of 1957, I was promoted to chief of the Computer Programming Section, I was in charge of all software development for the Data Reduction Branch. As time progressed, my programming staff increased and included a number of officers, airman, and additional civilian mathematicians.

Computer programming and software development (Public domain)

Programming and software development can be a long, arduous task. It requires the utmost care to break down a solution for a complex formula or a long series of computations. A computer is an extremely fast number cruncher, but it only does what you program it to accomplish.

An old expression—garbage in, garbage out—certainly applies. The computer is nothing more than a supersonic moron. The software must be programmed right. That is the programmer's job and responsibility. Vital in planning a software computer program is a flow chart.

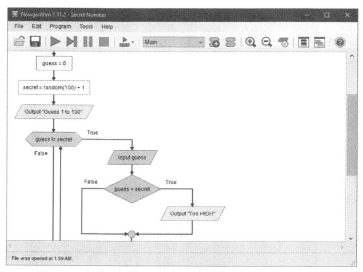

Flowcharting process (computer generated)

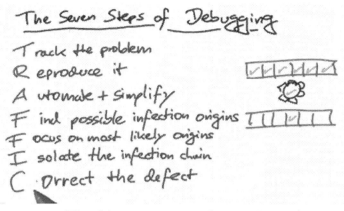

The debugging process (Public domain)

Debugging is the process of finding and resolving defects or problems within a computer program that prevent correct operation of computer software.

I can still visualize the various programmers going back and forth from the computer room, debugging their latest software. They would come back with smiles on their faces or wonder what went wrong. We all became aware of the vicissitudes of programming and software checkout and development.

When I would see their sad looks, I would sit next their desks and ask them how things were going. I would get all kinds of responses. "Everything is great, but that damn software program I was in the process of debugging went bananas. This computer doesn't know what it is doing." The mathematician turned out to be right on.

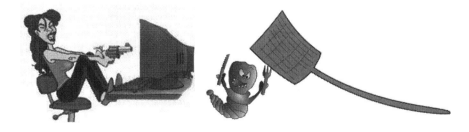

"You are absolutely right. The computer will only do what you tell it to do. The computer needs to be told every step of the way what to do. That is what computer programming consists of—and it is your job."

Think Again

IBM's "Think" motto is the best solution. I wanted them to think through a solution themselves. I would ask, "Did you flowchart the software before you began programming? Did you check the coding to see if you programmed the solution correctly?"

I had to learn my lesson by not properly flowcharting a program. That's like leaving on a long trip without planning a route, side trips, accommodations, restaurants, alternate trips, and unforeseen contingencies. You have to make many choices beforehand to get where you are going. If you don't plan your way, you are going to get lost. The analogy absolutely applies for developing computer software. I would say, "I have been there and done that. That's why we have to debug the software, and we all will definitely experience bumps along the way. Think it out and stick to it. You will work it out." This follow-up approach and technique proved very beneficial for me to get to know and understand my staff. We both benefited from these friendly exchanges.

Outstanding piece of work (Public domain)

Equation to Compute Mach Number (Test Engineering Manual)

$$M = \sqrt{5[(\frac{1}{\delta}\{[1 + 0.2(\frac{V_c}{661.5})^2]^{3.5} - 1\} + 1)^{0.286} - 1]}$$

M = Mach number

Vc is calibrated airspeed. The aircraft is configured with an airspeed-indicator sensor located at optimum locations near the nose of the aircraft, which records airspeed data. Thus, the need for an aircraft calibration. True Mach number depends on a unique aircraft calibration established by flying alongside another aircraft with known true established airspeeds. These results are tabulated and/or plotted. Aircraft calibrations are dependent on altitude due to different patterns of airflow over the aircraft. This calibration defines Vc, calibrated velocity, versus altitude. It was no longer necessary to program the calculation of Mach number if Vc was known for each aircraft being tested. The programmer needs to apply the proper calibration and prepare special code to interface with the software program, previously programmed, that computes Mach number. We developed a software library for use by all programmers in developing other software programs for a new test aircraft. I programmed the complicated solution to compute Mach number so many times I could almost program it from memory.

Computer Terminology, Acronyms, and Lingo

The mathematicians were referred to as computer programmers. Software was originally called computer code. Small computer programs that were developed and available for other programmers were called subroutines, meaning that certain formulas would not change, thereby not needed to be re-coded for other applications. Today, I would refer to this subroutine as mini apps. Completed computer programs are now referred to as computer software. Many of the components to a computer as well as a plethora of associated equipment were called hardware. Processing the data usually meant running the program. A language all of its own sprang up; for example, the digital data-processing system was called DDPS, an acronym that is formed by the first letter for each major word. The beat goes on today ad infinitum.

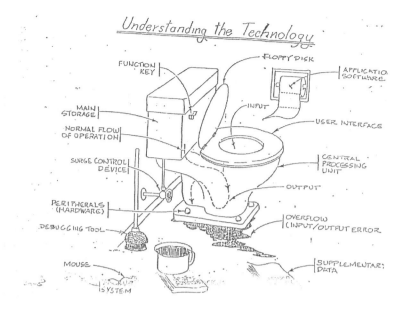

More Programming Support

The branch was very busy providing more and more support for aircraft tests. We had a continuing and expanding level of support for about ten to fifteen aircraft undergoing new or continuing flight tests. By that time, we had already developed various kinds of software for previous aircraft test programs. As section chief, I had all of these programs documented and available to other programmers for use, integration, and assembly by other to use in developing new application software. This eliminated any unnecessary reprogramming efforts. This was highly successful.

New Mathematician Orientation

When a new mathematician would come in—or anyone else for that matter—I gave them an orientation. This was not an interview. They already had been selected for the job. When I first arrived at Edwards AFB as a very young mathematician, I didn't really know what to expect. I would conduct the orientations for new arrivals who knew practically nothing about the job. I wanted to put them at ease. I remember how I felt when I was introduced to Mr. Paul Bikle, the civilian director of flight test. Some of the new personnel were intense, some were putting up a front, and others were very interested in their new jobs as mathematicians. The officers who were assigned were a little more confident; after all, they were officers and a gentlemen.

Counseling and Advice

I remember one time when a mathematician was interviewed. He had some concerns that he might not be able to solve all of those complex math problems. I didn't remember my response, until later when he told me that my response to his concerns really helped put him at ease. He said that I responded, "I have a PhD in mathematics sitting in the next room to help you and me with those big math problems."

I always tried to interview personnel at their level rather than trying to impress them with how much I knew. This served me very well throughout my career. There was plenty of time for them to know me and learn what I know and what I expect of them. There was a good working relationship among all the programmers. Many of them lived in base housing, and we socialized together with flight test engineers. Great fun.

Mathematician Staff

As time progressed, the sections programming staff increased, which included a number of very capable officers, airmen, and civilian mathematicians.

Military Officers Come and Go

I was extremely fortunate to have outstanding officers assigned to me for two four-year assignments. After the military officers completed their service as programmers, they were offered lucrative programming jobs in private industry. One became a vice president of cash register corporation. He was promoted above his contemporaries by significantly increasing sales of the company's products at a business conference. He took a bank teller's customer transaction and bounced it off the moon in the process. This sales technique used for marketing was accomplished prior to the moon landing in 1969. He was visionary and aggressive.

Another officer was assigned as a top software engineer for IBM to develop a new operating system for a new line of IBM 360 computers. One became a key programmer for Apollo Computer Systems, and one electrical engineer with a PhD formed his own company to develop new data-handling systems. Their Edwards AFB experience served them well. They were assigned at the right place at the right time to master their skills for future careers.

First-Class Airman John

I had a very excellent airman assigned to my section. I was offered his talents; even though he did not complete his BS degree in mathematics, he became one of our best programmers. I will anonymously call him John, but he had very interesting background. First of all, he stuttered far worse than I did as a kid. This didn't bother him; he would just spit it out. He had a very good singing voice, and he was able to sing without stuttering. I found that to be the case for myself. He was the son of a very famous minister who had a great fellowship church in Portuguese Bend in Southern California. I am sure that the reverend's son sang in their church choir. Being gifted, he had no trouble in getting into Harvard University. Even though he did not have any trouble getting into Harvard, he got himself into quite of bit of mischief while attending Harvard. He always seemed to be the instigator in mischievous pranks.

The one incident that led to his doom at Harvard University was when he and a few other students apprehended an electric streetcar about midnight on Main Street in downtown Boston. They attempted to solder the wheels to the tracks. Well, this prank did not go unpunished. Probably with the help of his minister father, he was dismissed from Harvard to join the air force. He never caused a problem working in my organization. He did his job in an outstanding manner.

My Greatest Section Chief Achievement

One of my major achievements as section chief was the preparation, justification, submittal, and subsequent approval of the latest and best IBM electronic computer available. The IBM 704 computer replaced the outdated Electrodata Datatron computer. Since the computer industry had a policy of renting its computers, it was easier to justify a new computer without a substantial increase in expenditure. A moderate increase in monthly costs was a minimal expense in comparison to the tremendous increase in computer power.

IBM 704 electronic computer installation (AF Photo)

I am located in the center in full view. Mr. Alfred D. Phillips, data reduction branch chief, is located close to the other side of the computer opposite me. Mr. Paul Bikle is the flight test director who is standing next to Mr. Phillips and Frank Ross, Technical Support Division chief, stands next to Mr. Bikle. Two other air force personnel are in the middle row on the left. Mr. Carroll Sweet, chief, Computer Operations Section and Mr. Dover. The remainder of the personnel are IBM dignitaries. The computer was installed in building 1408 located about one hundred yards from the Flight Test Engineering Division and very near the flight line.

IBM Sales Representative for Edwards AFB

It is interesting to note that the IBM sales representative, Dale Edwards, was the nephew of Captain Glen Edwards, the base's namesake. Dale and I became great friends. He was always available to assist with any problems in education and training. At his invite, I attended a high-level IBM executive seminar at Poughkeepsie, New York, to learn more about the potential of the IBM 704 and future developments in computer technology. At my expense, I saw the original production of *Music Man* on Broadway and had a drink at Sardis's Bar.

The Undisputed Leader of Scientific Computers

IBM was the leader in business as their name indicates. Under the leadership of Mr. Watson, president, IBM strongly invested in scientific computers. They developed the IBM 701 electronic computer with the production of nineteen systems, thinking it would saturate the market at the time. Very shortly thereafter, they developed the next generation of computers with the introduction of the IBM 704. When we obtained an IBM 704, we entered the modern computer age. IBM built excellent quality computers that were supported by outstanding customer service. I still remember the motto that IBM had at the time: "Think." Dale gave me a nice engraved memento with their motto, and I kept it on my desk for many years. IBM helped me think and live up to their reputation of great service.

Edwards AFB Entered the Modern Computer Age

As the lone mathematician heavily involved in flight testing the YF-100A Supersonic Sabre, I was instrumental, along with Dale Edwards, in the acquisition, modernization, and advancement of the computer technology at Edwards AFB. The YF-100A was the first military aircraft to fly supersonic in level flight. With the acquisition of the IBM 704 computer, Edwards entered the modern computer age of advanced technology. Breaking the sound barrier mimicked the new computer age.

God Expanded My Family and Horizons

I was able to work with many other engineers and branch chiefs from different engineering organizations and other section chiefs and branch chiefs within the Technical Support Division. In addition, I was able to work with other organizational personnel, supervisors, colleagues, test pilots, and other AFFTC staff members. I became a section chief when I was about twenty-seven years old.

Jennifer, Natalie, Meribeth, and Melissa

It was another great learning experience for me. It was a real challenge being a section chief, but also very interesting, career-broadening, and rewarding challenge. I always got support from Dorothy every step of the way. I was at the right place at the right time with God as my copilot.

Chapter 27

Mr. Bill Adams, Data Reduction Branch Chief

Mr. Bill Adams was assigned as chief to replace Mr. Ken Rich. He was previously assigned at the Rocket Propulsion Laboratory across the lake bed on Lehman Ridge. He was a very capable electrical engineer and had expertise in magnetic tape-recording systems and data-processing and handling systems. In addition, Mr. Adams was a captain in the United States Air Force.

Mr. Adams had considerable knowledge and experience in an area of electronics, which were badly needed. He spent most of his time concentrating on solutions to recording, handling, and processing aircraft test instrumentation onboard recording systems. He was able to acquire these systems and hire competent staff, including a new chief of the Data-Processing And Handling Section. Through his expertise and leadership, the Data Reduction Branch was able to accommodate onboard magnetic tape-recorded test data, utilizing off-the-shelf electronic systems.

Data handling and processing systems (AF Photo)
Initially this proved to be adequate to do the job. Regretfully,
Mr. Adam had to depart on a medical retirement.

T-38 class 2 mod installation (AF Photo)
Test recorded data incomp 6.

Reflections

When I reflect back on my career, God was and is my copilot. It had to be God's intervention that I accomplished and did the right thing. I believe it was God's intervention that guided a shy young man to marry the lovely person who God meant for me, sent me to the dean of students to change my major to mathematics while in the middle of eating a ham sandwich, provided me the job opportunity to be employed as a mathematician at Edwards AFB, allowed me to pursue my dreams of working with airplanes and computers, began my career working on two of the most important projects in the air force and the Department of Defense, the YF-100A supersonic aircraft and the XB-52 strategic bomber, promoted to a section chief at a very young age, and others. God opened many doors for me and helped me as I walked through them. Dorothy was very supportive in encouraging on the job and raising our first four young daughters before we were twenty-seven years old. I was able to concentrate on doing my job. When I would return home after a busy day, I could enjoy my family—even though I would occasionally take work home with me. Dorothy is a wonderful spouse and a great loving mother.

Chapter 28

As Chief, Mr. Phillips Applied His Vast Flight Test Knowledge

With the medical retirement of Mr. Bill Adams, Mr. Alfred D. Phillips was promoted as the new Data Reduction Branch chief. Yes, Mr. Phillips was the premier flight test engineer. Mr. Phillips was very instrumental in utilizing computers for the first time as a flight test engineer on two major programs at Edwards Air Force Base. I was fortunate enough to be assigned as his mathematician programmer on two of the most important air force programs: the YF-100A Supersonic Sabre and the XB-52 Advanced Bomber. I was very pleased with his new assignment as chief. Mr. Phillips was a visionary and very capable at getting things accomplished. His vast experience in flight test engineering coupled with his experience in utilizing the application of the most up-to-date computer technology made him an exceptional choice for managing the Data Reduction Branch.

Management Objective

His management objectives were quite clear: to promote the advantages of automation and computerization and enhance communications and understanding of flight tests among computer programming, processing, handling, and overall support operations among the various engineering personnel at the Air Force Flight Test Center (AFFTC). He expected me to be very instrumental in accomplishing these objectives.

Reluctance to Change

One of the major conflicts at the time was the reluctance of the flight test engineers to automate instrumentation systems. Using photo panels and oscillographs, recorders were the standard way of acquiring and recording flight test data onboard test aircraft. This simple approach to recording information for some test programs was adequate at best—but very laborious. You needed to develop the film, read the film, and record the information on data worksheets so the test engineer could manually compute the results with a slide rule and or on an adding machine. Flight test engineers are busy people.

Oscillographs are used to record high-frequency data and the photo panels were to record low-frequency information on display to the pilot in the cockpit. Test engineers had a somewhat strong resistance to change, which is understandable, and they were reluctant to lose control of the manner of recording onboard test and data processing and data reduction. Mr. Phillips's forceful management style was needed to computerize flight testing accomplished at Edwards AFB. For a few years, a conflict existed between Mr. Phillips and a key flight test engineer in management. However, cooler heads prevailed by management to update and modernize where absolutely necessary. Mr. Phillips had the vision, drive, guts, and courage to make it happen.

Consolidation of Branch Support Facilities

One of Mr. Phillips major accomplishments was to centralize all of the data-reduction facilities and capabilities in an ideal location close to the flight line. There was a two-story building that was built by the army's Ballistic Test Facility (BTF). Building 3940 was a two-story structure large enough to accommodate a large computer installation. This required a major renovation of the building to make it suitable for all the branch operations and functions. This took about six months to accomplish. The major task began to centrally relocate all the data systems under a single roof for better management, control, and accessibility for test engineers and support personnel to accomplish their many tasks and functions. The biggest task was relocating the huge IBM 704 electronic computer complex. Since the IBM computer was rented, IBM took on the major responsibility of accomplishing this relocation. Shortly thereafter, we were back in operation.

Major Increase in Support Workload

As all of the flight test engineers had to comply with the policy to modernize instrumentation systems, the buildup of computer software and computer operations increased manifold. I recruited a few additional mathematicians, civilians right out of college and officers who were assigned by military personnel. I went on a few recruiting trips to some of the major colleges and universities in California. Yes, I even went to Berkeley. Mr. Phillips gave me pretty much of a free hand. Even though Mr. Phillips could be very authoritative in his management style at times, he also managed by objectives. With our very successful working relationships in other major programs, he trusted me. I also tried my best not to let him or myself down. I later was promoted as his assistant division chief. Mr. Phillips certainly had a major role in allowing me advancement opportunities.

Hazards of Being a Flight Test Engineer

For thirty years, I worked very closely with Mr. Alfred D. Phillips. I was involved in many close working relationships as engineer/mathematician, branch/section chiefs, assistant division/branch chiefs, division/deputy chiefs, and division/technical director. It stands to reason that there are many stories to tell about Mr. Phillips and myself on and off the job. Flight testing is as risky and hazardous for test engineers as it is for test pilots. Engineers also fly on test missions that have a seat—or not. I have known at least three flight test engineers who have lost their lives during flight testing. They are honored—but not to the same degree as test pilots.

XB-52 Phase II Performance Incident

Al Phillips told me a story about when he almost bought the farm. He had a piece of metal on his desk, and I inquired about it. He told me that it was a piece of a J-57 engine that he recovered onboard the XB-52. It exploded in flight, and he survived a near miss. The onboard test crew was Lieutenant Col. Guy Townsend, project pilot, Captain Bill Magruder, copilot, Mr. Al Phillips, project engineer, and Marsh Mullens, test engineer. (Marsh flew P-38 aircraft during World War II performing reconnaissance missions over Japan during World War II).

P-38 Aircraft (Army Air Corps Photo)

On one mission, he noticed a bright flash of light. He was very curious. The P-38's cameras only pointed down, so he banked his aircraft and got a spectacular side view shot of the mammoth mushroom cloud as it plumed skyward. Al was a good storyteller. He went on to say that he was on a second attempt conducting the last light for the initial phase of the test program. It almost ended in disaster as the turbine and one of the engines came unglued, and the engine blew up just as we were being rotated. We didn't have an emergency fuel dump system, and it was very dicey for a while. Al said, "If it were not for the grace of God, I would not be able to tell you the story today." Mr. Phillips's story is a reminder that test flying has all kinds of risks and hazards—not only for test pilots but for all the crew members. The flight test engineers have to make do in makeshift cubbyholes or cargo bays to do their jobs as best they can. In my book, test pilots are fearless in what they do. The flight test engineer does most of the engineering, test planning, and conducting, writing, and reporting of fight test results in many onboard locations if required. They are kings in my book. They have the right test engineering stuff to faithfully support the right stuff.

XB-52 and flight crew (AF Photo)
Mr. Alfred D. Phillips is pictured on the left.

Chapter 29

My Promotion to Data Reduction Branch Chief

As I approached my eighth year at Edwards AFB, I was selected to become chief of the Data Reduction Branch within the Technical Support Division. I replaced Mr. Alfred D. Phillips, my mentor, who did an outstanding job as chief. I was still quite young, twenty-two, when I was first employed. I used to call lieutenants "sir." As a branch chief, I had a captain that was assigned as one of my section chiefs who called me sir. I wouldn't salute him, but I gave the officer a slight nod in acknowledgment out of respect. On the job, the officers always showed me their utmost respect. Off the job, I made sure that we were all one of the boys. Right or wrong, it worked fine for all of us.

Data Systems Branch

The Data Systems Branch was postured to support the needs of the Air Force Flight Test Center (AFFTC), but none of this would have been accomplished without the expertise of many dedicated mathematicians, engineers, operators, technicians, film readers, competent section chiefs, and my dedicated administrative staff. Last, but not least, I thank God, over and over again, for being my copilot. The following is a summary of some of my major accomplishments as chief of the Data Reduction Branch.

Canceled the IBM Graphics Device

One of the first decisions I made as branch chief was to cancel the rental of a very expensive IBM graphics device that rented for four thousand dollars per month. Mr. Phillips proudly had this plotter installed on the IBM 704 computer. It was obtained to automate graph presentations for flight test engineers. The software and plotting technology proved not to be suitable or cost-effective. The graphic display was presented on a small scope that did not lend itself to making suitable-quality graphs. This was a commendable goal to automate the presentation of engineering data in graphic form for analyzing, reporting, documenting, and publishing results for test and evaluation reports. This plotting device was a spellbinder when it came to conducting tours. IBM had a software package that depicted a crude-looking bomber launching and tracking a bomb on its way to blow a target to smithereens. The amount saved paid my salary for almost a month and a half. In later years, private industry eventually developed electromechanical systems that satisfactorily provided a solution to the problem.

Development of the Digital Data-Processing System (DDPS)

There was no appropriate equipment to adequately handle the new instrumentation magnetic-tape systems being installed on test aircraft. We had what one would call off-the-shelf equipment that proved to be inadequate. Fortunately, I had two very capable lieutenants who graduated with master of science degrees in electrical engineering from the Massachusetts Institute of Technology (MIT). After much discussion regarding cost, performance, design, and scheduling, I entered into a pact with the data-processing and handling chief to build the digital data processing system (DDPS). I said, "If you can build it economically, I will definitely support the challenging endeavor. I will do my utmost to obtain the funding and approval to proceed." I was sticking my neck out, but I was confident that we could accomplish this new development task.

DDPS System and Operators (AF Photo)

My organization's mission was to support flight testing and not to develop new in-house data-processing systems and capabilities. With the support from upper management, we proceeded according to plan. All the engineers, technicians, maintenance personnel, and operators chipped in and were very motivated to get the job done. I would show up quite often and show my presence. Of course, I was genuinely interested in their progress—without interfering. I would give them encouragement. I had an open-door policy to discuss any problems with the section chief, and I had complete confidence in all of them. The DDPS system became the backbone of our data-processing and handling section for years to come. This DDPS system postured the Data Reduction Branch to meet current and midterm requirements. It was well worth the effort and cost.

Branch Expansion and Reorganization

At the direction of the division chief, I reorganized the Data Reduction Branch to consolidate all the telemetry acquisition and display systems, both local and remote, at Edwards AFB. Building 3940 was a large two-story building adequate to provide office, personnel, and electronic equipment space to accommodate all Data Reduction Branch capabilities under single management and control. This provided the first range mission control (RMC) facility at Edwards AFB. We built three separate mini control rooms for displaying telemetry data in real-time and in support of the specific test programs. Since this reorganization expanded the organizations responsibility, I renamed the existing branch to the Data Systems Branch, which now consisted of five separate sections responsible for computer programming, computer operations, film reading, data processing and handling, and telemetry acquisition and mission control room operations.

XB-70 Valkyrie (AF Photo)

B-70 Mission Control Facility

The first flight was conducted by North American and the air force B-70 test force, utilizing a mission control room specially designed and built by our staff. This RMC was planned, designed, and built to the specifications and requirements imposed by flight test engineers and fabricated, constructed, and installed by the technical personnel within the

Data Systems Branch. The first flight was conducted very successfully on September 21, 1964, my birthday. What a birthday present as I watched the control room engineers, North American management, and air force brass smile with pride and joy! The branch received a special commendation for the outstanding support provided by Data Systems Branch personnel.

XB-70 Remote Off-Site Range Support

Later in my career, when I was head of the Edwards Flight Test Range, I had two colleagues who were pilots and were checked out for flying the C-130 Hercules aircraft. We had an occasion to use the C-130 to haul a truck and other gear to locate a mobile digital radar for tracking the XB-70 over the Great Salt Lake Desert.

Mobile radar system (AF Photo)

After we arrived at Wendover AFB in Utah, all five of us mounted a large all-terrain vehicle and motored off in the Great Salt Lake Desert to search for a suitable location to locate a digital tracking radar. We found location not far from Wendover. We also enjoyed lunch at the famous Wendover Casino.

Data Acquisition and Transmission System (DATS) Flyover

On the return trip back to Edwards AFB, we flew by all of the microwave sites (eight in all) that transmitted flight test and radar data over eight hundred miles that formed the north (DATS) link.

Typical microwave sites (AF Photos)

The DATS System (AFFTC User's Handbook)

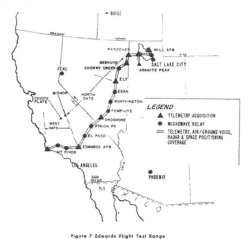

Figure 7 Edwards Flight Test Range

In addition, a western link, called West DATS, was installed and connected to the Vandenberg AFB and the navy's Point Mugu, California, range complexes. This inter-range net provided long-range flight testing along a thousand-mile corridor. This capability became an indispensable asset in carrying out various cruise missile tests. In addition, the DATS system was interconnected with a DOD worldwide net for all space shuttle missions recovered at Edwards AFB (more on the space shuttle recoveries later).

X-15 Support and Fatal Crash (NASA Photo)

First flight: June 8, 1957. The local area coverage was provided by the space positioning branch's FPS 16 digital radars. Speeds, altitudes, and other critical safety-of-flight information were also provided by use of local telemetry antennas, which are similar to a radio receiver but use far different frequencies. Since we didn't have sufficient personnel to operate and maintain the total DATS system, we entered into an engineering and technical services contract (ETTS) with Kentron, Inc. The DATS system proved to be invaluable in later years to support future programs. The North American X-15 was a hypersonic rocket-powered aircraft flown by air force and NASA test pilots. X-15 records are: top speed: 4,520 mph or m= 6. 72 set by William J. Knight. Range: 280 miles altitude 354,200 ft. or 67+ miles set by Joe walker. First flight: June 8, 1959, 199 flights completed. Twelve test pilots, including Neil Armstrong, later a NASA astronaut. Last flight: November 15, 1967, X-15 flight designated 191 crashed, piloted by Michael J. Adams.

Bonnie Watson and Fritz Miller in X-15 film (AF Photo)

Major Expansion of Computer Capability

With the tremendous increase in workloads, there was a pressing need to expand our computer capabilities. We increased our capacity by replacing the IBM 704 with an IBM 7090 computer, and then with an IBM 7094 computer.

Doug Tiffany, Lieutenant Col. Smith, myself,
and Al Dewitt (AF Photo)
Mr. Doug Tiffany, Computer Operations, chief
Lt. Col. Harold Smith, Technical Support Division, chief
Alfred F. Miller, Data Systems Branch chief
Alden Dewitt, Assistant Branch chief

IBM 7094 computer (AF Photo)

Since we were renting the IBM equipment, a minimum increase in rental costs resulted in a manifold increase in computer power. The IBM 7090 is a second-generation transistorized version of the earlier IBM 709 vacuum tube mainframe computer that was designed for large-scale scientific and technological applications. The 7090 is the third member of the IBM 700/7000 series scientific computers. The first 7090 installation was in November 1959. The IBM 7094 data-processing system featured outstanding price/performance and expanded computing power, built for large-scale scientific computing. Compatible with the IBM 7090, the advanced solid-state IBM 7094 offered substantial increases in internal operating speeds and functional capacities to match growing scientific workloads in the 1960s. The powerful IBM 7094 had 1.4 to 2.4 times the internal processing speed, depending upon the individual application.

Summary of Accomplishments

    Established multiple mission control rooms for real-time flight test operations under the control of a flight director.

    The DATS system was updated and expanded to form a thousand-mile test corridor for continuous remote coverage and flight operations.

    Supported all major air force test programs.

    The DDPS system was put into operation to accommodate modern magnetic-tape instrumentation systems for recording onboard flight test data.

    Consolidated telemetry acquisition systems for display and monitoring of safety-of-flight parameters and presentation of real-time test data under the watchful eye control by test engineers and mission control flight conductors.

    Reorganized the Data Systems Branch to more efficiently and effectively accommodate the scope and changes to support flight testing.

    Established a modern-age computer capability to meet the ever-growing needs driven by new developments in aircraft design.

Chapter 30

Share

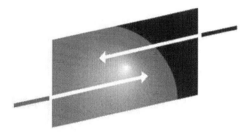

SHARE (IBM Photo)

SHARE Inc. is a volunteer-run user group for IBM mainframe computers that was founded in 1955 by Los Angeles-area users of the IBM 701 computer system. It evolved into a forum for exchanging technical information about programming languages, operating systems, database systems, and user experiences for enterprise users of small-, medium-, and large-scale IBM computers, IBM 701, IBM 704, IBM 7090, IBM 7094 and a whole series of IBM 360 computers. Despite the capitalization of all letters in the name, the official website says SHARE is not an acronym; it's what we do.

AFFTC-SHARE Membership

During the planning, acquisition, and implementation of the IBM 704 at Edwards AFB, I was instrumental in obtaining SHARE membership. Being the manager of all scientific computers at Edwards AFB, I was assigned as the key participant for Edwards AFB. SHARE has a fantastic library with all kinds of software that is available to members. A variety of start-up computer software routines are there just for the asking. Many overhead, housekeeping, assembly languages, and a whole variety of other computer programs were acquired and put into full operation and use at Edwards, which saved countless hours of valuable mathematician time. We could concentrate on applications software to support the center's mission.

SHARE Library and SHARE Conferences

A major resource of SHARE from the beginning was the SHARE library. Originally, IBM distributed its operating systems in source form, and systems programmers commonly made small local additions or modifications and exchanged them with other users. In 1959, SHARE released the SHARE operating system (SOS). Semiannual SHARE meetings were held at many strategic locations around the nation. The membership was able to meet face-to-face with many computer experts on their home grounds. A variety of computer installation tours proved invaluable. Many restaurant and bar encounters proved not only to be entertaining but highly informative. The opportunity to be a member of SHARE provided a monumental lift in computer understanding and education for me.

Computer Pioneers and Entrepreneurs

I met the famous Roy Nutt and Fletcher Jones who were the big movers and shakers in the computer industry at the time. Mr. Nutt was an American businessman and a computer pioneer. He helped build computer languages. He was a cocreator of FORTRAN—*formula translation*—a problem-oriented language (POL) that was utilized extensively for software development at Edwards AFB. Fletcher Jones was a well-known computer businessman. Mr. Jones and Mr. Nutt formed their own computer company, the Computer Sciences Corporation, which is known today as CSC and is currently on the New York Stock Exchange. I immediately recognized the potential in these two firehorses. I submitted an order to my broker to purchase some CSC stock just prior to John F. Kennedy's assassination. The stock purchase was not executed until after the assassination but the close of stock exchanges for the day. I was lucky to buy the stock at the low of the day after the panic sell-off.

Growing Family Begets Growing Home

About that time, due to our growing family, we needed a much bigger home with more bedrooms. Over the following year, I located a two-story home to exactly fit our needs. The gentleman who owned the home worked in aerospace and had a steady job with North American Aviation. After he bought the home, he had it all landscaped and added two bedrooms upstairs in the area reserved for later expansion and modification. In addition, he had a shrine installed in the middle of the backyard with plants, lighting, and a water system. It was installed with Saint Francis in mind. When I told him prior to buying his home that I planned to use the shrine for our Virgin Mary, he was very pleased. Mary still glows and resides in the Miller backyard—as a permanent resident now for more than fifty-five years.

The previous owner spent many days and hours locating enough rocks to build the shrine. He was transferred to another job within North American a few months after purchasing his new home. He quickly put his home up for sale, and I verified that the home was for sale and available. I immediately cashed out my CSC stock, contacted the owner, and told him that I was interested in possibly purchasing his home. He was interested in someone buying him out in order to recover his expenses. He was also a parishioner at Sacred Heart Church. He taught Christian doctrine as I did. There was not much negotiation that took place. He got what he wanted, and I got what Dorothy and I needed. I had enough cash available to execute a sweet deal for both of us.

Looking Back

Again, looking back, God provided for our needs. Dorothy and I raised all eight children in this wonderful 2,700-square-foot home. It is more than a coincidence that I made the right investment at the proper time to eventually purchase a badly needed home that became available at the right time. One might say that this mantra applies to my job opportunity but other important life situations. This theme prevails throughout my career. Dorothy and I made our way on a fantastic voyage, picking up eight children along the way. God held our hands and guided us as we ventured from cows to space with God as my copilot.

Coincidences or God's interventions

I write this from my office, in happy tears, and having difficulty, emotionally, continuing with my convoluted story. This office, which was once a bedroom in the home I bought fifty-five years ago, is now my working abode. I am glued to it almost 24/7. It might seem strange that I would submit to deep emotions talking about a very technical organization called SHARE. SHARE is one word that closely describes Jesus's mission as love of God in action, and it really moved me. In those terms, it is a wonderful definition of loving thy neighbor. The emotions started when I realized there are virtually no coincidences. As I grow older, my definition of coincidences is more interventions from God. As I grind through my life's story, there are too many coincidences that stacked up over time. God has been working overtime with me. As a mathematical statistician, I knew that my coincidences are impossible, from a mathematical viewpoint, without God pulling the strings. When I finally realized the full force as to what has taken place in my life with God's interventions, I couldn't help myself from crying. I just let it flow. Crying is not a crowd pleaser—but a fantastic healer for what ails you. As I reflect back on all the coincidences that have taken place in my life, I realize that there are no coincidences. "Coincidence is God's way of remaining anonymous," said Albert Einstein. God has certainly shared his blessings upon us. God is the way, the truth, and the life. Amen.

Chapter 31

Range Commanders Council

The Range Commanders Council (RCC) is a Department of Defense (DOD) organization comprised of all the test organizations within the navy, army, and air force and has test range capability to support their unique test missions. The air force systems command, located at Andrews AFB, has under its command many of the test organizations within the air force. Edwards Air Force Base, also called the Air Force Flight Test Center (AFFTC), has the Edwards Flight Test Range. The other test ranges include the Eastern Test Range (ETR), located near Cape Canaveral at Patrick AFB, Florida, the Western Test Range (WTR), located at Vandenberg AFB, California, which is used for over the pole launches as well as others over the Pacific to Barking Sands, near the Hawaiian island of Kauai, and the Navy Test Range located at Point Mugu, California.

The Range Commanders Council is organized into inter-range instrumentation group, called IRIG working groups. These groups include data reduction, telemetry, photo optics, communications, documentation, frequency, and range instrumentation. The purpose of these groups is to share and exchange classified and unclassified information among various range personnel who represent all the range operational functional elements. The IRIG organization proved to be extremely important in developing IRIG standards that have been used industry-wide. The RCC under the control of all the flag officers (general or admiral rank) has not only been very informative for range commanders as they meet biannually to share and exchange high-level management, command, and control issues and provide a highly effective IRIG working group structure to address common technical problems, standards, and range-operation issues.

Inter-Range Instrumentation Groups (IRIG)

The IRIG working groups would meet, separately, at a different range location twice a year. These working group meetings met to brief, share, and exchange information and included tours that proved to be most informative. Working group personnel had the opportunity to establish excellent working relationships. Many topics of mutual interest were range instrumentation accuracies, computer software, used for many range applications, radar and optical systems, time-space positioning information (TSPI) software, which are used to pinpoint aircraft, missile, bomb, or other test vehicles that need accurate tracking in space. In addition, working group members provide special technical briefings on various topics of job interest. These IRIG meetings proved to be an excellent mechanism for each range member to become very familiar with each other's test range operations. When I was a section chief, I participated in the data-reduction working group dealing with TSPI software and other data-reduction issues.

Range instrumentation (AF Photo)

IRIG Membership and Participation

Edwards AFB had membership in most of the groups. Over a period of about fifteen years, I was a member of three groups—the data-reduction, telemetry, and communications groups—and was designated as the range contact for Edwards AFB. In addition, I was selected to be a participant in an RCC study group to take a comprehensive look at the effectiveness of the RCC under the leadership of Colonel Sullivan from the USAF air force station in the greater Los Angeles area. Among other changes, the commanders approved the establishment of an executive committee, which was to consist of the top technical directors for each range and test organization. At that point in time, my function was to be the range contact when I no longer participated in the working groups for Edwards AFB. I remained as the assistant to the technical director for range issues.

Edwards Flight Test Range (EFTR) Range Contact

The range contact that I functioned as was a most interesting assignment. I accompanied the generals from Edwards AFB on a few RCC conferences. I assisted the Edwards AFB command structure to host an RCC meeting. I accompanied General Robert White, of X-15 fame, who was my neighbor when we lived on base as a major to attend RCC meetings at the Eastern Test Range (ETR) at Patrick AFB, Florida near Cape Canaveral, which launches most NASA and air force space vehicles, the Western Test Range (WTR) at Vandenberg AFB, California, and the Satellite Control Facility (STF) at Sunnyvale, California. General White introduced me to Davey Jones, now a two-star general, commander, ETR. He became famous as the fifth pilot to take off from the "Hornet Carrier" that participated in the famous Doolittle raid on their way to bomb Japan on April 18, 1942. When I accompanied General White to the SCF at Sunnyvale, we had breakfast together, and I entered into some small talk with the general by saying that they have thirty-two computers at the facility to keep track of all the satellites in orbit around the world. He half-jokingly said, "I wish that they were airplanes." That response ran me out of small talk and ended the conversation.

Chapter 32

Little Kids, Fun, Anniversaries, and Family Photos

When the kids were very young, I would have fun with the kids. I would do a lot of antics that my dad would do with my siblings. My dad would play funny games. For example, he would give us what he called a *Pops boomer*. He would put his fist on our nose and give us a little tap with his other fist. He would give us a *drucha*, where he would put his hands on each side of our cheeks and scrape a little bit. Then he would give us a *kneebly*, where he would put our nose between his thumb and index finger and give us a little pinch. Then he would give us a *steig*, where he would take his index finger from both hands and poke each side of our cheeks. As kids, we all enjoyed those small acts of endearment from our dad.

When my kids were very young, I would play the same foolishness, depending upon their ages. In addition, I would add my own embellishments. The kids enjoyed my antics immensely. The kids just loved for me to give them a banjo ride where I would put them on my hip and hold them with my upper arm and act like I was playing the banjo. I would shake, rattle, and roll like Johnny Cash, strumming and swaying around as I tickled them in the process. This was one of their favorites. I loved to give them my rendition of giving the kids pony rides. I would sit in a chair, position the kids on my feet, and give them gentle and bumpy rides. This is how the cowgirl rides, the lady rides, or how the lady goes horse riding. I would perform gentle and more advanced imitations of grown-up cowgirls. I would perform the same kind of antics with the boys, but I added a more aggressive galloping ride—as best I could sitting and getting all worn out.

We had a lot of pets at one time or another. We had cats, small dogs, and big dogs. My nickname for all the pets was Miserable. If one of the pets would annoy me, I would threaten the pet, knowing that the kids would hear me. "Miserable, I am going to throw you over Rasmussens' house across the street."

Kevin jokingly said, "Hey, Dad, the Rasmussens' backyard is full of cats and dogs—and there is no more room!"

Our Fiftieth Wedding Anniversary

At our fiftieth wedding anniversary reunion, we had about 150 guests to celebrate, including my siblings, relatives, kids, grandkids, and very close friends from both sides of the families. Our second son, Keith, as part of the entertainment, got up after a couple of beers and performed his version, entertaining the audience with my same shenanigans. This turned out to be a crowd-pleaser.

Our Sixty-Sixth Wedding Anniversary

We recently had a much smaller wedding anniversary celebration, and I had three priests attend the festivities. When Dorothy and I were married, we had three priests attend our wedding ceremony. During our sixty-sixth wedding anniversary, the highlight of the evening was roasting one of my priest friends to the delight of the priest and all in attendance. Usually, when I was asked how long I have been married, I would respond, "Sixty-six years—to the same woman!" That always got a laugh. Dorothy wouldn't say much. She would just sit there in the background and smile, as to say, "I've heard it all many times." What a wonderful spouse! She was a fantastic mother, grandmother, great-grandmother, and a great-great-grandmother. She was the rock-solid foundation for the Miller family. She was my long-standing support and my compassionate and devoted copilot. She was always at my side as we jointly maneuvered our way on an unbelievable journey from cows to space.

Family Photos

Cayucos Beach

Disneyland

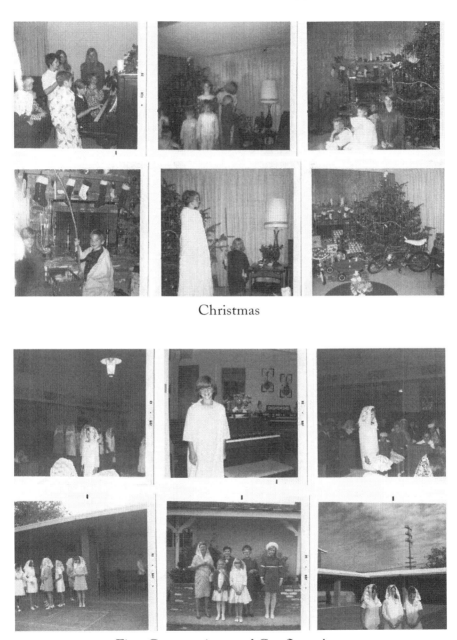

Christmas

First Communions and Confirmations

Easter

Other Family and Friends

Sibling Reunions

Dorothy and me in the Mountains and Back Yard at Home

Antelope Valley Poppies

Snow

Chapter 33

Long-Term, Full-Time Study

During the fall of 1965, I was selected to participate in the air force's long-term, full-time study program. I was the chief of the Data Systems Branch. I was pursuing a master's degree in aerospace operations management. To continue my studies in mathematics was not practical since I was in management with a broad supervisory assignment. It seemed much more appropriate to get a master's degree in management. Here again, I was at the right place at the right time in my career.

The University of Southern California had a program called systems management, which was perfect for my career and advanced education. Serendipitously, two of my very close colleagues were selected to participate in this program as well. Mr. Donald Smith, the chief of the Performance Engineering Branch, was responsible for most of the flight test engineering personnel. Engaged in aircraft performance and stability and control, he was selected. In addition, Mr. Richard (Dick) Harer was selected. Dick was chief of the X-15 program office for the Air Force Flight Test Center.

Captain Richard Harer, F-94C Test Pilot Tragedy

Dick Harer has a very interesting historical background. He was one of a very few test pilots who has survived an unfortunate test aircraft accident. He had a long painful recovery after he suffered severe burns that engulfed the cockpit in an unsuccessful landing of an F-94C.

F-94C (AF Photo)

He lost both of his legs from the knee down as a result. He was doing high-altitude drogue shoot testing. Upon completion of the test, according to the test plan, he tried to disengage the shoot from the tail of the aircraft. Unfortunately, the mechanism used to release the drogue shout malfunctioned and did not disengage. According to procedure, he lit the jet engine's afterburner, which provided an added burst of thrust and flame to burn off the shout, to no avail. The only options left were to attempt a forced landing on Rogers dry lake bed or bail out.

Captain Harer decided to land on the lake bed. He needed to stay in afterburner operation in order to maintain flight and maneuver to the lake bed. No one, to my knowledge, has ever attempted an afterburner landing. Dick was able to successfully approach the lake bed for an attempted landing. He experienced a hard landing, which resulted in a fire in the cockpit. Fortunately, another aircraft near the lake bed witnessed the crash landing. A test pilot, Captain Mel Apt, of future X-2 fame where he lost his life, was on aerial photography mission flying a C-45. He immediately flew over to the crash site and landed his aircraft close by. The pilot and aerial photographer pounded away on the cockpit to rapidly remove Dick from his burning craft. The only blunt instrument large enough to beat the hell out of the cockpit shielding was an expensive camera. They successfully removed Dick from the flaming cockpit in time to transport him, in a severely burned condition, to the base hospital for emergency treatment. This quick response, by all personnel, saved Dick's life.

My Roommate

I roomed with Dick in an apartment just west of the USC campus for the year. We had adequate accommodations. We would take turns driving back and forth to our Lancaster homes during weekends. Due to Dick's condition, we were able to park close to our classroom on campus. We had classes in a couple of portable buildings off the main campus area, near the football practice field, which made parking much easier.

Dick and I were very compatible. Dick was a very intelligent person who previously received an MS degree in aeronautics from the California Institute of Technology in Pasadena (Cal Tech). It took a while for me to get used to Dick taking off his artificial legs and throwing them into the corner. He would look at me and smile. I have heard it said that flesh burns are one of the most painful injuries that anyone can endure. Don Smith stayed in Long Beach, and the hunting grounds were very fruitful. He met his future wife, Margaret, a lovely person, prior to his graduation.

USC's Fantastic Program

I thoroughly enjoyed the systems management program. The courses were structured for managers in the aerospace field. I found the course on the psychological aspects of space flight most interesting, following the first Russian orbital space launch of Sputnik on October 4, 1957. I also had a course in aircraft structures and aerodynamics. The course I had in personnel management was most helpful. The course I had in biology, which covered the physiological aspects of space flight, had the most impact on my physical well-being. Dr. Barron was Lockheed's flight surgeon for Lockheed and helped develop the SR-71 Blackbird spacesuits and other flight gear for extreme altitude testing. He was the most outstanding university professor I ever had. He had the latest hands-on experience in physiology as it relates to extremely high-altitude flight operations.

My Fritzmobile

His biology course was absolutely enlightening and motivated me to begin jogging with Don Smith and many of my coworkers almost every day for a two-mile run at lunchtime. One of my sergeant's requisitioned a bicycle and labeled it the Fritzmobile, which was very handy going to and from the base gym. I continued that ritual until I retired and then well into my retirement years. I am absolutely convinced that this kept me in shape and extended my life.

How Much Skin?

Doctor Barron explained the amount of skin that covers the total body. He spoke in ninths as to explain the both legs account four-ninths of the skin. Each arm is one-ninth, the back, including the head and neck, is two-ninths, and the stomach and the face are the other ninth. One of the inquisitive students asked, "Dr. Barron, what about the other 1 percent?" I don't know if this was a planted question or not. The good doctor immediately smiled and commented rather excitedly, "Sir, that depends on how lucky you are!"

Other Related Courses

I had other courses in contract law, tort law, government aircraft acquisition procedures, and comparative management. The course we took in the psychological aspect of space flight was extremely interesting. Dick, with his handicap, would always sit in the front row with his artificial legs crossed. I would always sit next to him. Not very many people knew of his unfortunate aircraft accident, including the professor. In the course of demonstrating the patellar reflex reaction, the instructor tapped Dick just under the kneecap. His hand bounced after encountering a hard surface. The instructor was perplexed when he heard a loud thud and no reaction other than Don Smith and me squirming in our chairs and trying not to laugh. I noticed the instructor was totally stunned. After the class was over for the evening, Don had a pleasant powwow with the instructor about Dick's very unfortunate aircraft accident. We all got a good laugh regarding the circumstances of the situation, and the instructor apologized for his clumsiness. Dick as usual smiled and put the instructor at ease.

Government-Funded LTFT Education

The government funded all the tuition costs and our complete salaries for the year, including books and other miscellaneous office supplies. I obtained a master's of science degree in systems management. I found myself invigorated in returning to my assignment as Data Systems Branch chief, which I held for a short while longer until I was promoted to deputy division chief by my mentor, Alfred D. Phillips, chief, Flight Test Support Division.

Chapter 34

Promotion to Deputy Technical Support Division

The Technical Support Division is responsible for all airborne and ground instrumentation systems at Edwards Air Force Base. This included Edwards Fight Test Range (EFTR), all of the scientific computers utilized at Edwards AFB, photography laboratory, design of aircraft test instrumentation systems, and many other flight test functions and facilities. Mr. Alfred D. Phillips, my mentor, was the division chief. By this time, I had a long-standing work relationship with Mr. Phillips as a section chief and a branch chief, and I supported him as a young mathematician on two major high-priority test programs earlier in my career. Now, I was sitting in the same office and running a very large portion of Edwards Air Force Base technical support operations engaged in flight test.

As I came into work one morning, he asked me to go down to the weight and balance hangar. "I want to show you something."

We got into our staff car and entered a large hangar, and I noticed a weird-looking airplane that I never had seen before. Squatted on the scales was a U-2 reconnaissance aircraft. It was a breathtaking sight.

U-2 at USAF Museum (Government Photo)

The U-2 was a highly classified program at the time. All I could remember after taking a close and quick look was a long, slender fuselage with extended wings that made the aircraft appear to look wider than longer. We both had top-secret clearances. We figured that the U-2 was utilizing the weight and balance scales under our division management, and we decided to go on an inspection tour. Being in upper management does have its benefits and privileges. What an exciting important job with many responsibilities and headaches.

Functions of Management

Since I had recently graduated from USC in systems management, there was a challenging opportunity to practice what I learned. Being taught the functions of management provided me a much better understanding of management in general and how to approach and handle very large, diverse, and highly technical enterprises.

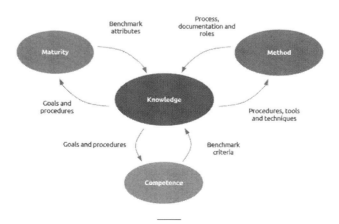

Management Activity

There is one important management function not identified: budgeting. We not only had to plan, budget, track, and allocate expenditures for operating and maintaining the Technical Support Division, using institutional sources of funds. We also had to plan, cost, track, and control all of the other funds and expenditures obtained from system program offices, known as SPOs. In other words, we had to perform a balancing act to make sure that we had sufficient operation and maintenance (O&M) funds to remain solvent. Budgeting was a very time-consuming and hands-on task to control expenditures. Due to the vicissitudes of flight test with all the delays, changes, and unforeseen events, it is sometimes very difficult for flight test engineers to plan accordingly. We had to make sure that our support would be available on demand. After all, the Air Force Flight Test Center existed to support flight test—not to support the AFFTC Support Center.

Other Support Capabilities

Even by looking at the organization chart, you would never know of some of the unique responsibilities. For example, besides the weight and balance hangar, previously mentioned, the installed thrust stand, the moments of inertia facility, the instrumentation-calibration laboratory, aerial photography, and other types of photography for all kinds of nonflight test activity to meet all requirements. The division had around-the-clock alert photography responsibility to photograph support many necessary mundane and detail needs at Edwards the city and Edwards AFB the flight test center: aircraft accidents, car accidents, family disturbances, suicides, special functions and activities, police activity, and many other unscheduled and unforeseen events.

Range Support Functions

In addition, a large variety of other range support functions, such as special gunnery ranges, special targets, precision impact range area (PIRA), sport and downfall, which are call signs for the range control officers (RCO) who are in direct and continuous contact with test pilots, conducting flight testing on the range. If anything went wrong, the RCO would be the first to know. There are a few ankle-biters in being responsible for safe range operations. The RCOs were on a first-name basis, but they did not communicate informally.

Randy Chestnut, range development engineer (AF Photo)

Chuck Yeager would visit the sport control folks on occasion and express his thanks for a job well done, which would be graciously accepted. Steve Kukic, the lead RCO, was an institution at Edwards, and they knew each other quite well. Colonel Yeager—now a retired brigadier general—was periodically assigned at Edwards AFB during his absolutely spectacular career. After all those years, he never forgot the guys in range control on the ground. It was comforting for him to know that there was a friendly voice on the ground.

Steve Kukic started to work at Edwards not very long after Chuck Yeager broke the sound barrier. Steve Kukic was an extremely well-known RCO for countless years. Our responsibility was twofold: flight safety and ensuring mission accomplishment. We operated in real time, which meant in the time domain, when it happens. There are no do-overs for range-support operations. We either did our job as it takes place—or we didn't. No slipups. Do-overs are anathema, which requires another go-around or schedule another mission.

F86-H Fatal Crash

The most notable tragic accident in my early days took place on August 25, 1954, taking the life of Captain Joseph McConnell, the leading Korean War ace with sixteen known scores over mostly MiG-15s.

F86-H Hawk (AF Photo)

The aircraft suffered a complete hydraulic failure by a missing bolt. Captain McConnell had to fly the airplane using the elevator trim rather than bailing out the airplane, and he flew his aircraft back several miles short of the lake bed. His attempt to save the aircraft failed—so Captain McConnell bailed out. He had to bail out too low for the parachute to open. He died upon impact with the desert floor. His H-86H Sabre went cartwheeling into a fireball a couple hundred yards away.

Captain Joseph McConnell (AF Photo)

Implications

For the purpose of this discussion, the instrumentation branch assigned to the division was responsible for the design of flight test instrumentation to sense and record test data obtained during a test mission. As a result, I personally witnessed all of these stringent procedures, however necessary, which are used in the design, documentation approvals, and check-out procedures that were required for each aircraft instrumentation installation. The air force did not want to experience another avoidable incident that killed a triple-ace hero. Three major organizations were involved in the design, installation, and approval process. The instrumentation engineers worked very closely with flight test engineers in order to obtain all the test data that is needed to be captured—hand-in-hand with the center's aircraft maintenance organization. The flight test engineering organization had to define all the flight test requirements for planning, designing, and documenting onboard instrumentation systems. This was a challenging task since no two airplanes were alike—and flight test data collection requirements are different from one aircraft to another. I was asked to conduct a comprehensive study with the task of how to improve and reduce the time for the overall process from beginning to ending with the center's final approval.

Defining the Problem

I approached the problem by using the scientific method. One of the first things I learned in one of my management courses was to define the problem, make sure that you are about solving the real problem. I started out by educating myself all about the process in much more detail.

Comprehensive Organizational Review

I made a rather comprehensive review of all the organizations involved and work assignments, including instrumentation supplies, purchases, and other overlooked activities that unnecessarily slow the program. I had to brief most of the managers all the way up to the headquarters staff. I identified a number of soft spots, delays, and inefficiencies and provided recommendations and improvements as best I could. Some improvements were made, but the largest contribution I made was presenting the overall interorganizational entanglements and interfaces that needed to take place in a clear fashion. They never fully realized all the organization interactions involved in the overall process. This stringent process was the air force's answer to ensuring that the bolt mishap would never happen again. Almost everywhere I gave briefings, management personnel were very surprised as to the magnitude of the problem. Despite the fact that it was absolutely necessary to conduct a totally safe flight test program, all the organizations involved in the process obtained a much better appreciation for installing a class-2 modification on an aircraft.

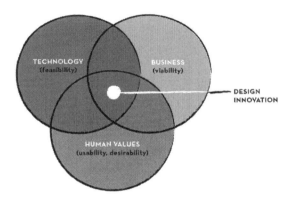

I used Venn diagrams to convey organizational interfaces and responsibilities. A Venn diagram is an illustration that utilizes circles—either overlapping or nonoverlapping—to depict a relationship between finite groups of things. This diagram was named after John Venn, an English philosopher and logician, in 1880. These diagrams can be applied within an organization, between two organizations, or for multiple organizations individually in more simple terms. When I briefed some organizations, I was asked "What the hell is a Venn diagram?" I would simply state that it was a way of identifying responsibilities and interfaces. When I finished the briefing, I heard someone say jokingly, "That's pretty good stuff." I like to think that this study had some benefit in improving the overall process. In addition, I witnessed less infighting and browbeating among organizations. I hoped Captain Joseph McConnell would be happy because I was sure that his demise was not in vain—and that many future accidents were prevented, saving many test pilots' lives.

Chapter 35

NF-104 Crash, President Reagan Policies, and New Developments

The Lockheed nF-104A was an American mixed power, high-performance, supersonic aerospace trainer that served as a low-cost astronaut training vehicle for the X-15 and projected X-20 Dyna-Soar programs. The third NF-104A (USAF 56-0762) was delivered to the USAF on November 1, 1963, and was destroyed in a crash while being piloted by Chuck Yeager on December 10, 1963.

Role	Aerospace trainer
Manufacturer	Lockheed Aircraft Corporation
Designer	Clarence Kelly Johnson
First flight	July 9, 1963
Introduction	October 1, 1963
Retired	June 1971
Primary user	United States Air Force
Number built	3
Unit cost	$5,363,322 (modification cost for all three aircraft)
Developed from	Lockheed F-104 starfighter

Data Reduction Branch Role in the Investigation

Due to the limitation of funding at the Aerospace Research Pilot School (ARPS) to provide for an onboard test instrumentation system for conducting NF-104 high-altitude testing, it was decided to rely on all ground-space tracking systems that are needed to determine and establish official high-altitude records. At the time of the crash, I was chief of the Data Systems Branch. The branch had the capability for receiving telemetry data, but it was not used because a telemetry transmitter was not installed onboard the NF-104. However, the Space Positioning Branch had all of their range ground-tracking systems operating in full force. Very fortunately, they recorded excellent long-range high-accuracy optical data. They had four very high-resolution German-made Askania cameras that can be used for triangulation, similar to the constellation of global positioning satellites (GPS), which had not yet been fully developed, only in a reverse fashion. In other words, the constellation of satellites are the receivers of information, whereas the Askanias are the receivers for tracking objects in space from the ground.

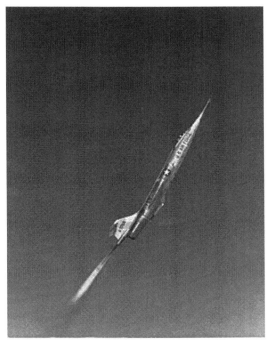

NF-104 in a steep climb (AF Photo)

Data Reduction and Analysis

The Data Systems Branch was faced with a problem. The branch was able to provide the aircraft-altitude data for the total mission profile in short order, but we were never asked to provide angle of attack, pitch, roll, acceleration, and other information that would normally be recorded onboard the aircraft. We were approached to see if we could provide this engineering data, optically. In addition to the Askania cameras, the space-positioning branch had long-range nonmetric tracking scopes that assisted in the data-reduction process. The real problem was we had a long way to go and a little time to get there. I had the whole staff of able mathematicians put to the task. Mr. Tom Simpson, Bob Ray, and others led the way. Overnight, they developed the software and computed the data-reduction process for subsequent analysis by the accident investigation board, the very next day.

Colonel Guy Townsend, of XB-52 test pilot fame, was the president of the board as well as the commander of flight test. He was absolutely amazed as to the thoroughness and timeliness of receiving this all-important data. This was the only meaningful computed test data that was used in the accident investigation. I advised my chief, Alfred D. Phillips, that Tom Simpson deserved a lot of the credit. He informed Colonel Townsend accordingly. He now refers to Mr. Tom Simpson as "Galileo." Upon having an audience with Colonel Townsend, Tom found out that they were both from Texas. They both are big, tall men who probably sang the famous Texas song "The Eyes of Texas Were upon You." Tom came back to my office with a big grin on his face. When I assigned him to undertake this formidable task, I wasn't sure that it could be done. The top speed of the NF-104 established by Chuck Yeager on this mission was 1,452 mph. Well done, Colonel Yeager and Tom Simpson, wherever you are.

Askania Theodolite (Manufacturer Photo)

Askania Mounted Theodolite (AF Photo)

As it turned out, it was extremely fortunate to have scheduled these highly accurate optical cameras. They played a significant role in the NF-104 investigation. These time-space positioning information (TSPI) systems provide very accurate tracking of an object in space.

President Reagan's Policy Changes

After the election of President Reagan, he changed Department of Defense department (DOD) policies. This initiated a tremendous push in the development of new offensive and defensive weapon systems. In addition, the B-1 test program was reinstated. This increased the workload for computer services and exposed the dire need to expand the long-range continuous coverage for remote flight test support operations.

B-1 Bomber (AF Photo)

Various types of new aircraft designs sprung up on the design boards, which continued throughout the remainder of the 1960s. In addition, a number of existing aircraft needed modification and updates with new state-of-the-art electronics and other aircraft modifications. In addition, DOD attempted to develop aircraft to meet requirements for the air force and other armed services. This also included swept wing technology.

FB-111 Multipurpose Aircraft (AF Photo)

The FB-111 was developed as a multipurpose fighter bomber. This approach required a design challenge, whereas, various design trade-offs were necessary. The major buildup of additional new aircraft developments along with all of the modifications greatly increased the flight test activity and Data Systems Branch workload.

Expansion of Inter-Range DATS System for Remote Testing

There was a great need to expand the capabilities of the Data Acquisition Transmission System (DATS) to form a major test corridor that extended from the Naval Test Center at Point Mugu to Vandenberg Air Force Base.

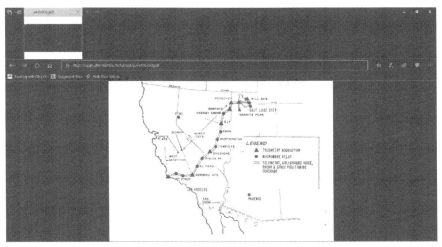

Data Acquisition and Transmission System (AF Diagram)

A microwave system transmitted the information from the West Coast to the Edwards Flight Test Range (EFTR) that interconnected with the facilities at Hill AFB, Wendover, and the army's Dugway Proving Grounds, Utah, all located in the Great Salt Lake area. This formed a major flight test corridor that provided continuous data acquisition and communications coverage that extended more than 1,200 miles from the West Coast to the Great Salt Lake. Our segments were known as West DATS (WDATS) and North DATS (NDATS). The NDATS system was originally installed before my tenure as branch chief, to support the X-15 vehicle research program. This provided the capability to transmit digital radar tracking data (space positioning) information and communications for complete coverage of an X-15 mission profile. The EFTR supported virtually all of the X-15 research tests.

X-15 Research Aircraft

First flight: June 8, 1957 the local area coverage was provided by the Space Positioning Branch's FPS-16 digital radars. Speeds, altitudes, and other critical safety-of-flight information were also provided by use of local telemetry antennas, which are similar to a radio receiver but used far different frequencies. Since we didn't have sufficient personnel to operate and maintain the total DATS system, we entered into an engineering and technical services contract (ETTS) with Kentron, Inc. The DATS system proved to be invaluable in later years to support future programs. The North American X-15 was a hypersonic rocket-powered aircraft flown by air force and NASA test pilots. X-15 records are: top speed: 4,520 mph or m= 6.72 set by William J. Knight. Range: 280 miles altitude 354,200 ft. or 67+ miles set by Joe Walker. First flight: June 8, 1959, 199 flights completed. Twelve test pilots, including Neil Armstrong, later a NASA astronaut. Last flight: November 15, 1967, X-15 flight designated 191 crashed, piloted by Michael J. Adams.

Home HYPERLINK "https://theaviationist.com/category/aviation-safety/" Aviationsafety/air crashes that time an X-15 rocket plane entered hypersonic spin at Mach 5 and broke apart killing USAF test pilot.
That time an X-15 rocket plane entered hypersonic spin at Mach 5 and broke apart killing USAF test pilot.
November 15, 2017 d a, s 5 comments

X-15 in powered flight (AF Photo)
(Narrative credits given above)

X-15 # 3 crash

This air force photo shows the X-15 ship #3 (56-6672) in flight over the desert in the 1960s. Ship #3 made sixty-five flights during the program, attaining a top speed of Mach 5.65 and a maximum altitude of 354,200 feet. Only ten of the twelve X-15 pilots flew ship #3, and only eight of them earned their astronaut wings during the program. Robert White, Joseph Walker, Robert Rushworth, John "Jack" McKay, Joseph Engle, William "Pete" Knight, William Dana, and Michael Adams all earned their astronaut wings in ship #3. Neil Armstrong and Milton Thompson also flew ship #3. In fact, Armstrong piloted ship #3 on its first flight, on December 20, 1961. On November 15, 1967, ship #3 was launched over Delamar Lake, Nevada, with Major Michael J. Adams at the controls. The vehicle soon reached a speed of Mach 5.2 and a peak altitude of 266,000 feet.

During the climb, an electrical disturbance degraded the aircraft's controllability. Ship #3 began a slow drift in heading, which soon became a spin. Adams radioed that the X-15 seemed squirrelly and then said, "I'm in a spin." Through some combination of pilot technique and basic aerodynamic stability, Adams recovered from the spin and entered an inverted Mach 4.7 dive. As the X-15 plummeted into the increasingly thicker atmosphere, the Honeywell adaptive flight control system caused the vehicle to begin oscillating. As the pitching motion increased, aerodynamic forces finally broke the aircraft into several major pieces. Adams was killed when the forward fuselage impacted the desert. This was the only fatal accident during the entire X-15 program. The X-15 was a rocket-powered aircraft fifty feetlong with a wingspan of twenty-two feet. It was a missile-shaped vehicle with an unusual wedge-shaped vertical tail, thin stubby wings, and unique side fairings that extended along the side of the fuselage. The X-15 weighed about 14,000 pounds empty and approximately 34,000 pounds at launch. The XLR-99 rocket engine was manufactured by Thiokol Chemical Corp.

US Air Force test pilot Major Michael J. Adams was killed during X-15 flight 191.

Chapter 36

Family Reunions and Memories

My youngest sister, Theresa, and her husband, Don, lived in very large mountainous homes in Sutter Creek, and Ione, California, which are located in Amador County in the western foothills of the Sierra Mountains. We had family gatherings at least once or twice a year for more than thirty years. All of my siblings are very indebted and most thankful to Theresa and her lawyer husband, Donald, for their wonderful hospitality and being great sports. We told lawyer jokes in jest—but totally politically incorrect, in today's parlance. Every family needs to periodically get together and remember recent memories and continue to generate many more.

Three sisters and three brothers
Left to right: Joe, Rose, Theresa, Richard, Mary, and Fritz

Sutter Creek Reunions

Theresa was a fantastic host and cook. I would kid Theresa about using every pot and pan in the house to cook gourmet dinners. We would wait until five o'clock to arrive—New York time, that is—to begin our libation and celebrations. Unfortunately, a time or two, dinner was late, and we did our best not waste our precious time. Our five o'clock hour, at times, would be extended an hour or two while we still engaged in New York time. On top of all that, the hosts would serve some of the best wines in Amador County. We all drank in moderation except for one occasion.

What Did We Talk About?

Many things: family, kids, illnesses, politics, church, world problems, teenagers, births, dating, schools, and many other topics. Suffice it to say, there were a plethora of stories to engage in, resulting in some very serious discussions. These family gatherings took place after the siblings were married. Decade after decade, amounting to more than thirty years, we talked about all the thirty-eight nieces and nephews: upbringings, graduations, marriages, offspring, serious illnesses, and many other events and subjects of mutual interest.

As time marched on, many other current life situations were cussed and discussed. We talked about doctors, surgeries, medications, diseases, and the trials and tribulations of raising teenage children in our current culture. Raising teenagers was the most difficult task for our siblings. Each family member had issues. A couple of kids struggled with alcoholism, drug abuse, serious illnesses, and difficulties finding their way.

Dorothy and I with our eight children experienced our share of problems with a premature pregnancy and serious drug abuse. We lost our third daughter, Jennifer, at the age of fifty-one, to the absolute horrors of both illegal and legal drug abuse, which resulted in an accidental overdose. She lived a horrible lifestyle. She lived at home almost continuously for the last fourteen years of her life. Dorothy took a very sane and sensible position with Jennifer. She made her choices. Despite her very mature outlook on the situation, Dorothy loved Jennifer very much and agreed to let her live in our home. I viewed the situation much differently. I did everything I could to rehabilitate her. Many times, I thought I was successful—and then the situation would get worse. Toward the end of the nightmare ordeal, I began suffering again from a very serious depression. God had mercy on her by ending her misery a couple of months later, despite very sad circumstances. This is a majorly convoluted story.

The Stories Continue

As the past memories unfold, we enter into grandkids era—having kids and then having their own kids and so on. The siblings and offspring experienced and suffered deaths, fatal accidents, major health issues, divorce, business conflicts, depression, anxiety, and a series of mishaps that confront large and small families.

Toward the end of the thirty years of fabulous family adventures, as we gathered together one last time, my oldest sister was in a wheelchair, and Joe and his wife, Pat, were in walkers, Theresa and Don were the only couple who was not handicapped. Robert was in a wheelchair after being handicapped by a terrible stroke. Sandi, Bobby's wife, was in fair health. Dorothy was in a walker with back issues. I was in good health. Aloise and Alicia (Alice) normally did not attend the reunions due to their involvement with a special and very unusual Catholic church mission: God's Word of today.

Final Thoughts about Family Reunions

Without a doubt, Theresa and Donald Garibaldi's strong family interests were paramount by instigating, encouraging, and sparking sibling interest in keeping the ball rolling for all thirty plus years. It is virtually impossible to comprehend the family's spiritual benefits. We all used each other to solve family problems—if no more than listening to each other's narration of our family problems. Family support abounded.

Family is what it is all about! It really bothers me that our society is not only becoming more and more godless and is chewing up families in the process. Heaven forbid. Our country faces a difficult task in surviving the continuous anti-God sentiment. Our last president advocated that Christianity is dead in the United States. This is absolutely hogwash and unbelievable in my opinion. It is a path to perdition and destruction. What is happening to the Constitution? We must return to the God's principles that our founding fathers so ably established and built the greatest society on the face of the earth. Enough said. My final thought is spoken by the Father in heaven. Thy will be done. Amen.

Coffee, Dinners, Local Gatherings, and Home Visits

There is much more to the memory stories associated with all the reunions that we attended at Teresa and Don's homes in the mountains. There were many other occasions where there were daily, weekly, monthly, and numerous other gatherings where the siblings living in Wasco would celebrate together. Mary and Ray's home became a second home for all of us. My brother Joe, when he farmed and was about town, would visit Mary for a cup of coffee. Robert and Rose would show up occasionally as well. Furthermore, Mary would entertain and prepare fantastic dinners for all the Catholic priests and family members. Rose and Howard would do the same on many occasions. Howard Bennett was the local pharmacist who knew many local businessmen. Howard was a great guy who was a very interesting conversationalist. All the priests viewed Mary and Rose's as their homes away from the rectory. They would all look forward to the next Miller gathering. Occasionally Mom would have similar gatherings at the ranch home on the farm. The priests would remove their collars and mix in very well. This provided the opportunity for the priests to really relax among true friends and forget about the rigors of being a pastor at a poor minority parish. These occasions provided therapy for everybody. Drinks and jokes were prevalent in good taste, and the booze flowed in moderation. The tops of the evening were both of my sisters' wonderful cooking with a large amount of conversation on a variety of political, spiritual, and family topics. It was difficult for one of the priests to leave. He enjoyed it so much that he would always be one of the last to leave. It would be a good time to go to confession.

Dad's Demise

After Dad died, Mom was left by herself in the large farmhouse that was located very close to my two older brothers' homes, less than a couple hundred yards distant. Basically, Mom was never alone. The two sons and their families would go see Mom at least two times a day. Joe and Aloise would visit mom very frequently, and Pat, Joe's wife, and Shirley, Aloise's wife, would take turns taking Mom shopping and visiting relatives. Joe had told me many times that he wished that he went to college. I had to remind him that God planted him and his family exactly where God wanted him to be. As a result, Joe, Mary, and Rose remained very active in the church as manifested at the fiftieth anniversary of Saint John's Grammar School.

Saint John's Grammar School's Fiftieth Celebration

Mom was so proud of Mary and Joe for being key leaders for Saint John's the Evangelist Church. They were the prime movers and shakers in promoting, planning, performing, and executing a very successful celebration event. Mary arranged for all the cooks, help, waiters, and kitchen cleanup. In addition to all the planning and setup, Joe was the master of ceremonies. I accompanied Mom.

As Swiss immigrants, Mom and Dad certainly have made their contribution to the Saint John's Parish and to the Wasco community and society as a well. I only wish that Dad was still alive to revel with Mom to witness their fruits grow. Thanks to God, we all attended Saint John's and got an excellent education from the Franciscan nuns. Joe was president of the school board. The siblings who remained in Wasco sent their children to Saint John's School. In addition, Mary was in charge and ensured that everything was ready to go for the celebration. If you wanted anything done right, Mary would respond and perform in an outstanding manner.

My Immigrant Parents

Mom was a very humble and meek person who, no doubt, underneath her very kind and sweet nature, was very happy and proud that her two oldest children performed a major role in the celebration. Mom added credence and meaning to the old biblical saying the meek shall inherit the earth, and Mom and Dad fully understood the importance of family. They came from very large families from Switzerland and were raised in a small community where church attendance and God-centered family life was centerfold for building strong family ties and togetherness. The Miller family certainly contributed to the formation of a vibrant parish at Saint John's. In addition, Dad was involved in many committee chairmanships and built two churches during his lifetime. Dad was a significant church donor who purchased the altar for the new church that was built during the mid-1930s. I talk about God working wonders through me. I submit that God worked wonders through Mom and Dad as they lived out their lives that accomplished many wonderful things for Saint John the Evangelist Church and the city of Wasco, California.

Home Visits

A few times a year, Dorothy and I and the family would venture back to the farm. The kids thoroughly enjoyed the farm. The kids liked to visit both grandmothers. My mother would be referred to as the Wasco grandma, and Dorothy's mother would be referred to as the beach grandma.

We didn't get to the beach as often. Wasco was a little over one hundred miles away. We made a point to visit and stay at the beach for two weeks every year. They roamed the beach every day and went swimming at will, sporting their skin protectant. On the farm, the boys wandered around the farm, went swimming in two reservoirs, and rode their bikes and motor bikes to their content. Mom's cooking was special. I would always kid Mom before we would all leave. "Mom, you mistreated us again." It got so that Mom accepted that criticism as a dear compliment. She would always laugh when I characterized our visits in that manner. I even use that same expression today in complimenting my siblings for a job well done.

Mary and Ray's Fiftieth Wedding Anniversary

On a very special occasion, the Miller and the Schroeder families and friends celebrated the fiftieth wedding anniversary of Mary and Ray. What a wonderful occasion. Mary was all smiles, and Ray was his happy-go-lucky self. Richard and I decided to act up a bit. Richard was funnier and more outgoing than me. We planned for a midevening gig with a dual comedy act. We both liked to sing. Richard was not bashful like me. If we got up together, I would have more courage to go along with the act, particularly after a couple glasses of wine. We decided to put together a few commercial jingles and excerpts from many of the songs of the day, particularly the ones Mary liked when she was growing up.

Songs and Jingles

We started off with the song "Drinkin Rum and Coke-a-Cola, go down to Point Koomahnah, both mother and daughter, working for the Yankee dollar," and " Managua Nicaragua is a wonderful town, you buy a hacienda for a few pesos down, you give it to the lady you are trying to win, but her papa doesn't let you come in." Then the Beer Barrel Polka: "Roll out the barrel we'll have a barrel of fun, roll out the barrel we've got the blues on the run." For our decorated World War II brother-in-law Purple Heart veteran, we included "Praise the Lord and Pass the Ammunition,"

"Remember Pearl Harbor," and "Right in Der Fuehrer's Face." We sang the Bob Hope and Bing Crosby rendition of Marizy Doats (Mares eat oats), "Mairzy doates and dozy doats and little lamzy divey, a kiddley divey too, wouldn't you?" Translation: "Mares eat oats and does eat oats and little lambs eat ivy" from a song by Merry Macs. Yes, I can still hear Mary singing the favorite song of the day: Rose O'Day. "Rose O'Day, Rose O'Day, you're my Filla-da-gusha, Filla-ma-rusha, Bah-da-rah-da-boom-foo-dee-ay to the delight of all her siblings. What a laugh! We ended up with the Ford commercial, "It's a Foooooorrrdd." Dad never owned a Ford. He would always characterize a tractor, some other mechanical device, or a car that wouldn't start as "All the same Ford." At the end of our so-called comedy act, we had everybody in stitches. Richard and I relished performing in a very uncharacteristic fashion. We enjoyed doing our act and had a hell of a time. Everybody enjoyed themselves immensely as the evening wore on in spirit and delight of everyone celebrating Mary and Ray's grand fiftieth wedding anniversary.

Chapter 37

Technical Support Division

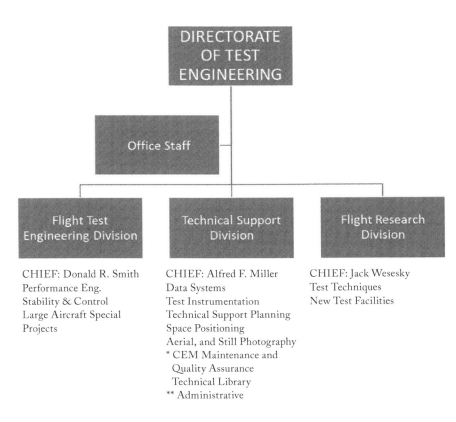

CHIEF: Donald R. Smith
Performance Eng.
Stability & Control
Large Aircraft Special
Projects

CHIEF: Alfred F. Miller
Data Systems
Test Instrumentation
Technical Support Planning
Space Positioning
Aerial, and Still Photography
* CEM Maintenance and
   Quality Assurance
   Technical Library
** Administrative

CHIEF: Jack Wesesky
Test Techniques
New Test Facilities

*CEM; Communications & Electronic Maintenance

AFFTC Reorganization

As a result of a new center reorganization, I was positioned as the chief of the Technical Support Division. I was assigned as a deputy chief on my previous assignment. The difference between a deputy chief and an assistant chief is that a deputy chief can act in full authority during the absence of the chief. I was deputy chief of the Technical Support Division under the leadership of Alfred Phillips. At this stage in my career, I had a long-standing working relationship with Al Phillips, my mentor. I used to kid him the next time he went hunting or fishing, I would cancel his job. Of course that was something I couldn't and wouldn't do, but it was a long-standing joke. A couple times a year I would jokingly ask, "Isn't it about time that I can cancel your position again?" He would always laugh and put me in my place. He would say, "When I get back, I will have a lot more power than you. So be careful what you ask for." This is indicative of the type of working relationship we had. I wasn't just a yes-man. He respected me, and I respected him. Working under my mentor, we accomplished many good things that truly enhanced the flight test mission. I can truly say that we both accomplished almost wonders. I speak about the real wonders elsewhere in my book (God's wonders).

Technical Support Division

All three of the three newly positioned and appointed division chiefs were established as division chiefs. All three of us were already at the GS-15 level. All three of the division chiefs, including me, were assigned additional responsibilities. There were approximately four hundred personnel who were employed in the Technical Support Division that encompassed the operation and maintenance (O&M) of specialized onboard instrumentation systems and ground data acquisition capabilities, still photography, and both aerial movie and video coverage in different gravity situations in addition to all Edwards Flight Test Range (EFTR) capabilities that utilize telemetry, radar, gunnery ranges, special targets, precision impact range area (PIRA), and special long-range optical devices used to track and record planned aircraft spins and other test maneuvers both locally and remote. In addition to all of the large-scale scientific computers and data-processing and handling systems, I didn't have a deputy division assigned to me, at the time. One of the reasons for the reorganization was to establish a promotional path for capable officers to advance in the directorate of test engineering, particularly in the highly technical and unique functional test areas. I finally got a lieutenant colonel assigned to be my deputy after about four months. I had to carry the load. I didn't have a deputy assigned yet to keep all the technical support activity on an even keel. Over the next seven of eight years, I had three different lieutenant colonels parade in and out of my deputy assignment position. My thanks to Lieutenant Colonels Warren McCormack, Dave Kincaid, and Roger Counts for keeping me sane.

For the rest of my career story, I don't plan to give a blow-by-blow account of the duties I faced as an upper-level manager employed at Edwards AFB. I plan to relate a number of stories about special projects and assignments that I worked on as additional duty, which I feel is of some interest without being too technical. Suffice it to say that the functions of management that I learned studying for my master of science degree, gave me a much better insight into management. The textbook approach to management is as follows:

Technical Support Planning

When Al Phillips went off to a year's Sloan scholarship program in executive management at Stanford, he came back with some great ideas about how to get a better handle on costs, schedules, workload, and associated planning. He formed a new Technical Support Planning Branch. I was his deputy at the time. He selected Charles Kroll, one of the premier engineers, to plan, establish, and implement this new branch. This organization needed knowledgeable support personnel to staff the organization who were very familiar with the many services provided by the division. Two very notable personnel come to my mind: Paul Anderson and Zac Zaccardi. Mr. Kroll's staff contacted all the major users of the EFTR. They prepared technical support plans—large and small—to document anticipated support requirements for the various facilities within the division. This was no small task since the flight test engineers were content with the status quo. They felt comfortable with the way things were where they would just ask for support services or schedule support accordingly. Mr. Phillips realized that this was no way to run a railroad. He was very bold in trying to force some engineers to get with the program. This resulted in some serious conflicts among the other divisions within the directorate of flight test. As Mr. Phillips's deputy, I had a major role in the approval and sighing many of these support plans. All this information by project was recorded in a database that, when fully developed, became a very important summary of most all of the Technical Support Division's workload for the present and the future.

Planning and Improvements

This had immense possibilities to plan, organize, staff, measure, and control a very large complex technical organization. One very important aspect, regarding these support plans, project engineers had to approve and certify their requirements. Even though this was a traumatic process at times, it proved a most valuable process to carry out the demands for division management. These plans worked both ways. We committed the division, put our reputations on the line, and gave the project engineers ample ammunition for us to provide the support or else. Both key divisions planned, worked, communicated far better, and carried out a much better paradigm in accomplishing the AFFTC mission. For most of my entire career, I was involved hand in hand, pounding the pavement, with all of the notable flight test engineers, managers, and test pilots engaged in flight test at Edwards AFB and assisting all of them in making aerospace history. In some ways, being a member of upper management was every bit as rewarding, but at times more frustrating, but the pay check made it worthwhile.

The Inter-Range Instrumentation Group (IRIG)

The very important IRIG Range Documentation Group established standards to plan and document requirements for inter-range support activity. Mr. Paul Anderson and Zac Zaccardi became members of that group, through my request, as the AFFTC's range contact. Paul and Zac were the division's top planners. This was a standard way of documenting inter-range requirements. These procedures were particularly useful to support all of the major inter-range test programs, such as the U-2, X-15, B-1A, B-2, SR-71, XB-70, cruise missile, and NASA's space shuttle programs. I will elaborate on two programs: the cruise missile and the space shuttle programs.

Space Shuttle Inter-Range Documentation Support

I have spoken somewhat briefly about what we had previously accomplished supporting the cruise missile program and all of the inter-range activity that took place supporting cruise missiles. What needs a little bit more elaboration is the worldwide range net used to support the space shuttle. Mr. Anderson performed a yeoman's job in accomplishing this horrendous documentation task from an EFTR perspective. This included documentation requirements, and he also assisted the establishment of inter-range, check, countdown, and readiness procedures, including the Ridley Mission Control Center (RMCC) and range control officer (RCO) functions for ensuring in-flight operations. This RMCC was named after Colonel Jack Riley. Chuck Yeager's trusted aerospace engineer guided him through the breaking of the sound barrier. Jack Riley was his "gum-chewy buddy," so well depicted in *The Right Stuff.* Upon construction of the new RMCC, I was honored to be the first occupant along with Lieutenant Colonel Roger Counts. My deputy and staff were to be the first occupants of the new RMCC in early fall 1981.

Additional Management Functions

There are a few additional functions of management that may be unique for managing a highly technical organization engaged in supporting a very unique one-of-a-kind air force flight test institution. For instance, General Slay signed up for what is called "institutional funding," which is a special way to accomplish financial planning, budgeting, allocating, accounting, reporting and managing various kinds of money. The money is still green, but it's kept and managed in a variety of different pots (categories) of funds that are used only for special purposes. In other words, you can't reprogram funds from one pot to another except for some categories. The center comptroller (known as the bean counter) has a nightmare job of keeping track of all the different kinds of dollars. The nightmare did not end in the comptroller's office; it came down in many ways. Since the Technical Support Division owned, organizationally, a significant share and portion of the center's operating funds, it stands to reason that Mr. Phillips and I had our hands full managing the division's allocation of various funds. We shared in the comptroller's nightmare. Since I was the mathematician in the office and Mr. Phillips was the managing engineering director, I had the continuous duty to keep our hands all around the budget to stay solvent.

Institutional Funding

Back to institutional funding, our operating budget came directly from the air force as institutional dollars that provided most of the funds to operate the Technical Support Division, supplemented by what is called "project money" that we earned by supporting all kinds of test activity. Many of our facilities were "firehouse manned," which means that it took a certain number of personnel to support scheduled flight operations—whether you had to support one or ten missions a day. During slow scheduling times, we couldn't generate sufficient project funds to sustain operations. My problem was making sure that we earned enough project money to supplement the institutional money that we would normally get. At certain times, the division could earn more than we expended. I had to employ many different functions of management to stay above water. Needless to say, I had to employ some functions of management more than others with a high concentration on budgeting, measuring, and controlling. It is surprising to me that many of the flight test engineers shied away from budgeting and budgets. I am not sure whether it was disinterest, didn't know how, couldn't care less, or just downright afraid of budgeting. With all the disciplined training I had in studying mathematics and statistics, as well as being computer knowledgeable, budgeting wasn't that difficult for me—but not simple. I did know how to prepare and handle budgets. Here again, I was in the right place at the right time.

Entrepreneur

When I was a kid during World War II, I would make small amounts of money doing all kinds of things. I would find and save rubber that I could take in for so much of a pound to supplement my meager bankroll. I felt good about supporting and contributing to the war effort. I would save the grease Mom had in the kitchen for little more extra money. I would walk down the streets near school and downtown to collect the silver-looking wrappings around cigarette packages. I figured if it looked good, it was worth something, I would save bottle caps and bottles, and I would dig up worms for my dad's fishing buddies for the coins in their pockets. I didn't collect enough to buy a small war bond, mainly because of having an occasional soda pop, ice cream bar, or candy bar that was too tempting to pass up. I did learn the value of money early in life. I was pinching pennies with purpose and delight. Now I was managing millions of dollars as a division chief. The little things you learn as a little boy translate to a much larger scale later in life. So, early in life, I knew how to do a very little planning, working, saving, spending, and enjoying the little things. All the sweets sure did taste good. Luckily, I was active enough to burn the goodies off.

Newly Assigned AFFTC Commander

About the twenty-year point in my career, Edwards AFB was assigned a replacement general, which happens about every two or three years. Some of the time, with a new star assignment for the Air Force Flight Test Center, some changes were made. Brigadier General Alton D. Slay, referred to above, made his mark in more ways than one. He had just become a flag officer and then was assigned to Edwards. Later in his career, he was awarded four stars. He became the commander, Air Force Systems Command, which was an extremely large responsibility in the United States Air Force. I would compare this general to General Patton as a hero. Their management styles were similar: no blood, but a lot of guts and sweat. It took a lot of guts to stand in front of him, give him a briefing, and be subjected to an occasional arrow—or a bullet or two as a division chief. As a result of his reorganization, I had the opportunity to attend project reviews given by test force directors, program directors, project officers, test engineers, and other management personnel. I had the scary occasion of having to brief the general three times. They were informational briefings, not a big project status briefing, so he was receptive to me and took it easy on me. Be that as it may, it was quite an experience. His interest was airplanes, of course, not all that other mundane stuff. He asked me a few questions that seemed to satisfy him. I felt that the questions he asked were to convince me that he was very interested, being the commanding general, in all the technical support stuff.

C5-A Test Force Director

I remember one time I attended the C5-A test force director's status briefing. There were issues as to the lack of storage space in the hangar and the scales that were not able to adequately weigh the mammoth aircraft, affectionately known as the "Flying Cloud." He found that out for the first time about the facility problems in order to support the C-5. The general got very upset, and he immediately got into General Patton mode. The general fiercely laid into his veteran and well-respected program director. He had all the graphs of hangar space and other backup information. Before he finished the briefing, the general picked up all the graphs and materials and tossed the whole bunch directly across the table, and it almost hit his chest.

The stunned colonel had a bewildered look on his face. After the general left, he said, "How in the world do you brief this guy?"

This got a little laugh from the other officers around the table.

The colonel gestured with his raised hands, gave a little relief smile, and dashed out of the gold room, licking his wounds. He went back to his office a little wiser. I heard later that he not only gave other colonels a bad time, but a young first lieutenant, knowing his reputation, had to give him a status briefing. I was told that the young officer got up and went to the podium and before he started his briefing, he passed out in fright.

The general simply stated, "Somebody call the medics so we can get to the next briefer." He had a few words emboldened on a gold-looking frame that stated: "Don't do anything dumb, I will decide what's dumb." I would characterize General Slay as the George Patton of the noncombatant era.

C-5 Galaxy and Weight and Balance Scales

The largest military transport in the American arsenal is also one of the largest planes in the world. This year marks the fiftieth anniversary of the aptly named C-5 Galaxy, and it's been five decades worth celebrating. With the ability to swallow fifty-ton main battle tanks and deposit them on another continent, the Galaxy is an essential part of the global logistics system. As air force historian John Leland noted, the C-5 symbolized the size, power, might, and majesty of the United States Air Force, and it still does to this day. For half a century, the Galaxy has kept America's armed forces, allies, and far-flung scientists well supplied in the most remote corners of the earth, and it will continue to do the job for the foreseeable future.

Scales Modification

The scales located just north of the huge maintenance and modification (MM) hangar, very near the flight line, were grossly inadequate to weigh such a large and heavy aircraft. The gross weight of the C-5 was designed fully loaded at 550,000 pounds. The scale's footprint was not designed to accommodate the wheel design of the very large transport aircraft. I was assigned to work with the C-5 System Program Office (SPO) located at Patterson AFB in Ohio to obtain more than $500,000 to defray the cost of the updated scales. The Engineering Development Branch, headed by Mr. Paul Sehnert and Lieutenant Bill Wise, accomplished the scales modification task on time to meet flight test requirements. The C-5 storage capacity will hold 24,844,746 ping-pong balls.

General Slay's Changes in Management Style

He instituted far-reaching changes regarding financial management and test reporting accountability with a strong emphasis on safety of flight and timelines of test results reporting. One of the major complaints by sister commands was the lack of timely reporting of test results for tactical, strategic, and transportation commands and many other operational units within the Department of Defense (DOD).

General Slay mandated the final test report was to be written, approved, signed, and published within ninety days after touchdown on the last flight. This raised all kinds of consternation. He put the burden on the flight test engineer to make it happen. The chief of flight test engineering, in my estimation, had a valid concern because his organization did not have full control to make it happen. He again emphasized that it's the engineer's job responsibility to make it happen—no matter what. To my knowledge, there was only one flight test engineer that accomplished this stringent reporting task: the world-famous Burt Rutan. He designed and built the fabulous voyager that successful traveled around the world with his brother David at the controls and Jeanne Yeager as the other famous crew member (no relation to Chuck Yeager).

Personnel Management and Discipline

The Edwards Flight Test Range (EFTR) had two office locations out on the range, about five to ten miles away from the main division office. I would occasionally go out to the range to visit these isolated personnel. They appreciated the visits by upper management and welcomed me. During one of my visits, one of the employees took me aside and complained about his supervisor at the far remote site. He was a sports enthusiast, and he would take long jogs around the range areas. He would exercise with the weights. It became too much for this employee, who complained that something had to be done. In addition, he informed me that he strongly suspected gas stealing from the motor pool facility that was on the range. He knew me, and I knew him. He also had heard that I was fair and honest and was an employee-centered manager. He reluctantly told me in detail that he had personally witnessed far too much abuse by the section supervisor. I immediately informed the branch chief and made him aware that I planned to conduct an independent investigation. I had to be very careful since all the employees in that section were unionized. In addition, the section chief was a veteran. I also advised and informed my commander, Colonel Brick Russell, directorate of engineering group.

Remote Range Investigation

I recommended that he assign a high-ranking officer to perform an independent investigation. He immediately responded by assigning a major from one of his other organizations. We wanted to conduct this investigation quickly without the accused knowing. If he was guilty of the charges, we didn't want him to cover his tracks prior to the major's investigation and recommendations. The major conducted a very though investigation. He was able to review all the gas consumption records and compare that to all of the aircraft range support schedules. He estimated that the amount of gas the range would normally consume was far less than the amount shown and consumed at the pumps, based on flight support schedules. It was easily determined that far more gas was being consumed than necessary. In addition, he verified, with a number of randomly selected employees, within the section, to substantiate, validate, or disprove the claims. The major's report was submitted to the colonel, and he forwarded it to me for recommendations and proposed action. I read the report. All of the abuse claims and gas stealing was verified. I got together with the major to review the report and go over recommendations and his proposed actions. I discussed the report with his range branch chief and came to an agreement as to the next course of action. I felt that he had to be removed from his supervisory position and reassigned to a position with close supervision or, in the worst case, be fired.

Closed-Door Meeting

The major and I had a closed-door meeting with the section supervisor. Since I was the division chief, the major asked me to brief him on the results of his investigation. I advised him to listen to what I had to say and that I would give him all the time he needed to respond. He listened very carefully. I knew him very well. He was a long-standing, capable employee with special skills of all the support activities on the far range. This included downfall, which was a call sign for all the test pilots flying over the range for tracking and guidance purposes. He responded, "What can I say?" He was very remorseful over what he had done. He expressed his deep sorrow. He was not too far from retirement. Losing his job would be devastating.

We needed to retain employees of his expertise and capabilities. I made the recommendation to retain him in a different range position with no supervisory responsibilities. I was establishing a new range control function to accommodate all the range support activities that culminate in the Riley Mission Control Center. He was ideal for the job and very happy with his new assignment. The colonel approved my recommendations and thanked the major for conducting an outstanding investigation and report. The major was very pleased to accomplish this assignment. Officers efficiency reports (OERs) that include outstanding additional duties are certainly looked upon most favorably for future promotions.

Upper Management

It became apparent to me that upper management had to deal with a wide variety of management problems and situations. Above is an example. Being a mathematician, the left side of the equation always equals the right side. When it comes to managing human beings, principles of math and the scientific methodology do not apply. When I went to management school at USC and six weeks of intensive executive development training at the University of Oklahoma in Norman, I learned that there was, most definitely, a human side of enterprise. In addition, I learned that there are a number of management approaches and styles that may be adopted depending on the myriad enterprises that exist in all forms of endeavors in our nation, society, and the military. McGregor's X-Y theory of management—where X is very authoritative and y is laissez-faire—really enlightened me about managing people. *The Human Side of Enterprise* was paramount for learning the most about managing people. In the serious personnel problem I confronted, I used the authoritative approach and solved the problem in a human manner to the benefit of all—thanks to the help of an independent ranking field officer.

The Hawthorne Effect

One of our management professors at USC told us about the study called the Hawthorne effect, which was conducted by Westinghouse. The object was how to improve productivity in a very repetitive work environment. They started off the experiment by simply increasing the lighting in the work environment, which increased productivity. Then, they increased the lighting slightly more with some additional improvements. Then they reversed the test procedure by reducing the lighting—behold productivity increased—and then upon lowering the lighting a little more, productivity continued to increase somewhat. They scratched their heads and came up with a very significant realization that "the Hawthorne effect is a type of reactivity in which individuals modify an aspect of their behavior in response to their awareness of being observed" (Wikipedia). This revelation was considered one of the most important findings in the early days of behavioral research. I never forgot that axiom. Pay attention to your employees—and don't treat them like robots.

Military Warriors

The United States military requires warriors, particularly in wartime and in preparing soldiers to fight wars, and the authoritative approach becomes an absolute necessity. However, these warriors need to make a transition and employ a different management style when they get back to the real world. Luckily, I worked mostly with very professional ranking officers. I sometimes had to put up with some high-ranking colonels who liked to strut their stuff. I had to put up with their military presence, realizing it would be temporary until their eventual reassignment. All of the management training I had certainly prepared me well as I advanced in my career.

Chapter 38

Hill/Wendover/Dugway Program Office (Utah Test and Training Range Formation)

Hill/Wendover/Dugway encompasses a vast expansion of land located in and surrounding the Great Salt Lake Desert area, west of Salt Lake City, Utah. This includes Hill Air Force Base about thirty miles to the north, near the town of Ogden, Utah, the army's Dugway Proving Ground, located about eighty miles to the southwest of Salt Lake City, and Wendover Army Air Base, California, to the far west of Salt Lake city that borders California's state line. This includes a land space of 1.8 million acres. Wendover is the base where Lieutenant Col Tibbets of Doolittle fame practiced simulated Hornet aircraft takeoff tests involving B-26 bombers in preparation for the Doolittle raid over Japan successfully conducted in the early stages of the war in April 1942.

Hill Wendover Dugway (HWD) Program Office

This program office was formed in January 1978 to organize and establish what was known as the Utah Test and Training Range (UTTR). Colonel Grazer was assigned as the program director. With myself as the ranking civilian as chief, Technical Support Division was responsible for the management and operation of the Edwards Flight Test Range (EFTR): Lieutenant Colonel Charles Aiello, one of my branch chiefs, Mr. Irvin Boyles, electronic engineer, specialist in the development and design of range instrumentation equipment, Mr. Charles Kroll, an accomplished flight test engineer, Mr. Richard Hector, flight research engineer with the assistance of range and staff personnel located at the major DOD facilities in the area.

The core HWD program staff hopped a commercial airplane and took off to Andrews AFB, just outside Washington, DC. We started the planning at AFSC command headquarters under the leadership of Colonel Arias. Little did we all realize the immensity of this program. The program took more than a year to accomplish and put into operation. The HWD program office pulled together range assets that existed from among all the organizational entities involved. We had to work with, coordinate, negotiate, formulate, organize, and obtain approval to establish the UTTR with range assets owned by all of the DOD installations involved. We were confronted with a number of sacred cows in the process. The UTTR is a Department of Defense major range and test facility base and provides an ideal location for operational testing and evaluation of weapons requiring a large safety footprint. It is the only location capable of supporting the overland testing of cruise missiles. In addition, it provided war fighters with a realistic training environment and provided testing and evaluation of overland, large-footprint weapons to enhance combat readiness, superiority, and sustainability.

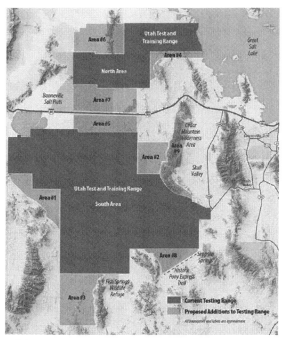

Utah Test and Training Range (UTTR) AREA MAP (AF photo map)

Cruise Missile Testing

A cruise missile is low-flying missile that is guided to its target by an onboard computer. There are surveyed wave points along the way to assist in the navigation to make midcourse corrections. Cruise missiles are designed to deliver a large warhead over long distances with high precision. I heard some of the engineers jokingly ask, "Do you want us to take out the large bathroom by entering the top or lower window?" That graphically shows its potential accuracy. It's all done by making midcourse corrections. That's how the Apollo spacecraft was guided to the moon. The difference between a ballistic and a guided missile are that ballistic missiles fly far above the atmosphere much quicker and deliver a much higher payload—over 10,000 kilometer is an example—whereas a cruise missile flies very close to the ground, undetected, and it has an onboard guidance system, propulsion system, and small wings and can be launched from the air, sea, or ground locations. Therefore, we have a sea-, ground-, and air-launched cruise missiles (SLCM, GLCM, ALCM). These missiles require very long-range areas to accomplish test and evaluations. Edwards AFB was an ideal DOD asset to meet this new challenge.

EFTR and the Utah Test and Training Range

The Edwards Flight Test Range (EFTR) controlled a thousand-mile test corridor that extended from the Western Test Range (WTR) at Vandenberg AFB to Wendover, California, just west of the Great Salt Lake area. This was technically provided by an extended microwave link called the Data Acquisition and Transmission System (DATS) with a west link to Vandenberg AFB and a north link to Wendover. There was a high-priority requirement to establish the Utah Test and Training Range to fill in the gap that existed in the Great Salt Lake area to accommodate a 1,200-mile corridor to support the three types of cruise missiles. The ALCM and GLCM desperately needed the added link provided by the new range. The navy had sufficient over-the-water testing areas without the use of UTTR, but the navy had to use a greater portion of the EFTR for testing their SLCM. Needless to say, the HWD office had its very high-priority work and responsibility laid out to complete the UTTR in sufficient time to support cruise missiles testing and evaluation.

Fact-Finding Tours and Briefings

The HWD program office made a variety of informational tours by jeep, helicopter, and all-terrain vehicle to survey the expansive Great Salt Lake area. In most of the area, nothing grows, which provides a well-protected area. I remember the bumpy helicopter ride that stirred a large herd of beautiful wild horses that surround the Dugway area. The horses seem to run fast enough to almost outfly the helicopter. What a wonderful sight of animal nature. There are geological geos, volcanic spit, that are hunted, located, polished, and cherished by many of the Dugway employees. I visited the officers' club one night, and it was one of the main topics of interest that they treasured. I was quite familiar with the range instrumentation systems that Hill AFB managed and controlled. In addition, I was aware of other instrumentation systems that were managed and controlled by other DOD installations in the Great Salt Lake area.

My thanks to Mr. Zac Zaccardi for all of his support and knowledge for advising me. In addition, Edwards AFB had the 6510th Drone Squadron located at Hill AFB, which used much of the range equipment in the area. Most of the organizations had standard range equipment, and some were adequate but outdated.

HAMOTS Range Improvement

Mr. Irv Boules was assigned as the lead electronic engineer to install a highly accurate multiple-object tracking system for tracking various aircraft targets. Mr. Kroll and Roger Crane were assigned to complete a comprehensive evaluation concerning HAMOTS accuracy. The HAMOTS system became the bread and butter for the UTTR. The UTTR was able to support all of the cruise missile programs—ALCM GLCM, and SLCM—and the flying red flag operations out of nearby tactical air force bases. The next big step was to determine what was available, what we needed, and how to acquire it over the organization's disapproval, if need be.

Army Dugway Proving Ground

The US Army Dugway Proving Ground (DPG) is the nation's leading testing grounds for chemical and biological defense to enable our country defenders. Many of the unknown weapons that the Nazis used during World War II were sent to Dugway during the war to determine the lethal elements. The areas that contain the remnants of these weapon systems are identified and strictly controlled. Being the senior range expert on the HWD program office, I was given the task to negotiate in a working meeting with the Dugway commander with everyone in attendance and the DPG staff.

Generic Range

I identified what I called a generic range that consisted of the elements that are needed to form and function as a range. Among many functions, I identified all of the space position range equipment: TSPI or time-space position information systems. These are radars, optical systems, communications, bombing, targets, available land space areas, other functions and capabilities, air traffic control capability for range operations, range safety responsibility over the land areas for bombing and strafing, and a vital range safety function.

Negotiations with the DPG Commander

This approach worked very well. When the commanders understood what a full-range capability consisted of, the generic range concept spoke for itself and did not come into question except for the crusty army commander. The very kind but firm commanding officer wasn't about to relinquish his assets and have his capabilities yanked out from under him without fully knowing the consequences. I respected him for that. We had to assure him that the new UTTR organization would definitely support his needs with the range instrumentation systems he would give up. He didn't like the answer, but he acquiesced. I had the advantage because I was much more knowledgeable on range matters than he was. I detected that he did not know much about some of the range instrumentation systems that he owned. After all, his primary interest had to maintain and sustain an extremely sensitive testing capability for chemical and biological testing. As I was informing him about what systems he owned on DPG that I was out after, he just kept glaring at me as if to say he knew more about his range stuff than I did. It wasn't a case of playing gotcha or one-upmanship, but I had a job to do. Needless to say, I took some daggers from the Dugway commander, but I got a lot of kudos from the program director, staff, and the air force systems command (AFSC) colonel in charge. Dugway mission complete.

DOD Pentagon Experience

Since the HWD program office was dealing with various organizational elements within DOD, we had to coordinate with the Pentagon. That was a great and frustrating experience. To relieve some of the pressure and frustration while we were working at AFSC headquarters, Colonel Arias exclaimed, "Let's all go to Balangao's Sandwich Shop in DC and pick up some tasty sandwiches and a bottle of nice red wine and have a picnic on the US Capitol grounds." Off we went and came back ready for the rest of the day and half the night to resume our work. Eventually, a very large implementation plan was prepared, coordinated, and approved with formation of the UTTR range squadron with Colonel Charles Alieo as the range commander.

Major Range Test Facility Base (MRTFB) (DOD narrative)

The Utah Test and Training Range (UTTR) is a major test range that is identified in DOD's list of very important test capabilities. Its mission statement provides war fighters with a realistic training environment and provide test and evaluation of overland, large-footprint weapons to enhance combat readiness, superiority, and sustainability. It is the only location capable of supporting the overland testing of cruise missiles. The UTTR is located in Utah's West Desert, approximately eighty miles from Salt Lake City. Interstate 80 divides the range into north and south sections. The range is used in a training capacity for air-to-air, air-to ground inert and live practice bombing and gunnery training by DOD aircrew. UTTR provides a vast area of realistic terrain for world-class testing and training scenarios to ensure the war fighter is prepared to deploy at a moment's notice to win any conflict with decisive air and space power. Originally the responsibility was assigned to AFFTC, located at Edwards AFB, but it has been headquartered at UTTR at Hill Air Force Base, which now operates and maintains the UTTR.

Fast facts

    Location: Tooele County, Utah (near Tooele)
    Land Area: 1.8M acres
    Special Use Airspace: more than 19,000 nautical miles
    Sorties/Year: 8,800 training; 1,101 testing

Chapter 39

Space

At this point in my career, the space shuttle began testing at Edwards Air Force Base. This began with the *Enterprise* shuttle terminal launch landing tests.

Shuttle Piggyback on the Boeing-Modified 747 (NASA Photo)

After launch, the space shuttle would land on the Edwards fifteen thousand-foot runway. I was the chief of the Technical Support Division that managed the Edwards Flight Test Range. The division responsibilities were to provide range tracking that included radars, optical trackers, long-range optics, and television coverage provided by a camera mounted on our FPS-16 digital radars. Two vital functions, referred to as sport control and downfall, direct, guide, and communicate with test pilots regarding the use of airspace over the EFTR while performing a test mission utilizing range assets and capabilities. Downfall, the other range control function accomplishes many of the same functions as sport control, but only for controlling test missions that utilize the precision impact range area, known as the PIRA, for close-in bombing runs. In addition, the division provides communications, black-and-white and aerial photography, computer software, and computation services. Of course, NASA provides for their own mission control functions. Many other base support services are provided, such as chase pilots and a full force of base support operational functions. The series of shuttle terminal landing tests were conducted and satisfactorily accomplished from the division's viewpoint.

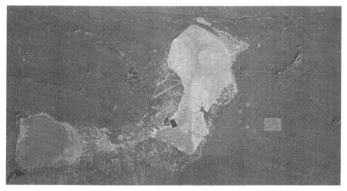

Rogers Dry Lake Bed

The following is taken from the AFFTC historical information available online:

The area of the lakebed was first used by the railroads, with a watering station for steam engines located nearby by the Atchison, Topeka, and Santa Fe railroad. In 1910, the Corum family settled on the lake bed; they attempted to create a small community called Muroc (the name reversed), but it failed. In 1933, the United States Army arrived, looking to establish a bombing range in the area. The lakebed's potential use as an airfield was then realized, and in 1937 the United States Army Air Corps set up Muroc Air Field for training and testing, which later became Edwards Air Force Base. During World War II, a 650-foot replica of a Japanese cruiser was constructed on the lakebed, nicknamed Muroc Maru. The ship was demolished in 1950.

Geology

Rogers dry lake is in the Antelope Valley, about one hundred miles (160 km) northeast of Los Angeles. It covers an area of about 65 square miles (170 km²) at the low point of the valley, forming a rough figure eight. It is the bed of a lake that formed roughly 2.5 million years ago, in the Pleistocene. It is 12.5 miles (20.1 km) long at and 5.5 miles (8.9 km) wide at its greatest dimensions. The lake bed is unusually hard, capable of withstanding as much as 250 psi without cracking, sufficient to allow even the heaviest aircraft to safely land on it. During the extremely brief rainy season, it is possible for there to be standing water on the lakebed, which pools at the approximate low-point elevation of 2,300 feet for the region. The lake is adjacent to the smaller Rosamond Lake, which through the Holocene, together made up one large water body.

First Orbital Flight of the Space Shuttle

The day finally arrived. No doubt, nearly everyone around the world was tuned in with eager anticipation. Employees at Edwards AFB were feverishly engaged, and the general public descended and congregated around both sides of the gigantic Rogers dry lake bed to get a close-up view of the approach landing. What a sight! Campers, motor homes, tents, motorcycles, all- terrain vehicles, and all sorts of contraptions were visible at a distance as far as one could see. Basically, I cocooned myself in the Range Mission Control Center (RMCC) from the wee hours of the morning until mission accomplished. It was white-knuckle time in the RMCC.

STS-1 Launch

I remember the day of the first space shuttle orbital mission. It was a particularly intense and exciting day. The Technical Support Division had an extremely important role in recovering the space shuttle during the terminal phase. Practically all of the resources within the division, including engineering and technical services (ETTS) contractor personnel, and Kentron, Inc., were eager and ready to strut our stuff.

Edwards Air Force Base and the EFTR Range

Edwards Air Force Base is an ideal location to function as a landing site for space shuttle orbital recovery missions. The huge Rogers dry lake bed provides an extremely large landing area for safe operations. In addition, Edwards AFB is the home of the Edwards Flight Test Range (EFTR), which was used as range terminus for space shuttle operations. The EFTR consists of a major microwave link that interconnects the Western Test Range located at Vandenberg, California, and the navy test facility that borders the central coast at Point Mugu, California. In addition, this microwave link extends to the Great Salt Lake area at Hill Air Force Base, California. This provides for an elongated flight test corridor of about 1,200 miles. We had previously established inter-range procedures for inter-range operations. As range terminus, it became absolutely necessary to interface and become a very important part of an inter-operable worldwide range internet for tracking and communicating continuously for the duration of the mission many hours before and some after the mission. We had conducted many local inter-range operations and were experienced. This served us—and the space shuttle program—very well in the planning, documentation, and development of worldwide range net procedures for such a large-scale support operation. Our experience with conducting cruise missile tests proved to be a godsend as becoming prepared to support the space shuttle at the right time and in the right place in space.

Photography Laboratory Support Services

The photography branch chief, Gerald Reece, and his band of photographers, including aerial photographers, lab personnel, graphics, and a first-class photo-processing lab played a very unique role in providing all of the pictures for NASA, the air force, Edwards AFB public affairs office, the media, and the general public. This was a gigantic task to meet the demands for documentation. Immediately after touchdown, the focus was on the astronauts and the spaceship *Columbia*—and also on the official shuttle landing pictures. As a courtesy to me, Mr. Reese brought over the first few photos of the landing that came off the photo printer. I immediately visited my boss, Colonel Brick Russell, commander of the 6510th Test Engineering Group. I advised him that the Technical Support Division had made everyone proud. I showed him the first pictures. He asked if he could have the first picture of the successful shuttle landing. I jokingly told him the picture was mine. He looked at me with a smile, wondering if I really meant it or not. I saw his body language, said, "Absolutely," and honored him with the first picture. I happily kept the second picture as a treasured memento as an honorable mention. I fully intended to give him the first picture anyway.

Target Acquisition and Data Collection System (TACDACS)

TACDACS was a one-of-a-kind in-house-developed systems engineered, designed, and built by the Range Development Branch and very ably assisted by one of our very outstanding electronic technicians,

Lefty Leftwich, who operated and maintained the system. TACDACS provided for the main interface between the range-tracking systems for real-time acquisition and computer processing. This accommodated the special real-time processing needs for displaying tracking in the RMCC. This system was about fifteen years old, but it still functioned properly. Electronic parts were scarce, and the equipment was obsolete. These were the days before computer workstations became prevalent. I was very fortunate that Lefty Leftwich had a position in the RMCC as an ETTS contractor. He had worked in my organization previously and was a good friend. During the space shuttle recovery mission, I positioned myself very near Lefty and kept an eye on the TACDACS system during the recovery portion of the space shuttle. Of course, everything was preplanned, and we were hopefully ready for this gut-wrenching historic event that was about to be made.

Complete RMCC Shutdown

Lefty and I had smiles on our faces as we observed the shuttle information flowing in from the Western Test Range (WTR). Then, very suddenly, the shuttle data completely dropped off the North DATS that links the EFTR to Vandenberg AFB. This untimely loss of data happened at the most critical time during the recovery operation as far as we were concerned—when the shuttle entered the atmosphere and was nearly halfway to Edwards for a safe landing. Lefty turned white, and I probably turned green as we gazed at each other. My immediate gut reaction was that we had a TACDACS failure. I began to think negatively. *What I will tell the boss and upper management about an EFTR catastrophic failure? How could TACDACS alone cause such a massive sudden data loss?* To make matters worse, I had the total responsibility for the RMCC and data-acquisition systems that collect and forward test data to the RMCC. No matter what failed, I was responsible. That was doubt why I turned all kinds of colors. Since I am color-blind, it all looks mostly gray anyway. Very suddenly, the shuttle data was restored. The RMCC came back to life online, and we all looked on with bewilderment. Here again, God was our copilot—with me as his proxy. As a result, we were able to provide the most critical tracking and vectoring information. Longitude and latitude coordinates were provided to the chase pilots to mate with the shuttle as the spaceship entered the airspace at Edwards AFB. The chase pilots would accompany the space shuttle on a long glide path and approach to the lake bed for a safe touchdown.

What in heaven's name went wrong? The problem was not at Edwards Air Force Base. In one sense, it was not a problem at Vandenberg Air Force Base, but the problem took place on Vandenberg. It was an unfortunate car accident that happened outside the huge range control center, resulting in a power outage. Fortunately, their RCC had an emergency power system called EPS that was put online. It took about five minutes to transfer and restore an alternate source of power. That explained our five-minute delay as we stewed at Edwards in our RMCC. Subsequently, an uninterrupted power system called UPS—not the mail-delivery operation—was installed at Vandenberg. It became transparent to the user of the facility. At that time, UPS systems were very expensive to put into operation.

Space Shuttle Landing

The first launch of the space shuttle occurred on April 12, 1981, exactly twenty years after the first manned space flight, when the orbiter *Columbia*, with two crew members, astronauts John W. Young, commander, and Robert L. Crippen, pilot, lifted off from pad A, launch complex 39, at the Kennedy Space Center.

Launch date: 12 April 1981, 12:00:03 UTC
and landing date: April 14, 1981.
Columbia first landing on Rogers dry lake bed on April 14, 1981.

Subsequent Space Shuttle Missions

I do not recall the number of additional landings that we supported for the space shuttle program after the first very successful orbital landing. The *Endeavor, Atlanta,* and *Discovery* were built subsequent to the *Enterprise, Challenger,* and *Columbia*. A total of six space shuttle vehicles were built. Five of them were space-worthy. The original enterprise was air-launched at Edwards Air Force Base to evaluate the shuttle's landing characteristics. Five space shuttles were recovered at Edwards. One mission was a night recovery mission, and I spent most of the night in the RMCC. I had the honor of escorting Father Edward Clark, the principal at Paraclete High School. I loaded him up with a variety of pictures. Father Clark has since become a bishop in the archdiocese of Los Angeles, assisting the archbishop, Jose Gomez, in the huge diocese. Since becoming bishop, I have met and reminisced with him about the days we spent together at the patrons club.

Range Control Officers (RCOs)

All the missions we supported had RCOs within the RMCC that were responsible for controlling all EFTR range assets during support operations when recovering the space shuttles. I remember Harold Klein, Wayne Kupfer and others. Harold Klein was assigned the RCO for a mission that had a toilet problem onboard. The next day, Harold rushed into my office and showed me a cartoon out of the *LA Times* that showed another shuttle in rendezvous with the stricken shuttle transporting a big plunger protruding above the upper doors on the long end of a shuttle arm. Everyone in the RMCC got a great belly laugh. Harold went about his business getting ready to support the shuttle recovery. All the personnel within the Technical Support Division were very proud to be involved in these very historic events. As for myself, I couldn't have been prouder. We had a wonderful jacket designed and produced for all members of the RMCC. I have worn it so many times over the years that it has faded and is now carefully stored in my closet.

Range Mission Control Center (AF Photo)

Chapter 40

God Is the Way, the Truth, and the Life

When I was young, of course, there was no internet and no TV, and most movies were great with G ratings. At least it was what I thought because that was all we are allowed to see. My internet was the books of knowledge.

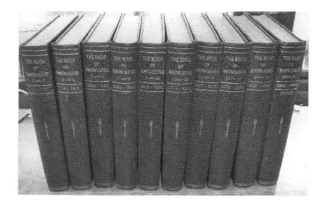

There was no concern about leaving my keys in the car, walking home, or riding my bicycle in the dark after seeing a movie with friends. The air was clear and pure. The stars at night sparkled brightly out in the big wide outdoors, which is certainly the case living out on the farm. We were far enough away from the streetlights, bright lights, and pollution to enjoy the pristine atmosphere during all seasons, particularly in the spring and summertime. At the time, I didn't realize I had it so good. Many times,

I would lay on the haystack, both at night and day, flat on my back, look up into the heavens, and wonder how large the universe was. The only interruptions I had would be the occasional mooing of a cow, crickets cricketing, the frogs croaking, an occasional car driving or racing a distance away, or the neighbor's large diesel water well pump extracting life-giving water, agriculture's life blood, to irrigate portions of the great San Joaquin Valley's breadbasket.

Natural Wonders and Babies

All these wonders about the universe, human nature, and mysteries of life made me thirsty for knowledge. Aside from the fact that faith is gift from God, there is a God accepted in faith. God's wonders are manifested in so many ways—both seen and unseen. For example, the unborn child in the mother's womb is where all the characteristics are stitched in the embryo using God's life-giving secrets, including the wonders of DNA. This is an absolute mystery to me. We were made in the image and likeness of God. I don't believe, in any way, all the false information generated by the media to support abortion, particularly when the media spins their prejudices. Furthermore, I don't understand why so many Catholics and Catholic politicians vote not to support life. What is more important than life? I believe in God as it says in the Good Book: "For you were formed my inmost being, you knit me together" (Psalm 139:13). Just think when we were impregnated, we were completely identified, formed, structured, and cocooned in our mothers' wombs nine months before we were born. We were made in the image and likeness of God and filled with God's infinite love and supernatural baptismal life. Astounding.

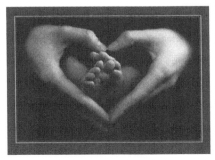

Wonders upon wonders (Care net and hurricane devastation)

The Haystack Experience

At times like this, when I lay on my back on the haystack about ten feet above ground, I feel blessed and glad to be born and living a very wholesome life on the farm. I was living well, safe, and loved by our parents and eating Mom's three home-cooked meals every day on time. I enjoyed being raised with my siblings. We all had our jobs and chores, worked hard, enjoyed each other, were all fit as a fiddle from all the farm labor, and were blessed by wonderful God-centered parents. These kind of life experiences can only be achieved by living—not just reading the books of knowledge or surfing the internet. This can only be achieved by encountering each other and interacting in a loving manner with every person you encounter. I am reminded of a very popular western song written by Allan Jackson: "I Am a Work in Progress."

Life is a living experience that cannot be duplicated or achieved by just reading books or being a slave to the internet. This kind of wisdom, knowledge, and experience can only be achieved by living and not just by reading all kinds of textbooks, encyclopedias, or novels. Knowledge does not make a person alone, but all the interactions, relationships, togetherness, church and community involvements, volunteerism, and helping poor people, incapacitated people, and the imprisoned, to mention a few. I was always a nonfiction reader. At my early age, I thought, *If it's not true, it's not worth reading.* Thankfully, this is not the case. We all need to be dreamers at some stage in our lives. We must have vision and strive to achieve beyond our reach. Don't get discouraged as you live out your journey. There are many ups and downs in life, and sometimes you may say to yourself, "Why me, Lord"? Nobody's perfect. Yes, we experience all kinds of ups and downs. Sometimes, it may result in too many downs strung together. I have gone through three very serious depressions during my very eventful journey. One depression is one far too many, believe me, where it seems and feels like all hope has been lost and has gone far out the window into the far empty space and beyond.

The Holy Bible and the Books of Knowledge

Fortunately, I learned early in life that the real books of knowledge and wisdom were in the heavenly book called the Holy Bible. Jokingly, someone told me that B-I-B-L-E stood for "biblical instruction before leaving earth." How true! No spin. Following my first depression, which was very debilitating, I studied Catholicism again from an adult point of view. I volunteered to teach Catholic high school students about faith in Confraternity of Christian (CCD) classes. I submit that if I had not gone through my serious depression, I never would have taken another hard look at my Catholic faith. As I said before, God works in many wonderful and strange ways. When I was in my deep depression, I felt like God let me down, but I didn't believe that. Unbeknown to me, at the time, when I struggled, hour by hour, day by day, week by week, God was preparing me for bigger and better things to come. Some days, I felt worse or it seemed worse, sometimes better, and then worse again. What a horrible experience and existence. If it wasn't for my true faith in God, I probably never would have made it. Dorothy was wonderful. She had her own severe struggles with our sixth child, Keith. She had gallbladder attacks most every other day. Dorothy worried about me and my condition. I had the added burden of worrying about my fantastic wife. Thank God for Dorothy's mother for seeing us through both of our serious troubles. The magnitude of the situation was understood when Keith was born. He was our sixth child in eight years. What a suffering year for both of us! God is good, and we survived for the better. Dorothy had her gallbladder removed after Keith was born, and I went back to work part-time and shortly after full-time just in time to install the new large-scale IBM 704 electronic computer.

The Catholic Church and the Bible

I found out with God's help that the books of knowledge were only part of the story. The whole and real story is found in the Bible, the Catholic Church, the pope's teaching authority, and the magisterium. The Bible was completed long after the Catholic Church came into existence, founded by Jesus Christ, with Peter as the head. The Catholic Church is the mother of the Bible with the authority of the pope to promulgate the final content and approval of the canon with seventy-two books. The Bible was written by the apostles and Christ's disciples who formed the early Catholic Church with the Holy Spirit as the church's guide. The pope, along with the magisterium, interprets the Bible as to its true meaning. After all, the Catholic Church was formed by Christ and personally established Peter as the head of the church. He speaks infallibility when he only speaks ex cathedra regarding faith and morals, which has been totally misunderstood, as to its real meaning.

Papal Infallibility

The following excerpt was taken from *Catholicism for Dummies*:

> Papal infallibility is a dogma of the Catholic Church that states that, in virtue of the promise of Jesus to Peter, the Pope is preserved from the possibility of error "when, in the exercise of his office as shepherd and teacher of all Christians, in virtue of his supreme apostolic authority, he defines a doctrine concerning faith or morals to be held by the whole Church." "Infallibility means more than exemption from actual error; it means exemption from the possibility of error.
>
> This doctrine was defined dogmatically at the f of First Ecumenical Council of the Vatican of 1869–1870 in the document Pastor aeternus, but had been defended before

that, existing already in medieval theology and being the majority opinion at the time of the Counter-Reformation.

According to Catholic theology, there are several concepts important to the understanding of infallible, divine revelation: Sacred Scripture, Sacred Tradition, and the Sacred Magisterium (Teaching Authority). The infallible teachings of the Pope are part of the Sacred Magisterium, which also consists of ecumenical councils and the "ordinary and universal magisterium". In Catholic theology, papal infallibility is one of the channels of the infallibility of the Church. The infallible teachings of the Pope must be based on, or at least not contradict, Sacred Tradition and Sacred Scripture. The doctrine of infallibility relies on one of the cornerstones of Catholic dogma: that of Petrine supremacy of the pope, and his authority as the ruling agent who decides what are accepted as formal beliefs in the Roman Catholic Church.[4] The use of this power is referred to as speaking ex cathedra,

Living a Catholic Faith

After my first serious depression, when I restudied and relooked at the Catholic faith, I finally realized the full meaning of living a Catholic life of faith. The books of knowledge cover physical, natural, biological sciences, and many other interesting subjects about life in general. They are necessary but not sufficient for living a God-fearing life. In my life, I had a good formal education and a wonderful upbringing with the help of the Holy Spirit to focus my life on God and be instilled, once and for all, most importantly, that the teachings of the church and the Bible are the real books of knowledge.

You may wonder about bad popes, cardinals, bishops, and priests. I wonder too. It is absolutely disgusting to read, listen, and watch TV about the continuous criticism that the Catholic Church endures, and unfortunately, is rightly admonished. The media relishes in selling airtime, newspaper copy, opinions expressed on TV, Facebook, Twitter, magazines, cartoon caricatures, and other forms of communication. I submit that the Catholic Church is the only institution in existence that is not controlled by political correctness. The major media repeatedly gloats that there is no media bias, but double standards are prevalent and prevail. The Catholic Church unfortunately does have very serious sexual abuse problem. So what is going on in the Catholic Church? The answer is concupiscence, which is a strong sexual desire, called lust. Lust is one of the seven capital sins. This is not a justification or spin for the many church scandals—but a sad commentary on the realities that all earthly humans face regardless of our states in life. Priests take vows of chastity prior to laying prostate near the cathedral altar, and some priests later struggle with their vows. Many are lonely, overworked, criticized, and become very discouraged and submit themselves to desired relationships. Many more ordained priests keep their vows despite their human weaknesses. There is not much media coverage about the vast number of faithful priests who float the Catholic boat, piloted by the many popes over two thousand years. The maneuvered a largely godless society through troubled and stormy waters.

The Good, the Bad, and the Ugly

The following are excerpts taken from the *Catholicism for Dummies* by Reverend John Trigilio Jr. and Reverend Kenneth Brighenti.

> Some colorful characters are interspersed among the bunch of 265 Popes. Seventy-eight of them are canonized Saints, and ten more are Beautified, which is one step short of Sainthood, so, approximately, 32% of the Popes have been really-good. Of all the rest, only twelve are considered morally evil and corrupt scoundrels. Although one bad Pope is one too many, Jesus himself picked 12 imperfect sinners to be his Apostles. The first

Pope, Peter, weakened and denied Christ three times, and Judas, one of the first Bishops, betrayed him for 30 pieces of silver. One repented, the other hanged himself instead of seeking mercy.

Final Thoughts

During the past year, I have been asked many times, "Why are you writing your book?" Here is where I get a little vain and selfish. I wanted my family, my siblings, and all the grandkids to know who their dad was, what he did for a living, and what he has accomplished. I wanted to inform them about what I did for a living—and how I lived. For those that get caught up in the maelstrom of today's misguided culture, it is the world's evil ways—not God's way. I also said many times that I have something to say, not really knowing what I meant by that statement. I felt that I have much to say about being exposed to today's warped society. What I have to say is being said my way, by the way I lived, to show all my extended family and friends that God is, in my judgment, the only way to fight off the devil with the evils in society with all of its entrapments. I hope that my life, as I have lived, can serve as an imprimatur for what it is worth. I think that I have proven my case. God has tested me, reformed me, instructed me, and enlightened me to witness the world around us for what it is. The devil is very smart and works a lot of overtime. In many subtle ways, he tries to convince us that there is no God or hell. The devil convinces some to believe there is no devil, and he grabs a few more of us. Finally, he states, "You have plenty of time to save yourself. You are still young." He snatches millions and millions more. The devil makes me mad. I would like to kick the hell out of him. I submit that now is the time to evaluate, readjust, if necessary, and ask yourself, "Am I living God's way, my way, or the world's way?" Our bodies are the temples of the Holy Spirit made wonderfully. Respect them. Our bodies are not amusement parks. Remember that God, most willingly, forgives our heartfelt sorrow and straightens us out no matter what. God is like a car body shop. You break it—and God fixes it. Regardless, as we live, God is not through with us yet. Yes, we are all on a journey and are works in progress. Make sure that its God's work during the process. I repeat that God is the way, the truth, and the life. God's will be done. Amen.

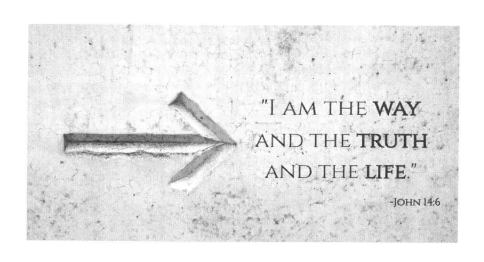

Chapter 41

My Last Day

My last day at Edwards Air Force Base was on the last Friday in the calendar year 1985. I turned fifty-five on September 21, 1985. This day was a very eventful day. I had to muster out by visiting the Civilian Personnel Office to start the process. The civilian officer gave a long checklist of things to accomplish. This included many different Edwards staff elements on base. Since I had a secret security clearance and other special clearances, I had to be debriefed, and I had to certify that I did not have any classified documents. This was not a problem, but there were many squares to fill to get released from my career assignment. All of the office equipment that was assigned to my organization and staff was handled by my administrative staff. Luckily, I didn't have to worry about many of the details administratively except for one thing: I had to sign for the mahogany desk because those items were strictly controlled. As I made the rounds to get all my clearances, I was able to say goodbye to the many people I had worked with at Edwards. I made a special intention to visit and say goodbye to many of the personnel who worked for me previously or under my current management. It was sad and joyful to visit all of my friends who I worked with over the many years. Needless to say, it took practically the whole day. Finally, I got signed approval from personnel.

Back at the Office

I had about forty-five minutes remaining in the day when I returned to my office. Unexpectedly, my office was a packed house. I was greeted with a bottle of Jack Daniels, all kinds of snacks, a video crew headed by Cyrus Crites, Chief of the Human Factors Branch, my staff, and many of the other management personnel who resided in the large test engineering building. We all had a great time. I decided to only consume one shot of Jack Daniels. I usually don't drink the hard stuff. I finally got out of my office about five minutes before five. I got in my car and drove slowly as I left the parking lot. I headed out to leave the base for the last time. As I was driving by the headquarters building, the United States flag was in the process of being retired for the day. "The Star Spangled Banner" is always played as the flag is being lowered and honored by the honor guard. Anyone in the military, upon witnessing the flag being honored, must stop, get out of their car, stand at attention, and salute. Civilians are expected to stop their cars, wait, and honor the flag accordingly. I usually worked late and did not participate in the flag ceremony, but on my final day, I gladly stopped the car, got out of the car, stood at attention, and saluted the flag with a tear in my eye. As I left the base on my way to Rosamond, which was about twelve miles, I had to drive by and observe many of the facilities I had been responsible for during my career. My final career glance of the large terrain of Edwards AFB. Very touching.

Dorothy and I Celebrate

Dorothy and I had decided beforehand that we were going to go out and have a nice dinner at the famous steak house located about halfway between Edwards Air Force Base and Lancaster, California. This restaurant was frequented by many of the astronauts who visited Edwards Air Force Base as well as all of the notable test pilots and visiting dignitaries. As I walked in the door, Dorothy was ready to celebrate. I was about an hour late in arriving at home. Dorothy understood, and she didn't mind at all. As I walked in the door, I stood there in awe as to how beautiful and wonderful she looked. She gave me a big hug and a kiss, and a short time later, we left for dinner. As we arrived at Mr. Bee's Steakhouse on time for our dinner appointment, we ordered our meals and a good bottle of red wine. We both thoroughly enjoyed the meal and our libations. The owner of the restaurant had a very nice orchestra and enjoyed playing them every evening. Dorothy and I listened to the music and danced. The owner always finished the evening with a very nice rendition of "New York, New York." As I listened to his orchestra blast out "New York, New York," I changed the ending in my mind: *Edwards Edwards Edwards is a wonderful place.*" I reminisced that I, unknowingly, had gotten mixed up with the right stuff. God sent me and honored me to be at the right place at the right time. I drove back home without saying a word. I was completely exhausted at the close of my last day. God bless America, the United States Air Force, the Air Force Flight Test Center, and Edwards AFB, California. I eagerly looked forward to a restful retirement.

Chapter 42

Contract Management and Party Time

When I was assigned division chief, I recognized the demanding need for additional contract monitors and managers. In addition, I found it necessary to develop promotion paths for women within the organization. I took the opportunity with a dual purpose to provide promotional paths for women and further expand the increasingly important function of contract management. We had a very large Engineering and Technical Services (ETSS) contract in existence, as well as the Systems Engineering Services (SES) contract that provided for highly skilled experts and professional engineers to augment the personnel shortages in range development and other flight test planning functions within the directorate of engineering. Tracy Hale and Mary Ann Kell did a superb job in performing these vital contract management functions. Tracy Hale was the contract manager for the very large ETTS contract, and Mary Ann Kell managed the SES contract. Additional capable personnel were needed to expand these functions to supplement and accommodate the growing need for managing and monitoring existing contracts and others to support the growing need for contract management in the present and foreseeable future.

Establishment of Upward Mobility Positions

I made a horse trade to exchange four military noncommissioned officer (NCO) positions, which were vacant and hard to fill by military personnel, into very scarce civilian positions. I established civilian upward mobility positions that allowed an entry-level person to be trained to eventually perform contract management functions with a pathway for later promotions. I knew that I had very promising women candidates that would accomplish the duties of becoming full-fledged contract managers. Debbie Latournow, Ardith Richardson, Maria Ann Smith, and subsequently Linda Chestnut come to mind. In my estimation, this was one of my better staffing decisions as a division chief. As of now, they are all retired and achieved the GS-12-13 level, which is a journey-person grade for most engineers and mathematicians. I am very happy that I provided opportunities for these very capable women to advance their careers.

My Retirement Party

Needless to say, they were very happy about getting their opportunity to excel. They once again excelled by putting on a fabulous retirement party for me. My compliments to the whole contract management team: Tracy Hale, Mary Ann Kell, Ardith Richardson, and Debbie Letourneau among others. They planned and executed a most memorable retirement party, which resulted in a fantastic affair. There were more than two hundred people in attendance, including my siblings and spouses, hometown friends, all of my children and their spouses, relatives and wives, and a complete spectrum of managers and supervisors I dealt with and/or worked in my organization. At Edwards AFB, I worked with a variety of air force personnel, including a few AFFTC staff personnel. Instead of buying a new suit, I decided to rent a tux. My son-in-law, Rick Warwick, a former first lieutenant officer assigned at Edwards AFB, provided a limo for the occasion. Someone got approval and refurnished my executive chair, which the master of ceremonies insisted I sit in while a parade of well-wishers came up to extoll their accolades and present me plaques, memorabilia, and computer software for my new IBM PC. Some roasted me, and others toasted me. Roger Crane was masterful at being the master of ceremonies. Mr. Richard Hildebrand, our technical director, presented me with an absolutely beautiful AFFTC album that had many pictures of test aircraft and Edwards Flight Test Range facilities, including the Range Mission Control Center. The theme for my final talk was "family," namely, my siblings' families, my family, and of course the wonderful family of friends and associates at the great Air Force Flight Test Center, located at the prestigious Edwards AFB. I was in the right place at the right time at the wonderful Edwards air patch.

AFFTC aircraft and technical and range facilities were taken from the great and wonderful AFFTC album that was presented to me at the retirement celebration.

XF-102A

F-101A

Early 1950s aircraft

Flying Wing

Helicopter Refueling Operation

An Attack Aircraft

SR71, F-104, U-2, F-100A, C-130 Turboprop, C-141

F-16 Aircraft

B-47 JATO Assist

North American F107A

Aerial Refueling Operation

Air Launch Cruise Missile

SR-71 flying above the clouds

B1-B

Fairchild Republic A-10 Thunderbolt Attack Aircraft

McDonald Douglas F-15 Eagle

Aircraft Missile Launch

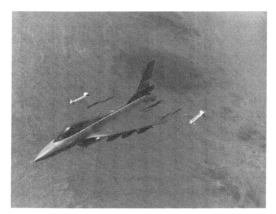

F-16 Launching Missiles

Aircraft Launching Rockets

Aircraft Rescue Helicopter

F-15 Approach Landing

F-20 Tigershark

Space Shuttle *Challenger*

F-117A

Astronaut in Space

Earth Shot from Space

Other Side of the Earth from Space

5780 Range Terminus Building for North & West DATS, West of Main Base Area

German-Made Askania High Precision Camera

Receiver located at Building 5780 for West DATS

The North DATS Data Receiver from the UTTR

Ridley Mission Control Center located near the flight line

Control Data Corporation Cyber Computer Network

Air Traffic Control System within the RMCC

Range Communications within the RMC

More Computer Equipment with the RMCC

Aerial View of the Main Edwards Air Force Base Flight Line and Environs Surrounded by a Collage of Aircraft

Epilogue

2018 Sacred Heart Countesses

2019 Sacred Heart Church Countesses

My Siblings,
Wasco 1947
Front row: Theresa, Aloise, Dad, Mom, and Joe
Back row: Fritz, Mary, Ray (Mary's spouse), Rose, Richard, and Bobby

2002
My Family

1968

2002
Front row: Melissa, Mom, Dad, and Jennifer
Back row: Natalie, Charles, Meribeth, Keith, and Kevin

Dorothy and I had eight children: four girls, Melissa, Natalie, Jennifer and Meribeth, and four boys, Kevin, Keith, Karl, and Charles, born between 1953 through 1965. Our children have given us thirteen grandchildren, seventeen great grandchildren, and two great-great-grandchildren.

Our oldest daughter is Melissa. She has been married to her husband, Rodger, for forty-three years. They have four children. Franklin has a doctorate in education and is a university lecturer. Sarah is a busy mom of four of her own children and works at the children's school. Their daughter Gwendolyn is a young mother of two and has been an elementary school teacher for nine years. Their youngest son, Gordon, is a customs officer for the Department of Homeland Security. Melissa spent most of her married years as a homemaker raising their children and volunteering in their activities. Melissa and Rodger have nine grandchildren.

Our next daughter, Natalie, has been married to Rick for more than four decades. Natalie has worked most of her life as an analyst. They have one daughter, Lindsey, who is working on her doctorate degree in counseling psychology.

Our third daughter, Jennifer, never had children. She passed away when she was fifty-one years old.

Our last daughter, Meribeth, has two grown children. Joshua is a construction superintendent, and Arinda is a medical assistant. Meribeth has seven grandchildren. Meribeth lives in the family home with us and assists with our daily needs.

Kevin is our first son. He works in the aerospace industry as an aerospace engineer for Scientific Applications International Corporation. He is a widower and has one son, Philip. Philip is working on his master's degree in cinema and media studies at the University of Southern California in Los Angeles.

Our second son is Keith. He and his wife Karen have three children. Keith is a retired automotive mechanic. Karen is a clinical laboratory scientist. Their sons, Brian and Tim, work in the medical industry. Brian is an MRI technologist, and Tim is a certified surgical technologist. Their daughter, Denise, is a special education teacher.

Our next son, Karl, lives in North Carolina with his wife, Helen. He had a long and distinguished career working for the air force and the army corps of engineers in Fayetteville, North Carolina. Karl and his wife, Helen, have two children. Jasmine is a certified nurse's aide, and one of our great-grandsons is Seth. Jesse is married and teaches at Florida State

University, Tallahassee, pursuing his PhD in anthropology. Jesse and his wife, Beena, also pursuing a similar PhD, are going to spend two years in Burkina Faso in West Africa to complete their dissertations.

Charles, our youngest son, lives in the family home along with Meribeth. They see to our daily needs by cooking, cleaning, running errands, and performing many other caretaker duties for their mother and father.

After Retirement

After my retirement in January 1986, I had a four-month reprieve. I relaxed, joined a gym, continued walking about two miles a day, and accomplished a few honeydews. The very broad Engineering and Technical Services (ETTS) contract was ready for re-competition for an additional five years. I had a major role in the previous competition and was in charge of the management evaluation team for source selection. I performed this additional duty while assigned as the chief of the Technical Support Division. Many of the contractors who were going to bid on the request for bid knew me very well. I expected that the same companies would again submit a proposal in response to a very detailed and comprehensive statement of work. Knowing that I had retired, many of the contractors were very interested in my source-selection experience. They would invite me for lunch and discuss employment, and I would turn them down. My loyalty was to the air force.

AFFTC Calls

I got a call from Colonel Marty Bushnell in early May, after I retired. Colonel Bushnell was a premier test pilot who flew all the initial and follow-on flight tests for the new F-16 fighter. He was recently assigned to accomplish the ETTS re-competition. He asked me to work as a consultant to assist him. I told him that I had retired and was enjoying my freedom. He pressed me to at least come out to the base for a meeting. I told myself, *Since I've been away from the base for about three months, it will give me an opportunity to see some of my colleagues and friends.* I acquiesced. I jokingly commented, "The contractors at least took me to lunch—but all you can offer me is to go to a meeting. At least you could've invited me for lunch at the officers' club." I detected that he was very concerned and needed help. I went to the base and attended the meeting. To my dismay, they were in need of guidance and assistance. He asked me to work a couple days a week. They assigned me to the systems engineering contract as a consultant. As it turned out, in about a week, I was working practically full-time, planning, staffing, and consulting, in order to establish a source-selection team that included a complete organizational structure and establishment of a secure and protected area for a very sensitive procurement. I assisted him in establishing a management and technical team, including the identification of a broad spectrum of technical personnel to assist in the overall evaluation. The source-selection process took about a year to accomplish. I was asked to stay on as a consultant for other technical acquisitions. This included a major contract for the civil engineering squadron, base photography laboratory, and a major computer acquisition to update and modernize the computer capability at AFFTC. After I completed a handbook that documented source-selection procedures at Edwards Air Force Base, not unlike those used for major weapon system acquisitions, I decided to hang it up for good. I retired again with very little fanfare—the way I wanted it.

Prison Ministry

I volunteered for prison ministry to assist troubled youth detained in youth camps. About three years before I retired, I volunteered to administer in detention ministry, representing Sacred Heart in my hometown of Lancaster California. I was asked to join the ministry by Mike Dante, a close friend. About the time I retired, he transferred to another position in the government on the East Coast. He gladly recommended me to take over his duties as a volunteer lay chaplain. I ministered as a chaplain for the next twenty-eight years. I was in charge of all the other volunteers from the Antelope Valley. I was a chaplain for the Catholic community, ministering at two Los Angeles County probation department camps. Camp Munz and Camp Mendenhall are located side by side in the mountains near Lake Hughes, California. I made the sixty-mile mostly mountainous round-trip ferrying volunteers twice a week. On Saturdays, whenever a priest was available, we would celebrate Mass and the sacraments. Otherwise, I would conduct a communion service and provide reflections on the liturgical readings for Sundays. I was very fortunate to know and become great friends with the internationally famous Fr. Gregory J. Boyle, SJ, the founder and director of Homeboy Industries in downtown Los Angeles, California.

Father Greg always made it a point to celebrate Mass at the various camps. He was very faithful celebrating Mass and the sacraments monthly at Camps Munz and Mendenhall for more than twenty years. Father and I became great friends. I consider him the most outstanding priest I have ever encountered. He is a nationally known priest for his notable work in addressing gang violence issues that are prevalent in all major cities in the United States. He is called upon to present numerous talks and lectures throughout the country and the world.

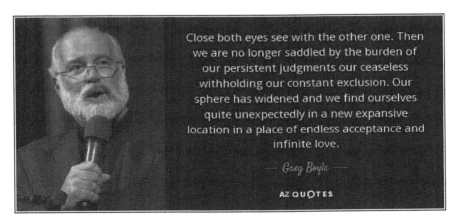

In April 2014, I was awarded the "Adult Hero of the Year Award" for the Los Angeles County Probation Department.

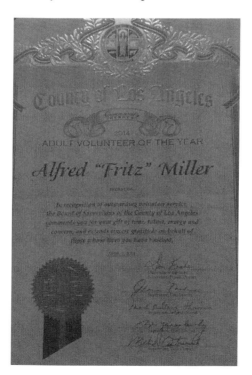

I received no monetary recompense for the many years I served in prison ministry, but I cherish this award just as much, if not more, than all the accolades I received during my career at the great and famous Edwards Air Force Base, California. I thank the Lord a hundredfold for putting me at the right place at the right time and for having known and ministered with Father Gregory J. Boyle, SJ.

Amen

I originally retired from the AFFTC after thirty-two years. I worked after retirement for an additional five years as a consultant at AFFTC, and then I completed thirty-two years as a volunteer lay chaplain under the auspices of the Los Angeles diocese of Los Angeles, Department of Social Justice. I then resigned my chaplain assignment in June 2015. Now after about three years, I began to write my memoir: *From Cows to Space with God as My Copilot*. Thanks be to God. Amen. Mission complete.

WWW WEB SITE REFERENCES

www.edwards.af.mil/home/R-2508　　　(Others)

www.thisdayinaviation.com/tag/muroc-army-air-field/　　　(This day in aviation)

www.warbirdsnews.com/warbird-articles/century-series-fighters (Conquest of the unfriendly sky)

www.airspacemag.com/flight-today/the-edwards-diaries-32471　　(The Edwards Diaries)

htpps://thisdayintechhistory.com　　　(IBM 701 introduced)

www.ibm.com/ibm/history/exhibits/space/space//card　　　(Card Programmed Calculator CPC

https://www.space.com/16709-breaking-the-sound-barrier.html (Breaking the sound barrier)

www.check-six.com/crash_sites/F86H_site.html　　(The F86-H Crash)

www.columbia.edu/cu/computinghistory/701.html　　(The IBM 701 Defense Calculator)

www.historyonthenet.com/the-b-52-bomber　　(The Air Force's Workhorse)

www,airforcemag.com/magazinearchive/pages1957　　(The last flight of the X-2)

www.boeing.com/history/products/b-52-stratofortress.page　　(The B-52 Stratofortress Historical Snapshot)

www,cityofsignalhill.org/422/the-oil-field　　(The Oil Field)

WWW WEB SITE REFERENCES (Continued)

https://mybaseguide.com/air-force/73-1834/edwards-afb-history (Edwards AFB History)

www.militarymuseum/edwardsafb.html   (Edwards Museum)

www.ibm.com/ibm/history/exhibits/mainframe/mainframe-PP7090. Html   (The IBM 7090 Data Processing System)

www.ibm.com/history/exhibits/mainframe/mainframe/-PP7094.html (The IBM 7094 Data Processing System)

www.islapedia.com   (Cattle Santa Rosa Island)

Made in the USA
Middletown, DE
25 February 2020

85333924R00203